IMPROVING

AMERICA'S

SCHOOLS

The Role of Incentives

Edited by

Eric A. Hanushek
and
Dale W. Jorgenson

Board on Science, Technology,
and Economic Policy

National Research Council

NATIONAL ACADEMY PRESS
Washington, D.C.   1996

NATIONAL ACADEMY PRESS • 2101 Constitution Ave., N.W. • Washington, DC 20418

NOTICE: The conference from which the papers in this publication were drawn was approved by the Governing Board of the National Research Council, whose members come from the councils of the National Academy of Sciences, the National Academy of Engineering, and the Institute of Medicine. The members of the board responsible for the project were chosen for their special competences and with regard for appropriate balance.

This publication was supported by the Kellogg Endowment of the National Academy of Sciences and the Institute of Medicine and by the Alfred P. Sloan Foundation.

Library of Congress Cataloging-in-Publication Data

Improving America's schools : the role of incentives / edited by Eric
    A. Hanushek and Dale W. Jorgenson.
        p.   cm.
    Includes bibliographical references and index.
    ISBN 0-309-05436-2 (alk. paper)
    1. School management and organization—United States.
2. Educational change—United States. 3. School improvement
programs—United States. I. Hanushek, Eric Alan, 1943- .
II. Jorgenson, Dale Weldeau, 1933- .
    LB2805.I434   1996
    371.2\00973—dc21   96-44606
                                                                            CIP

Cover: The emblem appearing on the cover of this publication is an illustration of the bronze medallion in the floor of the Great Hall in the National Academy of Sciences building in Washington, D.C. The medallion is the wellhead placed in the floor when the spectroscopic case over which the Foucault pendulum swings is lowered below floor level. The design is based on a map of the solar system published in 1661 by Andreas Cellarius Palatinus. The array of the planets is the Copernican system as known to Galileo.

Printed in the United States of America

iii

The **National Academy of Sciences** is a private, nonprofit, self-perpetuating society of distinguished scholars engaged in scientific and engineering research, dedicated to the furtherance of science and technology and to their use for the general welfare. On the authority of the charter granted to it by Congress in 1863, the Academy has a working mandate that requires it to advise the federal government on scientific and technical matters. Dr. Bruce M. Alberts is president of the National Academy of Sciences.

The **National Academy of Engineering** was established in 1964, under the charter of the National Academy of Sciences, as a parallel organization of outstanding engineers. It is autonomous in its administration and in the selection of members, sharing with the National Academy of Sciences the responsibility for advising the federal government. The National Academy of Engineering also sponsors engineering programs aimed at meeting national needs, encourages education and research, and recognizes the superior achievements of engineers. Dr. William A. Wulf is interim president of the National Academy of Engineering.

The **Institute of Medicine** was established in 1970 by the National Academy of Sciences to secure the services of eminent members of appropriate professions in the examination of policy matters pertaining to the health of the public. The institute acts under the responsibility given to the National Academy of Sciences by its congressional charter to be an adviser to the federal government and, upon its own initiative, to identify issues of medical care, research, and education. Dr. Kenneth I. Shine is the president of the Institute of Medicine.

The **National Research Council** was organized by the National Academy of Sciences in 1916 to associate the broad community of science and technology with the Academy's purposes of furthering knowledge and advising the federal government. Functioning in accordance with general policies determined by the Academy, the council has become the principal operating agency of both the National Academy of Sciences and the National Academy of Engineering in providing services to the government, the public, and the scientific and engineering communities. The council is administered jointly by both academies and the Institute of Medicine. Dr. Bruce M. Alberts and Dr. William A. Wulf are chairman and interim vice chairman, respectively, of the National Research Council.

Contents

Preface   vii

1   Introduction   1
Dale W. Jorgenson

2   Research-Based School Reform: The Clinton Administration's Agenda   9
Marshall S. Smith, Brett W. Scoll, and Jeffrey Link

3   Outcomes, Costs, and Incentives in Schools   29
Eric A. Hanushek

4   Changes in the Structure of Wages   53
Brooks Pierce and Finis Welch

5   The Effects of School-Based Management Plans   75
Anita A. Summers and Amy W. Johnson

6   Management Decentralization and Performance-Based Incentives: 97
Theoretical Considerations for Schools
Jane Hannaway

7   Signaling, Incentives, and School Organization in France,   111
    the Netherlands, Britain, and the United States
John H. Bishop

v

8 Public School Partnerships: Community, Family, and School Factors   147
in Determining Child Outcomes
Rebecca Maynard with Meredith Kelsey

9 Using Student Assessments for Educational Accountability   171
Daniel Koretz

10 Value-Added Indicators of School Performance   197
Robert H. Meyer

11 Economics of School Reform for At-Risk Students   225
Henry M. Levin

12 Staffing the Nation's Schools with Skilled Teachers   241
Richard J. Murnane

Index   259

Preface

With the exception of the Introduction, the papers in this volume were presented at a conference, "Improving the Performance of America's Schools: Economic Choices," held at the National Academy of Sciences in Washington, D.C.,
on October 12 and 13, 1994, with the support of the Kellogg Endowment Fund of
the National Academy of Sciences and the Institute of Medicine and the Alfred P.
Sloan Foundation. This conference was organized under the auspices of the Board
on Science, Technology, and Economic Policy (STEP) of the National Research
Council, by a committee that I chaired and that included Eric A. Hanushek,
professor of economics and public policy at Rochester University, and Stephen
A. Merrill, executive director of the board.

The STEP board was established in 1991 as a long-delayed response to a
decision by the National Academy of Sciences to admit economists as members
almost three decades ago. The principal objective of the new board was to harness
the interests and abilities of economists, industrial technologists, and scientists in
advising policymakers on issues of science, technology, and economic policy.

The first report of the STEP Board, *Investing for Productivity and Prosperity*, was published in June 1994. It called for policies that foster investment in the
nation's future economic capacity. The main focus of the report was the taxation
of income from capital. The principal recommendation was to shift the base for
taxation from income to consumption. This recommendation and the rationale
presented in the board's report proved to be important harbingers of the recent
revival of interest in consumption-based tax reform.

The conference on "Improving the Performance of America's Schools: Economic Choices" was the STEP board's second effort to articulate policies to

enhance investment in human capital, in the economic jargon now fashionable among policymakers. The point of departure for the conference was the nearly contemporaneous publication of a report by a group of 13 economists, the Panel on the Economics of Education Reform (PEER), supported by the Pew Charitable Trusts and headed by Eric Hanushek. The intention of the PEER group's report, *Making Schools Work: Improving Performance and Controlling Costs*,[1] was to initiate a serious intellectual debate over education policy by supplying a new, and previously absent, economic dimension. The chapters in this publication explore several aspects of that dimension, including the relationship of education to future earnings, the effects of school organization and management, school and community influences on student outcomes, measuring student achievement and school performance, and recruiting and retaining skilled teachers.

Dale W. Jorgenson
Cambridge, Massachusetts

---

[1]Eric A. Hanushek et al., 1994, *Making Schools Work: Improving Performance and Controlling Costs*, The Brookings Institution, Washington, D.C., 1994.

IMPROVING
AMERICA'S
SCHOOLS

CHAPTER 1

Introduction

DALE W. JORGENSON
Frederic Eaton Abbe Professor of Economics
Harvard University

The achievements of American education in the post-World War II period are rarely appreciated. The proportion of American workers who have completed four or more years of college education quadrupled from around 6 percent in 1948 to more than 25 percent in 1990. The proportion of workers with some college tripled from 14 percent to more than 46 percent over the same period. Finally, the proportion of workers who completed high school more than doubled from 37 percent to 85 percent.

The notion of investment in human capital provides a helpful framework for analyzing the economic consequences of the massive upgrading of levels of educational attainment of the American population. Investment may be defined as the commitment of current resources in the expectation of future returns and can take a multiplicity of forms. The most straightforward application of this concept is to investments that create property rights, including rights to transfer the resulting assets and benefit from incomes that accrue to the owner.

Economic research, beginning with the Nobel Prize-winning contributions of Gary S. Becker and Theodore W. Schultz, has successfully quantified the notion of investment in human capital. This concept encompasses investments that do not create property rights. For example, a student enrolled in school or a worker participating in a training program can be viewed as an investor. Although there are no asset markets for human capital, investments in human and nonhuman capital have the common feature that the returns can be appropriated by the investor.

The mechanism for translating investments in human capital into impacts on economic growth is well understood. Although these investments do not create

1

assets that can be bought or sold, the returns to higher educational qualifications or better skills in the workplace take the form of higher incomes. An individual who completes a course of education or training adds to the supply of people with higher qualifications or skills. The resulting income stream can be decomposed into a rise in labor services and the price of these services or wage rate. The increase in labor services contributes to output growth in proportion to the wage rate.

Investments in tangible assets were the subject of the STEP board's first report, *Investing for Productivity and Prosperity* (Board on Science, Technology and Economic Policy, 1994). These investments appear on the balance sheets of firms, industries, and the nation as a whole as buildings, equipment, and inventories. The benefits of these investments appear on the income statements of these same economic units as profits, rents, and royalties. Investments in tangible assets accounted for more than 45 percent of U.S. economic growth over the postwar period.[1]

Investments in human capital, especially through formal education, are a very significant source of U.S. economic growth. These investments do not appear on the balance sheets of individuals receiving the education or the institutions providing it. However, increases in labor incomes make it possible to measure the investments and assess their contributions to economic growth. Investments in human capital accounted for almost 30 percent of U.S. economic growth over the postwar period.

Another way of quantifying the role of investments in human capital is to compare them to investments in tangible assets. Barbara M. Fraumeni and I have shown that investments in human capital in the United States have been more than three times those in tangible assets during the postwar period. We also compared wealth in the form of human capital with wealth in the form of tangible assets. Given the long-lasting character of investments in human capital, affecting the incomes of investors throughout their working lives, it is not surprising that human wealth is more than 10 times nonhuman wealth. (Jorgenson and Fraumeni, 1995)

Investment in education has been one of the great, if almost unheralded, achievements of the postwar American economy. This investment program has taken place "off the books," represented by the U.S. national income and product accounts, the measuring rod of the U.S. economy. However, investment in education has been quantified and compared with other forms of investment. The magnitude of the benefits of higher educational attainments to American society has been truly staggering!

The year 1983 was an important milestone in charting the course of educational investments. The proportion of the youngest of the "prime-age" cohorts of workers aged 25-34 years who had not graduated from high school reached a low

---

[1]For further details, see Bureau of Labor Statistics (1994).

of 10 percent. Only one year later the proportion of this group with four or more years of college peaked at more than 29 percent. Since 1983 the distribution of this age group by educational attainment has been essentially stationary. As the individuals who made up this group in 1983 progress through the age distribution and eventually retire, increases in educational attainment will disappear as a source of U.S. economic growth.

The year 1983 also marked the publication of the federal government's report on the state of America's schools, *A Nation at Risk* (National Commission on Excellence in Education, 1983). This report initiated a vigorous debate over education policy that has produced more than 50 additional reports. This debate led President Bush to convene an educational summit in Charlottesville, Virginia, in 1989. This meeting assembled the governors of all 50 states; it was only the third presidential summit in American history.

In March 1994 the U.S. Congress passed and President Clinton signed into law legislation embodying the eight National Education Goals for the year 2000 established in 1990 by then-President Bush and the governors, chaired by then-Governor Clinton:

1. All children would start school ready to learn.
2. The high school graduation rate would be raised to at least 90 percent.
3. Students would leave grades 4, 8, and 12 having demonstrated competency in several specific subjects.
4. U.S. students would be first in the world in mathematics and science achievement.
5. Every American adult would be literate.
6. Every U.S. school would be free of drugs and violence.
7. The nation's teaching force would have access to programs for the continued improvement of their professional skills and the opportunity to acquire the knowledge and skills needed to instruct and prepare all American students for the next century.
8. Every school would promote partnerships that would increase parental involvement and participation in promoting the social, emotional, and academic growth of children.

The Goals 2000 legislation included a grant program aimed at supporting state-level reform driven by education standards. Goals 2000 also provided the framework for the five-year $60 billion Elementary and Secondary Education Act (ESEA) reauthorization enacted by the Congress and signed into law by President Clinton in October 1994. The principal architect of this legislation in the U.S. Senate, the senior senator from Massachusetts, Edward M. Kennedy, characterized the Senate vote as "the culmination of two years of impressive bipartisan cooperation and accomplishment in all aspects of education." (*The Boston Globe*, 1994)

The reaction to the National Education Goals was not one of unalloyed enthusiasm. The senior senator from New York, Daniel Patrick Moynihan, a former professor of education at Harvard University, summarized his reaction in a book jacket endorsement of Eric Hanushek's PEER group report:

> In 1991, the International Assessment of Educational Progress (IAEP) measured achievement levels in science and mathematics for a number of participating countries. Thirteen-year-old U.S. students scored at the bottom of both examinations. In 1994, Congress proclaimed that by the year 2000 American students would be first in the world in mathematics and science. Some would call this fantasy. Others denial. Either way, it is a formula for social calamity. The only remedy at hand is the rigor of economic analysis which Eric Hanushek and his associates have brought together in *Making Schools Work*. A magnificent achievement.

Senator Kennedy's characterization of the ESEA establishes the fundamental point that the main directions of federal education policy were not subject to partisan political disagreements in 1994. In this respect education policy is totally different from health policy, which was also debated in the Congress throughout much of 1994. However, Senator Moynihan's observations underline a second point, namely, that there remains a serious intellectual disagreement over the role of economic considerations in improving performance and controlling costs, the subtitle of the PEER report.

It is important to emphasize that the debate over the role of economic considerations in education policy reflects intellectual more than political disagreements. There has been a bipartisan consensus on the importance of clear objectives for national education policy, embodied in Goals 2000 and the ESEA legislation, if not for assigning the federal government partial responsibility for achieving the goals.[2]

The first contribution to the present volume is by Under Secretary of Education Marshall S. Smith, former dean of education at Stanford University, and two of his associates at the Department of Education—Brett W. Scoll and Jeffrey Link. This is an edited version of Smith's keynote address at the conference on "Improving the Performance of America's Schools." Smith's address provided a detailed summary of the recent accomplishments of the Congress and the Clinton Administration, including Goals 2000 and the ESEA legislation.

Smith and his colleagues describe federal education policy in terms of systemic school reform. The first element in systemic reform is to support the development of academic standards by the states, as specified in Goals 2000. The second element is to target the resources of ESEA at helping educationally disadvantaged students and other children with special needs to reach the standards.

---

[2]In the aftermath of the 1994 elections there have been efforts by members of the new Republican majority to repeal the Goals 2000 legislation or eliminate funding for it. This reflects a fundamental disagreement about the federal role in education but not about the need for school reform and thus does not detract from the relevance of the debate about how to improve school performance.

The resources will be made available to local school districts rather than retained at the state level. The third element is to align the education system to support reform through curriculum development, teacher training, and student assessment consistent with the content standards.

The detailed rationale for systemic school reform, as summarized by Smith and his colleagues, is based on eight major research findings:

1. All students can learn to far higher levels than we ever imagined in the past.

2. What you are taught matters.

3. The quality of teaching matters.

4. Teachers are more likely to teach well things that they understand well and that they have been taught to teach.

5. Schools, and the teaching and learning within them, are more likely to change when the school staff has ownership and some control over the nature of the change.

6. Teachers and the public, in general, do not have a common conception of what is meant by high international competitive academic standards.

7. Individual school reform has a long, complex, and unhappy history in the United States.

8. The education system often does little to support change or to sustain schools that appear to be effective.

These research findings support the proposition that the performance of the education system can be improved if its major elements are aligned to help all students meet more demanding content and performance standards. Since teachers and the general public do not have a clear conception of the goals of education, the role of federal and state governments is to articulate the goals through standards developed by the individual states. Achievement of these goals will require higher-quality teaching and better teacher training. With the addition of resources provided by the federal government through Goals 2000 and ESEA, schools will improve through systemic reform.

While previous school reforms have not been notably successful, the diagnosis given by Smith and his colleagues is that teacher training and educational assessments have not been properly aligned to support reform. This will be remedied under systemic school reform by inculcating content standards through teacher training and aligning assessments with performance standards. However, optimism about the effectiveness of the new approach to reform must be tempered by the fact that the education system does little to support change or even to sustain individual schools that appear to be effective. Persistence and time will be required for success.

The research findings that undergird systemic school reform have been produced by psychologists, sociologists, and political scientists. School performance research by economists has not been used in designing a new approach to reform. Smith and his colleagues emphasize the limitations of economic research rather than its potential contribution to the design of education policy. Although they can conceive of research on school performance that could support the systemic approach, this has not been carried out because of the unavailability of appropriate measures of school performance or "output" and because of deficiencies in existing measures of school resources or "inputs."

Smith and his colleagues conclude that school performance research revised along the lines they suggest would support systemic school reform. A properly aligned system would provide a clear focus through state education standards. These standards would increase accountability by making it easier to assess the performance of students, teachers, and schools. Alignment would also promote efficiency by providing incentives for greater achievement and coordinating the actions and decisions of educators and policymakers at all levels. However, systemic school reform does not include specific policies for providing incentives beyond monitoring performance more effectively.

In short, the rationale for Goals 2000 and the ESEA legislation builds on 25 years of research on the performance of students, teachers, and schools. The systemic approach to education reform has evolved out of the political debate of the past decade, initiated by *A Nation at Risk*, and culminating in the impressive legislative achievements documented so persuasively by Smith and his colleagues.

The second contribution to this volume is a summary of the PEER report by Eric Hanushek, "Outcomes, Costs, and Incentives in Schools." Hanushek characterizes *A Nation at Risk* and more than 50 subsequent reports as almost totally devoid of economic content. In particular, efficient use of education resources, the central focus of the PEER report, is missing from earlier reports.

The economic issues in education are twofold: Are we investing the right amount? Are the resources devoted to schooling used in the best way? In order to answer these questions, benefits must be compared with costs. The results of investment in education summarized above are based on benefits that are internalized by individual students through higher lifetime incomes. Hanushek also suggests that some of the benefits may be external, consisting, for example, of the contributions of education to better citizenship. With respect to using resources more efficiently, the PEER report advocates introducing performance incentives and basing changes on systematic evaluations of school performance while holding spending constant.

The issue of efficiency in the use of education resources is the nub of the disagreement between Hanushek and Smith and his colleagues. One source of skyrocketing education expenditures per pupil during the 1970s and 1980s was a substantial decrease in average class size. Although this is an important goal of teachers, especially in collective bargaining efforts, it has had little or no payoff over time in enhancing the average performance of students. School performance research or, in economic jargon, education "production function" studies show that cross-section variations in performance are uncorrelated with pupil-teacher ratios. This finding has been reinforced by the results of a substantial education experiment conducted by the state of Tennessee and summarized by Hanushek.

Another important trend during the 1970s and 1980s was a rise in the level of teacher training, as measured by the percentage of staff with master's degrees. In addition, the average level of experience for teachers has risen with the decline in enrollments. Both contribute to higher teacher salaries and add to the costs of education. Again, studies of school performance show no effect of additional teacher training and experience on student performance. While Hanushek agrees with Smith and his colleagues that past education reforms have not been successful, the PEER report diagnosis is that the nation's school system has failed to provide appropriate incentives for teachers and students.

Hanushek, like Smith and his colleagues, emphasizes the importance of explicit goals and of developing measures of performance that relate to these goals. However, Hanushek also emphasizes the creation of specific incentives directed at improving student performance, a matter Smith would leave to state and local officials. Examples of performance-based incentives include merit pay and hiring, promotion, and retention of teachers on the basis of classroom performance. The core of this approach would be performance-based contracting between school districts and teachers. This would be phased in through a two-tiered contracting system, leaving the existing seniority-based contracts in place for teachers already in the system. Given anticipated rates of retirement, this could produce a rapid transition to the new system.

Some of the incentives would be for schools rather than individual teachers. For example, merit school programs could key school budgets to student performance. School choice could provide incentives for better student performance by engaging the interest of parents and students in good schools. Mechanisms that permit choice, possibly including private as well as public schools, could align better student performance with the allocation of school resources. Hanushek emphasizes that incentives for performance are largely untested, since they have been introduced so infrequently. One attractive approach is to experiment with different incentive systems, coupled with evaluation of the resulting impact on school performance.

A final point of disagreement between Hanushek and Smith is the measurement of school performance. Hanushek and Smith agree that better assessments are essential. Hanushek observes that schools resist evaluation; this is echoed in Smith's negative evaluation of existing education assessments. Smith and his colleagues propose to align these assessments with education standards established at the state level. Hanushek propounds a "value-added" approach, based on differences in performance between students entering the school system and those leaving the system.

Under Goals 2000, federal education policy charges states with standard setting. Hanushek would have states promote incentive schemes for performance as well as establish standards and set overall education policy. Education policy would be implemented through incentives rather than regulations. Both authors would have states deregulate choices among education inputs and teacher certification, providing much enhanced discretion for local school administrators in selecting the best mix of education resources for achieving higher performance.

The economic perspective provided by the PEER report provides an important new dimension for deliberations about future education reform. This dimension was omitted from the lengthy debate that led to Goals 2000 and the ESEA legislation. Costs and benefits have not been compared in determining levels of support for education at the federal level. Evidence of substantial inefficiencies in the allocation of education resources has been ignored. Incentive schemes are notable by their absence from the resulting program for school reform.

The conclusions of economic research on education summarized by Hanushek and the conclusions of education research summarized by Smith and his colleagues represent different ways of abstracting from the same reality about American education. Education research focuses on the goals of education; economic research concentrates on the means of achieving those goals. Viewed from this perspective, the two points of view produce a more complete framework for future education reform.

Nevertheless, the policy recommendations of the PEER report go well beyond the education policies described by Smith and his colleagues. A budget crisis arising from rapidly growing enrollments is already enveloping school systems around the country. The new challenges facing America's schools will require balancing the costs and benefits of education and enhancing performance while realizing efficiencies in operation. In meeting these challenges it will be critical to make effective use of economic research in improving America's schools.

REFERENCES

Board on Science, Technology and Economic Policy. 1994. *Investing for Productivity and Prosperity.* National Academy Press, Washington, D.C.

Bureau of Labor Statistics, July 11, 1994, "Multifactor Productivity Measures, 1991 and 1992," News Release USDL 94-327, and Dale W. Jorgenson, 1995, *Postwar U.S. Economic Growth,* The MIT Press, Cambridge, Mass.

Jorgenson, Dale W., and Barbara M. Fraumeni. 1995. "The Accumulation of Human and Nonhuman Capital 1948-84," reprinted in Dale W. Jorgenson, *Postwar U.S. Economic Growth,* The MIT Press, Cambridge, Mass., pp. 273-332.

National Commission on Excellence in Education. 1983. *A Nation at Risk.* U.S. Department of Education, Washington, D.C.

The Boston Globe, October 6, 1994, p.10.

CHAPTER 2

Research-Based School Reform: The Clinton Administration's Agenda

MARSHALL S. SMITH,[1] BRETT W. SCOLL, AND JEFFREY LINK
U.S. Department of Education

THE CLINTON EDUCATION AGENDA

The Clinton administration's legislative accomplishments in education in the 103rd Congress span preschool, elementary, and secondary education through higher education and job training (See Figure 2.1). Let us consider the key pieces of legislation in roughly the chronological order that they became law.

Student Aid

The first Clinton education bill, passed early in the 103rd Congress, created a program designed to facilitate student access to postsecondary education while reducing the overall cost of loan programs to taxpayers and students. The Direct Loan program provides an attractive alternative to the existing Guaranteed Student Loan (GSL) program. The new program borrows money from the Treasury to lend to college students, rather than paying for the use of private money from banks as in the GSL program. Eliminating the middlemen reduces costs, which creates savings that are shared with students through lower interest rates and with taxpayers through returns to the Treasury. By 1996, the total savings to taxpayers

[1]This paper is an edited version of a keynote address given by Marshall S. Smith, Under Secretary, U.S. Department of Education, at the conference on "Improving the Performance of America's Schools," sponsored by the Board on Science, Technology, and Economic Policy, National Research Council, October 12 and 13, 1994. Brett Scoll and Jeffrey Link assisted in the preparation of this version.

9

Policy	*Desired Results*
• School Preparedness	All children healthy and ready to learn
Head Start and parent education	A reauthorized Head Start upgrades quality and opportunity; encourages intergenerational learning
WIC and Immunizations	Nutrition and immunizations for all children through increased appropriations
• School Reform	High standards and opportunity to achieve for all students
Goals 2000	Coherent strategy and framework to support state and local school reform based on high standards
ESEA reforms	In context of common high standards for all students: • Resources for those least able to help themselves • Improved teacher preparation • Safe and drug-free schools • Innovation and flexibility for local districts and schools and performance accountability
School-to-Work	Support state and local reforms to develop workplace-based and classroom learning to earn nationally recognized credentials in high-skilled occupations
• Learning for Everyone	Workers have the skills to compete
College student aid reform	A simplified, more efficient loan program; new payment options; reduced overhead costs; savings for students and taxpayers
Improved education and training opportunities	Consolidated and simplified programs; increased information and accountability; easier and earlier access to training

FIGURE 2.1   Lifelong Learning: The Clinton Agenda.

will be roughly $1 billion a year. Between 1995 and 2000 we estimate the total scored savings to be $12 billion for taxpayers and at least $2 billion for students.[2]

Established with the Direct Loan program is a set of repayment provisions, including the Income-Contingent or "Pay as You Go" Loan Repayment Provision. Income-contingent loans allow graduates who do not make a high salary in a given year to pay back only a small amount that year. Others with the same loan responsibility but higher earnings would make larger loan payments and thus pay off their loans faster. Income-contingent loans will give young people a chance to "get going" after college or graduate school without having a heavy debt repayment burden while taking entry-level or public service jobs or by starting their own businesses. A variety of other payback strategies are included in the legislation to provide flexibility and choice for students. These include the option for a student to consolidate his or her new or existing loans with standard repayment provisions into a single income-contingent loan.

Improving Occupational Opportunities for All Students

A second major piece of legislation passed by Congress is the School-to-Work Act. The School-to-Work program is designed to serve students who do not take a high school course of study that would lead them directly to a four-year college. It promotes the kind of rigorous alternative to traditional academic training that exists in a number of European countries. What we envision, and what is now being implemented in various states, is something like an occupational major that students could choose at the end of the tenth grade. An occupational major might be in health care, finance, or 25 to 30 other areas.

State standards for occupational majors that set out content and performance expectations would be developed or adopted by representatives of industry and vocational educators. Eventually, the standards would be common across the states. Students would be assessed after a couple of years in high school and one or two years in a community college. If students passed the assessment, they would receive a certificate that would carry weight when they sought employment anywhere in the country. Widely recognized, portable certification is not only valuable to job seekers but also helps employers identify qualified workers, thus saving hiring and training costs.

As part of their education programs, students would receive on-the-job training in their selected occupational areas. For example, if a student majored in health, he or she might hold a job or multiple jobs in a hospital, health maintenance organization (HMO), or public health clinic. At work, students would see what the occupational ladder looks like and understand what it means to work in

---

[2]Taxpayer savings are estimated by comparing the costs of the Clinton administration's program, including both the student loan reform of 1993 and the proposed FY 1996 amendments to the program, to the cost of the GSL program as it operated in 1992. Student savings derive from reduced origination fees and a reduced interest rate to become effective in July 1998.

a job. In school, students would learn academic content in the context of their occupational major. Health majors, for example, would learn something about the physics, biology, and chemistry of health care. They would also learn about the economics and politics of health care and might study how health affects the lives and stability of families.

All 50 states have received planning grants for the School-to-Work program. State implementation grants are being awarded on a competitive basis. Twenty-two states applied for implementation grants in 1994 and eight won. In 1995 another nineteen states won implementation grants. States are using different strategies. Some, such as Maine, focus more on the community college postsecondary system. Others, including Oregon, integrate academics and occupational programs to reform high schools for all students. What we have, in effect, is a large variety of different, rigorous, standards-based experiments going on around the country in the area of school-to-work education.

School Reform Focused on Challenging Academic Standards

The third major Clinton legislative victory was the passage of the Goals 2000: Educate America Act, the cornerstone of the administration's K-12 reform initiative. Goals 2000 codifies into law the National Education Goals established in 1990 by President Bush and then head of the National Governors Association, Governor Clinton. More importantly, the Goals 2000 legislation creates a stimulus for states to initiate reforms that are focused on all students meeting challenging academic standards established by states and local education agencies—standards that set out in clear prose what all students are expected to be able to know and do in a subject (content standards, illustrated in Figure 2.2) and what level of performance they should be expected to achieve (performance standards).

The aims of Goals 2000 are 1) to encourage states to establish their own challenging standards for reform; 2) to assist states in developing support systems, such as better teacher training; and 3) to help ensure that the resources, flexibility, and authority necessary to bring reform to all students are pushed down to the local level, so that teachers, principals, and parents have the primary voice in how to achieve the high-quality teaching and learning necessary to help all children learn to the challenging standards.

Revamping All Major Federal K-12 Education Programs

Reauthorization of the Elementary and Secondary Education Act (ESEA) of 1965, signed into law in October 1994, was the last major piece of the Clinton education agenda to be passed by the 103rd Congress. Called the Improving America's Schools Act (IASA) of 1994, the legislation restructures ESEA programs. In the past these programs supplemented the existing school system.

Levels K–4

- Characteristics of organisms
- Life cycles of organisms
- Organisms and environments

Levels 5–8

- Structure and function in living systems
- Reproduction and heredity
- Regulation and behavior
- Populations and ecosystems
- Diversity and adaptations of organisms

Levels 9–12

- The cell
- Molecular basis of heredity
- Biological evolution
- Interdependence of organisms
- Matter, energy, and organization in living systems
- Behavior of organisms

FIGURE 2.2 Life Science Content Standards. SOURCE: National Research Council (1994), Table 5-2, p. v-5.

The new ESEA is designed to help change the overall system by supporting state and local reforms for all students—the same reforms reinforced by Goals 2000. For the first time, the U.S. Department of Education will coordinate its major elementary and secondary programs so that they are in tune with each other and with state and local education reform efforts. Instead of having Title I, the massive compensatory education program, heading in one direction, Goals 2000 in another direction, and a professional development program in yet another direction, we are letting states pull these programs together to focus them on the same ends. Those ends are to support state and local reforms to bring all students up to demanding state and local academic standards. In addition to the $100 million allotted for Goals 2000 in 1994 and the $400 million in 1995, ESEA will leverage about $9 billion in support of those reforms.

Title I of ESEA, the largest of the ESEA programs, reformulates "compensatory aid" by focusing on academic standards as a means to promote both quality and equality for children in high-poverty areas. Under the new law, Title I students, like all other students in a school or a state, are expected to have an opportunity to achieve to the *same* standards set by states and local districts under Goals 2000. No longer can we encourage two different sets of expectations for what students should know and be able to do—one for children in high-poverty rural and inner-city schools and another, often more challenging set of expectations, for children in the suburbs (Knapp, 1992). Both groups of children deserve challenging, worldclass standards.

Other changes in ESEA include new programs designed to support widespread reforms in teachers' professional development, in technical assistance, and in promoting safe schools. In addition, the federal government will support, for the first time, a major technology effort in education. Finally, the Secretary of Education has a new waiver authority so he or she can respond to state and school district requests for relief from statutory or regulatory requirements that the states argue get in the way of local reforms. States will simply need to make the case that they or their local schools need extra flexibility to carry out reforms in the most efficient way.[3]

This has been a brief overview of four of the major education initiatives of the Clinton administration. Let us now consider some of the theory and detail of the K-12 reforms.

SYSTEMIC SCHOOL REFORM

The Department of Education hopes to stimulate state and local reforms through Goals 2000 and then to reinforce those efforts using the added resources of the newly reauthorized ESEA. A central idea behind this "systemic" school reform strategy is to establish at the state and local levels challenging content and performance standards that serve as clear academic expectations for the system and for all students. A second part of the strategy calls for states to provide maximum resources and flexibility to the local education agency, so that teachers, parents, and schools have the wherewithal and responsibility to decide how best to educate their students to those standards (Smith and O'Day, 1990). Toward those principles, 90 percent of Goals 2000 resources are pushed down to the local level, and in IASA's Title I program the figure is well over 95 percent.

Standards and local flexibility are two parts of systemic reform. The third challenge is to align the system to support the reforms. A fundamental step is to change the teacher training process. Institutions that train teachers must make sure that the teachers they graduate understand the content and skills set out in the academic standards and that they are able to teach to those standards. Furthermore, state and local assessment must be aligned with the curriculum standards

---

[3]Detailed descriptions of these EASA titles, the Eisenhower Professional Development Program, the Safe and Drug-Free Schools and Communities initiative and the Technology for Education initiative can be found in U.S. Department of Education fact sheets available on-line in the department's gopher site or in hard copy by dialing 1-800-USA-LEARN.

so that tests will measure achievement of the content and skills of those curricula. As it is, many standardized, norm-referenced tests created by profit-making organizations are strikingly independent of what is taught in schools, particularly in areas such as science. A rich performance assessment system that is aligned with student content standards and consequently with schools' curricula would serve to reinforce both student and teacher efforts and would operate as a much more legitimate accountability mechanism (O'Day and Smith, 1993).

To create an environment of support for teaching and learning to the challenging new state academic standards, school and state administrators should ask themselves: Are our strategies for resource allocation and other key administrative decisions focused on supporting all students to learn to higher standards? Are existing resources being used in the most efficient way to bring all students to high standards? If the answer is "no," then the strategies and decisions should be reconsidered.

The implementation of systemic reform will happen differently in school after school, district after district, and state after state. The fundamental idea is that if a state takes advantage of the Goals 2000 money it should set very challenging standards for all of its students and work diligently to help them achieve to those standards. But, just as the federal government should avoid prescribing how states should structure their reforms, the states should provide school districts with the flexibility and resources they need to improve teaching and learning based on their standards.

The administration's K-12 education legislation embodies a marked change in the federal role in public education. In the past the federal role focused almost exclusively on categorical programs for defined populations, such as the poor, migrants, or students with limited English proficiency or on specific subjects such as reading, science, or drug prevention. Goals 2000 and the School-to-Work program are attempts to help strengthen the functioning of the entire system rather than only a particular aspect of it. This is a new way of thinking about the role of the federal government. It means getting the federal government to support, rather then operate independently of, the goals of state and local education agencies.

A Research Base for Reform

These reforms were not invented out of whole cloth. They grew out of a generation of research, much of which has implications for how we go about changing our education system as well as how we conceptualize and measure educational effectiveness. Research on education and educational effectiveness of the past 25 years has taught us a great deal, especially in eight key areas.

1. *All students can learn to far higher levels than we ever imagined in the past.* Jim Greeno, Lauren Resnick, Howard Gardner, and others have carried out

research in cognitive science, anthropology, and other areas that has begun to provide real support for this notion in careful studies spanning a broad range of content (Gardner, 1991; Glaser, 1984; and Resnick, 1988). In addition, there are an extraordinary number of "existence proofs," of examples of teachers such as Jaime Escalante, who inspire "average" or "below-average" students to intellectual heights others would not have thought possible. It was not just Jaime Escalante, it was the teacher next door to him, and the one next door to her, and the people and schools throughout the nation who emulated Escalante, who help to expand our understanding of the learning potential of all kinds of students. Nationally, we have the beginnings of strong evidence from surveys of advanced placement (AP) course taking. The number of AP courses taken and succeeded in by all types of kids has skyrocketed in the last eight or 10 years.[4]

We also have existence proofs from other sources such as studies of international achievement. Many Americans have been amazed and appalled that so many Japanese students score well on algebra tests in eighth grade while Americans fail miserably (Crosswhite et al., 1985; Stevenson and Baker, 1991; and UNESCO, 1983). It is not so amazing at all. In Japan most students take algebra in seventh grade, so they score pretty well in eighth grade. This makes a certain amount of sense. In most cities in the United States, however, we do not let our students take algebra in seventh grade. In fact, we greatly limit the percentage of students taking algebra in eighth grade because we—"we" being the general public and the people in the schools—do not believe that American students can learn it.

2. *What you are taught matters.* Again, we can look to the example of algebra, among other subject areas. If you are not taught a foreign language, you are probably not going to learn one. It is not just a matter of teaching a particular subject area, however; *what* is taught in a given subject area is equally important. If a student is taught only a tiny bit of mathematics or science in the first three or four years of elementary school, he or she is not going to score very well on a mathematics or science test. If a student is taught a great deal of math, in terms of both breadth and depth, he or she is likely to know more and to demonstrate that achievement on appropriate assessments. Despite the seeming simplicity of this logic, our schools have been slow to either deepen their courses or make other changes that would connect what is taught to what is tested (Madaus, 1991; UNESCO, 1983; and Resnick and Resnick, 1985).

---

[4]Since 1989, the number of AP tests taken in all subjects has increased by 150 percent, from approximately 456,000 to 684,000. The growth was even more pronounced for black, Hispanic, and Asian students, whose participation rates nearly doubled. The mean grade achieved also rose across all groups (College Entrance Examination Board, 1994). From 1984 to 1992, the percentage of students in the eleventh and twelfth grades who took the exams rose from 2.4 to 5.7 percent, almost a 240 percent increase. The participation rates of blacks and Hispanics in AP testing have increased by even greater margins to 3.5 and 3.7 times the 1984 levels, respectively.

3. *The quality of teaching matters.* Ann Brown, Lee Shulman, David Cohen, Maggie Lampert, and many others have provided a great deal of recent data on how children are taught complex skills (Brown, 1985a and 1985b; Shulman, 1986 and 1987; Cohen, 1989 and 1990; Cohen et al., 1993; and Lampert, 1988). These studies and others clearly indicate that teachers with mastery of the content and knowledge of how to engage students in hard intellectual work can have a dramatic effect on student achievement. Magically, studies have shown that children who are interested in what and how they are learning and who have some control over the nature of the learning environment actually learn more. Students' motivation and commitment, like teachers', are heightened when they have ownership and are engaged in complex tasks for sustained periods of time. Depth of content and a potential understanding and relevance of experience help promote engagement. Combining challenging content and engaging instruction almost certainly has a multiplier effect on the quality and quantity of student learning (Sizer, 1992; Tomlinson, 1990c and 1991; and Newman, 1989).

4. *Teachers are more likely to teach well things that they understand well and that they have been taught to teach.* Today, in many American elementary schools few teachers feel comfortable teaching mathematics or science beyond a very basic level, in large part because they believe they do not understand the content well enough. Consequently, in many American elementary schools students are taught little more than routine arithmetic and almost no science. If teachers are going to be expected to teach to the kinds of science standards under development by the National Academy of Sciences, or the mathematics set out in the National Council of Teachers of Mathematics standards, they will need ongoing and sustained support, beginning with preservice training and continuing through a lasting system of professional development opportunities and technical assistance (Cohen, 1989; Cuban, 1984; Darling-Hammond and Berry, 1988; Darling-Hammond and Green, 1990; Lieberman and Miller, 1991; National Council of Teachers of Mathematics, 1982 and 1989; and National Research Council, 1994).

5. *Schools, and the teaching and learning that occur in them, are more likely to change when the staff of the school has ownership and some control over the nature of the change* (Conley, 1991). Social psychologists have long known, and organizational theorists have discovered over the past decade, that control over one's environment can increase investment in it and thus lead to greater participation in shaping and improving that environment (Mosteller and Moynihan, 1972). The lessons we learn from the private sector about pushing responsibility for implementation decisions to the lowest levels applies in schools as well (Brown, 1993).

6. *Teachers and the public do not have a common conception of what is meant by high and internationally competitive academic standards.* Some data suggest that the nation does not have a common understanding about performance standards, despite widespread support for such standards. Many teachers

have little current understanding of challenging content and skills or effective methods of teaching to them, in part owing to a national history of low expectations and low-level curricula, particularly for minority and low-income students (Louis Harris and Associates, Inc., 1992). Disparities in grading procedures have contributed to a lack of comparability of grades, especially between schools in high-poverty areas and those that are more affluent. For example, achievement test score surveys have shown that students who receive "A" grades in lower-income schools score at about the same level on independent tests as "C" students in higher-income schools (U.S. Department of Education, 1993). Thus, while students in lower-income schools believe they are succeeding to some high level, as do their parents and presumably their teachers, in fact they are scoring at what would be an average to low level in middle-income schools (Tyson-Bernstein, 1988, and U.S. Department of Education, 1993).

7. *Individual school reform has a long, complex, and unhappy history in the United States.* School reform has looked much like a field at twilight with some 85,000 fireflies in it—one for every public school in the country. For each effort at "reform" or "restructuring," a light blinks on, only to blink off again in a relatively short time. What does the metaphor suggest? To us it suggests that schools blossom into change under the right circumstances, under the charismatic leadership of the right principal, or under the guidance of a change agent, such as Hank Levin or Ted Sizer or Jim Comer (Sizer, 1992; Levin, 1987; and Comer et al., 1987-1988). Over time, however, most such schools lose the support system that helped them begin the change process. Principals change jobs, supportive teachers move away, school district policies change, financial support dwindles, schools lose their momentum, and the light goes out. Study after study indicates that schools in which quality and effectiveness increase over three to four years have trouble maintaining those gains long term (Cuban, 1990; David, 1990; Elmore and McLaughlin, 1988; and Fuhrman and Elmore, 1990). We believe this pattern is not simply one of regression but a phenomenon of the lack of organizational structure and of consistent goals and purpose that is endemic in our fragmented education system—thus, the last general finding.

8. *The education system often does little to support change or to sustain schools that appear to be effective.* Our education system is highly fragmented, dominated by belief in "magic bullets." New reforms constantly replace one another as new governors, secretaries of education, district superintendents, and school principals take office. Simultaneously, leaders at the federal, state, and locals levels may each adopt a different reform strategy, creating further confusion throughout the system. Sometimes these changes are made for thoughtful substantive reasons, sometimes for entirely political reasons. It is little wonder that many teachers are skeptical of reforms and prefer to close their doors and continue business as usual (Smith and O'Day, 1990).

These eight findings and others helped shape the rationale behind Goals 2000 and the new ESEA. Both pieces of legislation were conceived to support state- and locally-based reforms that are built on high expectations. Operational-izing these high expectations requires challenging content standards that describe what all students should know and be able to do and performance standards that measure the level students have achieved in each subject area. The legislation also emphasizes local resources, autonomy, and responsibility and promotes strong professional development and technical assistance to prepare teachers to help students meet the standards.

Building on a Decade of Education Reform

Goals 2000 and the new ESEA also build on the knowledge and experience gained in a variety of states and local districts over the past two decades. Vermont, Colorado, Delaware, Kentucky, California, Oregon, Ohio, and South Carolina, for example, have begun to set standards for what all students should know and be able to do and to reshape their education systems in support of those standards. The shape of reform varies greatly among states, as it should.

The federal government has supported these efforts in a variety of ways. The Statewide Systemic Initiative, a program operated by the National Science Foundation that addresses math and science, is helping 24 states develop math and science standards and provide professional development for teachers to teach to those standards. The U.S. Department of Education has provided 18 states with grants for generating state standards, and Goals 2000 planning and implementation grants are helping 46 states and the District of Columbia devise strategies for developing state improvement plans, including standards. The reauthorized ESEA will put the weight of $9 billion in federal programs behind these reforms, by linking ESEA to state standards rather than erecting separate federal requirements.

Simultaneously, in many communities across the nation local schools are undergoing privately initiated reforms to improve teaching and learning and to engage students. Sponsored by the New American Schools Development Corporation, the Annenberg grants, the New Standards Project, and many other organizations, local teachers, principals, and superintendents are changing the quality of teaching and learning. A great challenge of the middle and late 1990s will be to use the energy of all of these groups to multiply rather than divide their productive effects of reform on the U.S. school system.

Some Persistent Issues in Education Reform

Let us shift now to a few of the many issues that constantly challenge education reform. First, time and persistence are clear requirements, especially as a constantly changing political landscape brings new ideas and new methods with each new leader. Real reform takes years of hard focused work that does not capture headlines. The lure of promising "magic bullets" is very difficult for many politicians to resist.

Second, to make standards-based reform come to life, we need clear examples of high-quality standards and of the caliber of student work that we hope to see in the future. For example, while the Goals 2000 and ESEA legislation make it clear that states will develop or select their own content standards, exemplary standards can provide ideas about the content and structure of standards. The science standards that are being developed by the National Academy of Sciences will become a model for the states, as have those produced by the National Council of Teachers of Mathematics. Even if they are not directly adopted by states, they will have a substantial impact on how states think about and develop their own standards for science.

Useful standards must describe not only good content but also good performance. This should take the form of showing good student work. Too many parents, students, and even teachers in our country have little information about students' potential or what good school work looks like. To understand what good student work looks like and how it can be generated, experts have spent a great deal of time in different schools talking with many students, teachers, and parents. Unfortunately, most teachers and principals do not have that luxury. So often, they do not have a good conception of top-level student work. Parents do not either. Standards laced with examples of high-quality student work can help provide and disseminate information about what good work actually looks like.

Third, we need to address the professionalism of teachers through many strategies. Support for learning the content and strategies for how to teach students to achieve to the new standards are critical. As a by-product, mastery of the standards will mean that teachers know more in a particular subject than most of the population; it can provide teachers with the prestige that goes along with special knowledge, the kind of prestige that builds and reinforces professionalism.

Finally, we need to address both quality and equality. Concern about equality can tempt a state or local district or even a nation to lower its standards to reduce the likelihood of clear disparities between groups, especially between those that might have different kinds of advantages than others. Creating rigorous standards may, in the short run, exacerbate present disparities in student achievement. In the long run, however, unless we challenge all students to meet higher standards, it is likely that low-achieving students will continue to be taught less and learn less, both in terms of quality and quantity, than their higher-achieving peers. We need to create a system based on high standards and then provide the support that all students need to reach those standards, so that we can move at the same time and as quickly as possible toward both quality and equality.

OBSERVATIONS ON SCHOOL EFFECTIVENESS RESEARCH

Now we turn to the issue of measuring school effects. In particular, we will consider the work of Anita Summers and Amy Johnson on school-based management (chapter 5, this volume) and Eric Hanushek on a broader set of school reforms. The principal conclusion of Summers and Johnson's work is that the invention or implementation of any new management system or organizational structure in schools does not of itself necessarily lead to any improvement in education outcomes. Without organization around content-defined objectives for student performance, neither improved student achievement nor efficiency will follow willy-nilly from a governance change. In accord with the findings of the Panel on the Economics of Education Reform, an international study conducted through the Organization for Economic Cooperation and Development (OECD) reports that there are no clearly demonstrated links between increased school autonomy and student learning (OECD, 1994). School-based management may improve certain complementary aspects of schooling, not the least of which may be teacher morale and enthusiasm for the reform effort; however, little empirical evidence can be mustered to support the assertion that greater stakeholder participation directly improves student performance.

The OECD report goes on to suggest, however, that to the degree that a reorganization effort is conducted with a clarity of purpose to improve classroom teaching and learning, positive outcomes may accrue. In other words, to improve student learning, the content and instruction delivered to students must change as well as the organizational structure of the school. They complement each other.

This is not rocket science. Included in the administration's reform agenda discussed earlier are features intended to facilitate school responsibility in resource management by pushing resources down to schools, by granting waivers, and by other strategies. At the same time, incentives are provided so that schools will focus on challenging content standards and aligned performance assessments that together raise expectations for student learning, hopefully leading to increased efficiency and improved student achievement.

Eric Hanushek, too, finds no positive relationship between a variety of measures and school performance.[5] How does one reconcile this with the eight different sets of findings we described earlier that, taken collectively, suggest we know a lot about how to change the opportunities for children to achieve to higher levels. How do we balance these different perspectives?

A close look at the survey/production function studies Hanushek examines shows that those studies by and large neglected to consider any of these eight research findings. There is no measure of whether the teachers and schools in the surveys were focusing their instruction on bringing all students to achieve to high

---

[5]In addition to his paper in this volume, see Hanushek (1979, 1981a, 1981b, 1981c, 1986, 1989, and 1994), Hedges et al. (1994a and 1994b), and Spencer and Wiley (1981).

standards. There are not even any measures of the curriculum coverage or the depth to which material was taught. There are no adequate measures of teachers' quality, their knowledge of curriculum, or their ability to engage students. There are no measures of the degree to which schools have the autonomy and responsibility they need to design effective strategies or of the degree to which the overall district and state systems support the efforts of the schools.

These lapses are not unexpected. The school survey data used by most researchers generally do not include these measures. Very little of what has been found to influence achievement by psychologists, sociologists, and political scientists who actually get into and study classrooms and the education system is ever evaluated as an "input" in surveys.

Note that the variables that make up the backbone of the classic production function—number of years of experience of teachers, class size, proportion of teachers with master's degrees, or even school expenditures—are not among the research findings we listed as important for improving the quality of learning in U.S. schools. The number of years of experience a teacher has does not necessarily tell us anything about her or him as an educator. More relevant questions might probe: What does this teacher know about the content of science or math? Does this person know how to teach children who are difficult to teach? Can this teacher handle a child with Down syndrome who is mainstreamed into the classroom and make it a rich experience for everyone in the class?

Class size or teacher-student ratios are not always informative predictors of student achievement either. Depending on the climate of the school, discipline issues, a teacher's skills in making learning interesting, or even the student-tutoring assistance potentially available in heterogeneous classrooms, the impact of class size can vary greatly. No matter what the size of the class, if the curriculum is watered down, the teacher is not competent to teach the material, and the students are not engaged, learning will be minimal.[6] The central evidence for the effect of class size comes from studies of extremely small classes where intensive tutoring can take place. Much carefully collected data suggest only marginal benefits to smaller class sizes (Robinson, 1990; Tomlinson, 1990a and 1990b; and Mitchell et al., 1989).

By the same token, the number of teachers with master's degrees is not a predictor of student achievement. A very large percentage of U.S. teachers now have master's degrees. Many teachers, acting rationally, pick up their degrees at night school to boost their salaries. Unfortunately, because the courses for a master's degree are typically not aligned with the classroom activities of teachers, higher degrees do not necessarily increase teachers' capacity to teach, or their understanding of the curriculum they are to teach, or their way of dealing with children.

---

[6]The tendency for smaller class sizes to exist at either end of the ability distribution as well as the proliferation of noninstructional staff may also confound results depending on reporting procedures and the controls applied.

Per-student expenditures are an extremely poor measure of education re-sources applied to students' learning. How money is spent is far more important than how much is spent. Moreover, the accounting of expenditures has become so complicated in recent years that it is difficult to focus on its classroom applica-tions. The many services provided by schools in response to the demands of a changing society require increasing percentages of school budgets without any concomitant return in student achievement. In particular, a large percentage of the increases in real expenditures over the past 20 years has gone into special education and much of that into special procedures for health and other related services that special education students are entitled to by law (Chaikind et al., 1993). Often, the more difficult the teaching conditions, the larger the expendi-tures; in many production function analyses this may have led to the erroneous inference that expenditures have a negligible or even a negative effect on achieve-ment.[7]

In our view the independent variables presently in use are deficient. Instead of abandoning production function work altogether, however, we need to look at schooling inputs differently. In particular, we need to think about how to mea-sure variation in inputs that we expect from other research to have some plausible relationship to student performance.

On the other side of the equation, the dependent variable in most production function research is also problematic. The measure most commonly used is a score on a national standardized exam. These tests are purchased from private publishers who devise them to be as widely applicable as possible so as to sell the most copies. The generic quality of the tests tends to make them insensitive to variations in the quality of any particular curriculum used by a school or school system. In other words, the most common dependent measure in education production function research is largely independent of the instructional and cur-riculum content and quality in any particular school, district, or state. Tests that are developed to suit many different curricula and instructional approaches will be inappropriate for any single approach. In the language of systemic school reform, if the dependent variable is not aligned with the teaching and learning going on in the school, it is no wonder that it does not pick up variations in school resources.

Yet the standardized norm-referenced tests have to be sensitive to variation in student performance, for they are required to be psychometrically reliable instruments. What variation do they pick up if they do not systemically assess variation in curricula or teaching quality or engagement of students? There is a clue in many studies (Coleman et al., 1966). These studies show far larger variations in achievement within classrooms and schools than across schools,

---

[7]Many federal and state programs *impose* an inverse relationship between spending and achieve-ment by targeting resources to assist low-achieving students. For evidence that schools tend to spend more money on disadvantaged students, see Carter (1983).

systems, and states. This suggests that much of the variation in these standard-ized test scores is caused by experiences outside schools, especially experiences that vary with social class and environmental opportunities. This in turn is not surprising since the tests are designed to be independent of particular curriculum experiences.

So, when Eric Hanushek reports there is no systematic evidence that re-source differences among schools have a large effect on student achievement, we should not be shocked given his outcome measures. We should, however, care-fully scrutinize the policy implications that might be drawn from these results.

We might also think about improving the current model by changing the dependent variable as well as the independent variables. It seems much more reasonable to have an assessment device that is designed to measure what is being taught. That is what happens in many countries. That is what happens in college classes. Examinations are designed to assess student learning in the course taught, not in some generic course.

Imagine, then, a new scenario for a K-12 education production function. We carry out our new study in a state that has challenging content and performance standards. For our dependent variable we use student performance on a state assessment that is aligned with challenging state standards. For our independent variables we use measures of the resources that our theory of schooling indicates are critical to providing students with the opportunity to learn to the challenging new standards. Our study could analyze, for example, the relationship between student achievement and variations in teachers' knowledge and the quality of their teaching of the substance and skills in the content standards. It could explore the impact not of having computers in a classroom but of using comput-ers and software to support students in their efforts to achieve the state's stan-dards. And it could examine the relationship between students' control over their learning and their actual achievement.

Our objective in examining production functions would be subtly different from the old version. We would no longer be interested in the global question "do variations in school resources and practices influence student achievement?" Of course, they do! We know that from many other studies. Few students learn French or calculus or plate tectonics unless they are taught it in school. Few students learn much science in their elementary years if their teachers lack the expertise to teach it effectively. The new production function should clearly show such effects.

Our interest would be in understanding how, to what extent, and under what circumstances the variations in specific circumstances and resources in class-rooms relate to student achievement. One of the great advantages of an aligned system should be the efficiency that follows from having all of one's ducks in a row. The incentive would finally be right—hard work by students and well trained teachers would result in higher assessment scores. In addition to improv-ing the quality of teaching and enhancing students' opportunities for learning, an aligned system will make it easier to determine the performance of students, teachers, and schools. It will provide them with incentives based on this performance and more effectively support their needs. Our purpose in using the new production function would be to help understand how best to target the resources necessary to make the education system more productive for all children.

REFERENCES

Brown, Ann L., Bolt, Beranek and Newman, Inc. 1985a. *Reciprocal Teaching of Comprehension Strategies: A Natural History of One Program for Enhancing Learning.* Technical Report No. 334. Illinois University Urbana. Center for the Study of Reading, Cambridge, Mass.

_____. 1985b. *Teaching Students to Think as They Read: Implications for Curriculum Reform.* Reading Education Report No. 58. Illinois University Urbana. Center for the Study of Reading, Cambridge, Mass.

Brown, Clair. 1993. "Employee involvement in industrial decision making: lessons for public schools." Pp. 202-231 in *Decentralization and School Improvement,* J. Hannaway and M. Carnoy, eds. San Francisco, Calif.: Jossey-Bass.

Carter, Launor F. 1983. *A Study of Compensatory Education: The Sustaining Effects Study,* Final Report. Systems Development Corporation, Falls Church, Va.

Chaikind, Stephen, Louis C. Danielson, and Marshal Brauen. 1993. "What do we know about the costs of special education? A selected review." *The Journal of Special Education* 26(4):344-370.

Cohen, D. K. 1989. "Teaching Practice: plus Ca change..." Pp. 27-84 in P.W. Jackson (ed.), *Contributing to Educational Change: Perspectives on Research and Practice.* Berkeley, Calif.: McCutchan.

_____. 1990. "Revolution in One Classroom." Pp. 103-123 in S.H. Fuhrman and B. Malen (eds.), *The Politics of Curriculum and Testing.* Philadelphia, Pa.: Falmer Press.

Cohen, D. K., Milbrey W. McLaughlin, and Joan E. Talbert. 1993, *Teaching for Understanding: Challenges for Policy and Practice.* San Francisco, Calif.: Jossey-Bass.

Coleman, James S., et al. 1966. *Equality of Educational Opportunity.* Washington, D.C.: U.S. Government Printing Office.

College Entrance Examination Board, Advanced Placement Program. *AP National Summary Report, 1989-1994.*

Comer, James P., et al. 1987-1988. "School power: a model for improving black student achievement." *Urban League Review* 11(1-2):187-200.

Conley, Sharon. 1991. "Review of research on teacher participation in school decision making," Pp. 225-266 in *Review of Research in Education*, Vol. 17, Gerald Grant, ed. Washington, D.C.: American Educational Research Association.

Crosswhite, F. J., et al. 1985. *Second International Mathematics Study Summary Report for the United States.* Champaign, Ill.: Stipes.

Cuban, L. 1990. "Reforming again, again, and again." *Educational Researcher* 19:3-13.

_____. 1984. *How Teachers Taught: Constancy and Change in the American Classroom, 1890-1980,* New York, N.Y.: Longman.

Darling-Hammond, Linda, and B. Berry. 1988. *Evolution of Teacher Policy.* Report of the Center for Policy Research in Education, Eagleton Institute of Politics, Rutgers University, and the Rand Corporation, Washington, D.C.

Darling-Hammond, Linda, and J. Green. 1990. "Teacher quality and equality." Pp. 237-258 in *Access to Knowledge: An Agenda for our Nation's Schools.* J. I. Goodlad and P. Keating, eds. New York: College Entrance Examination Board.

David, J. 1990. "Restructuring in progress: lessons from pioneering districts." Pp. 209-250 in *Restructuring Schools: The Next Generation of Educational Reform*, R. Elmore and Associates, eds. San Francisco, Calif.: Jossey-Bass.

Elmore, R. F., and M. W. McLaughlin. 1988. *Steady Work: Policy, Practice and the Reform of American Education*. Santa Monica, Calif.: Rand Corp.

Fuhrman, S. H., and R. F. Elmore. 1990. "Understanding local control in the wake of state education reform." *Educational Evaluation and Policy Analysis* 12(1):82-96.

Gardner, Howard. 1991. *The Unschooled Mind: How Children Think and How Schools Should Teach*. New York: Basic Books.

Glaser, R. 1984. "Education and thinking: the role of knowledge." *American Psychologist* 39:93-104.

Hanushek, Eric A. 1979. "Conceptual and empirical issues in the estimation of educational production functions." *Journal of Human Resources* XIV(3):351-388.

_____. 1981a. "Education policy research — an industry perspective." *Economics of Education Review* 1(2):193-223.

_____. 1981b. "Throwing money at schools." *Journal of Policy Analysis and Management* 1(1):19-41.

_____. 1981c. "The continuing hope: a rejoinder." *Journal of Policy Analysis and Management* 1(1):53-54.

_____. 1986. "The economics of schooling: production and efficiency in public schools." *Journal of Economic Literature.* XXIV(Sept.):1141-1177.

_____. 1989. "The impact of differential expenditures on school performance." *Educational Researcher* 18(4):45-51.

_____. 1994. "Money might matter somewhere: a response to Hedges, Laine and Greenwald." *Educational Researcher* 23(4):5-8.

Hedges, Larry V., Richard D. Laine, and Rob Greenwald. 1994a. "Does money matter? a meta-analysis of studies of the effects of differential school inputs on student outcomes." *Educational Researcher* 23(3):5-14.

_____. 1994b. "Money does matter somewhere: a reply to Hanushek." *Educational Researcher* (23)4:5-8.

Knapp, Michael S., ed. 1992. *Better Schooling for the Children of Poverty: Alternatives to Conventional Wisdom. A Study of Academic Instruction for Disadvantaged Students. Volume I: Summary.* SRI International, Menlo Park, Calif.: Policy Studies Associates, Inc., Washington, D.C.

Lampert, M. 1988. "What Can Research on Teacher Education Tell Us About Improving Quality in Mathematics Education?" *Teaching and Teacher Education* 4(2):157-170.

Levin, Henry M. 1987. "New schools for the disadvantaged." *Teacher Education Quarterly.* 14(4):60-83.

Lieberman, Ann, and Lynne Miller, eds. 1991. *Staff Development for Education in the '90s: New Demands, New Realities, New Perspectives*, New York, N.Y.: Teachers College Press.

Louis Harris and Associates, Inc., for the Metropolitan Life Insurance Company. 1992. *Reaching for New Standards: The Teachers' Perspective.* Washington, D.C.: American Association for Higher Education.

Madaus, G. 1991. "The Effects of Important Tests on Students." Phi Delta Kappan 73(3):226-231.

Mitchell, E. Douglas, et al. 1989. "Modeling the relationship between achievement and class size: a re-analysis of the Tennessee project STAR data." *Peabody Journal of Education* 67(1):34-74.

Mosteller, Frederick, and Daniel P. Moynihan, eds. 1972. *On Equality of Educational Opportunity.* New York, N.Y.: Random House.

National Council of Teachers of Mathematics (NCTM). 1982. *Road to Reform: A Mathematics Education: How Far Have We Traveled?* Results of a pilot study conducted for the NCTM. Reston, Va.: NCTM.

National Council of Teachers of Mathematics (NCTM). 1989. *Curriculum and Evaluation Standards for School Mathematics.* Reston, Va.: NCTM.

National Research Council. 1994. National Science Educations Standards Table 5-2, p. v-5. http://www.nas.edu/nap/bookstore.

Newman, Fred M. 1989, "Student engagement and high school reform," *Educational Leadership* 46(5):34-36.

OECD, Directorate for Education, Employment, Labour and Social Affairs, Education Committee. 1994. *Effectiveness of Schooling and of Educational Resource Management: Synthesis of Country Studies.* Points 22 and 33. Paris: OECD.

O'Day, Jennifer A., and Marshall S. Smith, 1993. "Systemic reform and educational opportunity." In *Designing Coherent Policy: Improving the System,* S. Fuhrman, ed. San Francisco: Jossey-Bass.

Resnick, L. B. 1988. *Education and Learning to Think.* Washington, D.C.: National Academy Press.

Resnick, D. P., and L.B. Resnick. 1985. "Standards, Curriculum and Performance: A Historical and Comparative Perspective." Educational Researcher 14:5-20.

Robinson, Glen E. 1990. "Synthesis of research on the effects of class size." *Educational Leadership* 47(7):80-90.

Shulman, Lee S. 1986. "Those who understand: knowledge growth in teaching." *Educational Researcher* 15(2):4-14.

_____. 1987. "Knowledge and teaching: foundations of the new reform." *Harvard Educational Review* 57(1):1-22.

Sizer, Theodore R. 1992. *Horace's Compromise: The Dilemma of the American High School.* Boston, Mass.: Houghton Mifflin Co.

Smith, Marshall S., and Jennifer A. O'Day, 1990. "Systemic school reform." *Politics of Education Association Yearbook 1990.* pp. 233-267.

Spencer, Bruce D., and David E. Wiley. 1981. "The sense and the nonsense of school effectiveness." *Journal of Policy Analysis and Management* 1(1):43-52.

Stevenson, D., and D. Baker. 1991. "State control of the curriculum and classroom instruction." *Sociology of Education* 64(1):1-10.

Tomlinson, Tommy M. 1990a. *Class Size and Public Policy: Politics and Panaceas.* Washington, D.C.: Office of Educational Research and Improvement.

_____. 1990b. "Class size and public policy: the plot thickens." *Contemporary Education* 62(1):17-23.

_____. 1990c. *Hard Work and High Expectations: Motivating Students to Learn. Issues in Education.* Office of Educational Research and Improvement, Programs for the Improvement of Practice. Washington, D.C.

_____. 1991. "Student effort: the key to higher standards." *Educational Leadership* 49(1):69-73.

Tyson-Bernstein, H. 1988. "The Academy's contribution to the impoverishment of America's textbooks." *Phi Delta Kappan* 70(3):193-198.

UNESCO. 1983. *Course of Study for Lower Secondary Schools in Japan.* Tokyo: UNESCO, Education and Cultural Exchange Division.

U.S. Department of Education. 1993. *Reinventing Chapter 1: The Current Chapter 1 Program and New Directions.* The Final Report of the National Assessment of the Chapter 1 Program. Washington, D.C.: U.S. Department of Education.

CHAPTER 3

Outcomes, Costs, and Incentives in Schools[1]

ERIC A. HANUSHEK
University of Rochester

The production of school reform reports is big business in the United States. The current push for reform is commonly traced to *A Nation at Risk*, the 1983 government report that detailed the decline of America's schools (National Commission on Excellence in Education, 1983). Since its publication, new reports have come so frequently that it is rare for a major institution not to have its own report and position on education reform. Yet it is startling how little any of the reports, or the reform movement itself, draw upon economic principles in formulating new plans. At the same time, little appears to have been accomplished in terms of fundamental improvements in the nation's schools.

The movement to reform our schools is motivated in large measure by economic issues. Concerns over the strength of the U.S. economy, the incomes of our citizens, and gaps between the standards of living for different racial groups are consistently grounded in questions about the quality of our schools. A parallel issue seldom addressed in the reform reports but increasingly a matter of public concern is whether the steady increase in funds devoted to schools is being used effectively. These economic issues are at the core of interest in and apprehension about the state of the nation's schools.

Not only are economic results a key motivation for improvement, but economic principles are an essential means of achieving improved performance of the education system. Economists have studied the role that education plays in developing worker skills since before the United States declared its independence and have learned a great deal on the subject. More recently, economists have

[1]This work has been supported by the Pew Charitable Trusts.

considered how schooling affects such diverse things as the character of international trade and the choices families make about investments in their own health. The results of this work have not been adequately incorporated into the nation's thinking and policies toward schools. Most strikingly, standard economic principles are seldom applied to policymaking or to the administration of schools.

This paper grows out of the efforts of a panel of economists to bring economic thinking in its various forms to the reform of American schools.[2] Its purpose is to develop the policy conclusions that logically flow from existing evidence about the role and operation of schools. It does not point to a specific program or reorganization of schools that will solve all of the problems, in part because single answers do not appear to exist. Instead, it points to an overall approach, strengthening performance incentives, and a set of decision rules, comparing benefits with costs, that have proved extremely useful in enhancing business performance, even if they have been largely ignored by schools. It also highlights the necessity of learning from experience enriched by a well-designed program of experimentation. These ideas seem noncontroversial, yet they are noticeable in their absence from current education debate and policy.

Reform—in education as in other areas—is often thought of as the process of securing more resources. Here our panel breaks with tradition. Analysis of the history of schools in the twentieth century does not suggest that American society has been stingy in its support of schools. Quite to the contrary, funding for schools has grown more or less continuously for 100 years. The fundamental problem is not a lack of resources but poor application of available resources. Indeed, there is a good case for holding overall spending constant in school reform. Not only is there considerable inefficiency in schools that, if eliminated, would release substantial funds for genuine improvements in the operation of schools, but there also is a case for holding down funding increases to force schools to adopt a more disciplined approach to decisionmaking. Schools must evaluate their programs and make decisions with student performance in mind and with an awareness that trade-offs among different uses of resources are important.

The plan is not a substitute for goals and standards—the centerpiece of much recent policy discussion—but a way of achieving those goals. In simplest terms, the identification of curriculum, assessment, and achievement goals will not in any automatic way lead to achieving them. Instead, new and different approaches that actively involve students and teachers in attaining these goals are required.

---

[2]The Panel on the Economics of Education Reform (PEER), which met over the period 1989–1993, included Eric A. Hanushek (chair), Charles S. Benson, Richard B. Freeman, Dean T. Jamison, Henry M. Levin, Rebecca A. Maynard, Richard J. Murnane, Steven G. Rivkin, Richard H. Sabot, Lewis C. Solmon, Anita A. Summers, Finis Welch, and Barbara L. Wolfe. Its final report, *Making Schools Work: Improving Performance and Controlling Costs*, was published in October 1994 (Washington, D.C.: Brookings Institution).

WHY SOCIETY WORRIES ABOUT EDUCATION

Because the system of schooling allows little room for individual preference or competition among alternative suppliers and because of the special nature of education in the economy, there is no guarantee that society's interests are best served. The central questions are straightforward: Are we as a nation investing the right amount in schooling, and are the resources devoted to schooling being used in the best possible way?

Economists tend to focus on the trade-offs between alternative uses of resources. Money spent on schools cannot be used for buying health services, consumer goods, or national defense and vice versa. Economists do not devote much attention to evaluating choices that individual families make, such as whether to purchase a television or a car, because it is assumed that individuals make informed choices about things that directly affect them. But when government is heavily involved in the decisionmaking, the possibility of under- or overinvesting is more likely. Moreover, if resources are not used effectively, as is more likely when there is little competition, society gives up too many other things to get its schooling.

Analysis demonstrates clearly that education is valuable to individuals and society as a whole. The economy values skilled individuals, and this is reflected directly in the high relative earnings in the labor market and low relative unemployment rates of the more educated. Over the past two decades, the earnings advantages associated with more schooling have soared.[3] These facts on their own justify general investment in schooling, but they are only part of the story. More educated members of society are generally healthier, are more likely to become informed citizens who participate in government, are less likely to be involved in crime, and are less likely to be dependent on public support (Haveman and Wolfe, 1984; and Wolfe and Zuvekas, 1994). Moreover, the education level of the work force affects the rate of productivity growth in the economy and thus the future economic well-being of society (Lucas, 1988; Romer, 1990; and Jorgenson and Fraumeni, 1992). These latter factors, while further justifying schooling investments, also provide reasons for government financial support of education (as opposed to purely private financing), because individuals cannot be expected to take them sufficiently into account in making their own schooling decisions.

Why then, if schooling has been such a good investment, is there so much concern, consternation, and outright dissatisfaction with our schools? Much of

---

[3]The growth in rewards to skill, measured by years of schooling, is analyzed by Pierce and Welch (1995), who show broad-based increases in the demand for more educated workers. The largest gains have been for college-educated workers, with rates of return for further schooling calculated to have increased from 8 percent in the early 1970s to 12 or more percent in the 1980s. The returns to high school graduates have also increased, although not as dramatically. See also Murphy and Welch (1989), Kosters (1991), and McMahon (1991).

the analysis of the effects of education on earnings and the economy relates exclusively to the amount of schooling obtained by the population. The previous growth in school attainment of the population has virtually stopped, however, and with it the debate has shifted to quality differences. In simplest terms, the issues have centered on whether students are learning sufficient amounts during each year of schooling and whether the distribution in learning outcomes across individuals is appropriate and desirable from society's point of view.

The strongest evidence about the effects of school quality relates to individual earnings. Higher cognitive achievement, which is directly related to school quality, is rewarded through higher wages. There is also evidence that such skills are becoming more important over time as an increasingly technical workplace looks for people to fill jobs.[4] Finally, school quality directly affects the amount of schooling an individual completes, with students from better schools seeking postsecondary education and thus enjoying the added rewards of increased schooling. These benefits again justify investments in school quality.

It is also important to understand some of the macroeconomic implications of schooling investments because the public debate has been particularly confused about these issues. In the past quarter century, as questions have been raised about what is happening in schools, the national economy has also gone through extraordinary changes. The rate of increase in the productivity of the labor force, an important determinant of the economic well-being of society, fell dramatically in the 1970s and the 1980s. The importance of international trade over this period dramatically affected the U.S. economy, causing some citizens and policymakers to be alarmed about our ability to compete internationally as foreign producers have taken over markets previously dominated by U.S. firms. And, most recently, the economy has languished with slow growth of the gross domestic product.

Which of these issues are related to the perceived falling quality of schools during this period, and which are likely to be turned around by quality improvements? Current research suggests that school quality helps determine the overall productivity growth of the national economy, although there is considerable uncertainty about the exact magnitude of the effect. It is clear that *past* decreases in productivity could not have been caused by the recent declines in student performance, because these students were not in the labor force in sufficient numbers to have influenced the observed productivity changes.[5] Any direct effects of current student quality on national productivity growth will be felt only at some time in the future. Moreover, the direct effects of changes in American school quality on the level of trade deficits or on the character of international trade are almost

---

[4]Although the evidence on the effects of cognitive achievement is sketchier than that for amount of schooling, recent work suggests an increasingly strong impact on individual earnings. See Hanushek (1994a, 1994b).

[5]See, for example, Bishop (1989).

surely very small, since international trade is driven much more by comparative advantage and other aspects of world economies that evolve slowly. Finally, there is no reason to believe that business cycles and macroeconomic fluctuations are influenced by the schooling of the labor force. Thus, claims about the effects of schooling, past or future, on the overall aggregate performance of the economy appear exaggerated and do not provide direct justification for significant expansions in public schooling.

In sum, schooling is important. Investing in more and better schooling has been profitable for individuals and society. The case for supporting education is not without bounds, however. Other investments, such as in more modern plants and equipment, also have significant payoffs, so that the potential for schooling investments should be kept in perspective. Benefits must be compared to costs. Moreover, even a perfectly functioning school system will not solve all problems of society and the economy.

The change in focus from how much schooling individuals receive to how good the schooling is is also important to policy deliberations. The economic and social returns to more years of schooling do not translate easily into arguments for specific policies or spending actions related to improving the quality of schools (Hanushek, 1995). The latter issue lies at the heart of today's discussions.

WHAT IS KNOWN ABOUT SCHOOLS

A considerable body of documentation has been gathered about the economics of the education sector itself. Education is, after all, a sector that is noticeably larger than, say, steel or automobiles, and, as noted, it has strong links to other parts of the economy. As such, education has received its share of analysis and attention. The results of this economic analysis have, at best, been ignored, and at worst contradicted, in many of the popular versions of school reform.

The overall story about what has been happening in schools is clear: the rapid increases in expenditures for schools of the past three decades have simply not been matched by measurable increases in student performance. Moreover, detailed studies of schools have shown a variety of inefficiencies, which, if corrected, could provide funds for a variety of improvement programs.

There has been a dramatic rise in real expenditure per pupil over the entire century. Figure 3.1 shows that, after allowing for inflation, expenditures per pupil have increased at almost 3.5 percent per year for 100 years (Hanushek and Rivkin, 1994). This remarkable growth is not explained away by such things as increases in special education or changes in the number of immigrant students in the school population, although these factors have had a noticeable impact on school expenditures.

The spending increases have been driven by three basic factors. In terms of direct instructional staff expenditures, both declines in pupil–teacher ratios and increases in the real salaries of teachers have been very important. These two

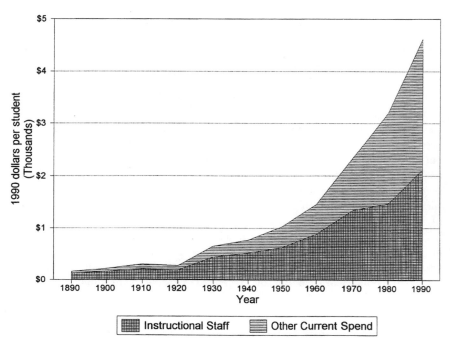

FIGURE 3.1   Real expenditures per pupil, instructional staff and other spending, 1980–1990.

elements are the primary elements behind the lower portion of the graph in Figure 1, which plots instructional staff and other expenditures per student. Throughout the century, teachers have been used more intensively, as a result of both direct efforts to reduce class size and the introduction of new supplementary programs that expand on teacher usage. Real teacher salaries have also grown, although in a somewhat complicated way. The increases in teacher salaries have not been uniform, as periods where salaries have not kept up with inflation are offset by periods of more rapid increase. Moreover, even with general improvement, salary growth has not kept up with the growth in salaries for college-educated workers in other occupations. Thus, while teachers' wages have put cost pressure on schools, school salaries have been competitive with a smaller proportion of outside jobs over time.[6]

---

[6]Hanushek (1995). An additional complication is that the competitiveness of teachers' salaries differs for men and women. Teaching has historically offered better relative salary opportunities to women than men, but this is ending, as outside opportunities for women expand. For men, teaching has kept up with outside wages over the past two decades. For women, there have been sharp declines over the same period.

The top portion of Figure 3.1 identifies in a general way the third source of cost increases. Expenditures other than those for instructional staff have increased even more rapidly than those for instructional staff. Between 1960 and 1990, instructional staff expenditures fell from 61 percent to 46 percent of total current expenditures. Unfortunately, what underlies this is unclear, because there are very poor data on those expenditures. While it is often convenient to label this simply "increased bureaucracy," the available data neither confirm nor deny this interpretation, because these expenditures include a variety of items that are legitimate classroom expenditures (such as teacher health and retirement funds or purchases of books and supplies), in addition to administrative and other spending. The aggregate effects are clear, however; if these expenditures had grown between 1960 and 1990 at just the rate of instructional staff spending—which itself includes significant increases in resource intensity—total spending per pupil would have been 25 percent lower in 1990.

The pattern of spending changes in recent years points to an upcoming fiscal crisis for the nation's schools. During the 1970s and 1980s, the U.S. student population fell dramatically. During that time, increases in per-pupil expenditures were offset by falls in the student population, so that aggregate spending on schools rose much more slowly than per-pupil expenditures (Hanushek and Rivkin, 1994). But the situation is now changing, and the student population is again rising. As rising student populations combine with growth in real spending per student, aggregate spending will be up at a much higher rate than over the past decade. These prospective expenditure increases are likely to collide with public perceptions that school performance is not rising. If this happens, local taxpayers, who continue to play an important role in American school finance, are likely to resist future expenditure increases with unprecedented insistence, perhaps putting schools into a real fiscal squeeze. Moreover, many major urban districts face fiscal pressures from competing demands for public revenues, such as welfare or police funding, suggesting that the worst of the fiscal crisis might appear in the already pressured schools of major cities.

Matched against the growth in spending, student performance has, at best, stayed constant and may have fallen. While aggregate performance measures are somewhat imprecise, all point to no gains in student performance over the past two decades. The path of achievement on reading, math, and science exams, shown in Figure 3.2, provides a visual summary of the pattern of performance for the population (U.S. Department of Education, 1994). These figures display the performance over time of a representative sample of 17-year-olds on the various components of the National Assessment of Educational Progress (NAEP). While there has been slight movement, the overall picture is one of stagnating performance. Moreover, since substantial decline occurred before the beginning of these series (see Figure 3.3, below), this chart understates the magnitude of the problem.

There has also been a series of embarrassing comparisons with students in

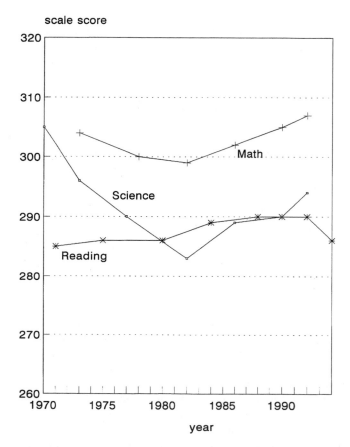

FIGURE 3.2   National Assessment of Educational Progress (NAEP), performance of 17 year olds, 1970–1994.

other countries. Comparisons of U.S. and Japanese students in the early 1980s showed, for example, that only 5 percent of American students surpassed the average Japanese student in mathematics proficiency (McKnight et al., 1987, and National Research Council, 1989). In 1991 comparisons, Korean 9-year-olds appeared closer to U.S. 13-year-olds than to U.S. 9-year-olds, hardly the kind of performance that would put U.S. students first in the world in mathematics performance (U.S. Department of Education, 1994).

The problems of performance are particularly acute when considered by race or socioeconomic status. Even though there has been some narrowing of the differences in performance, the remaining disparities are huge and incompatible with society's goal of equity. Figure 3.3, for example, displays the history of

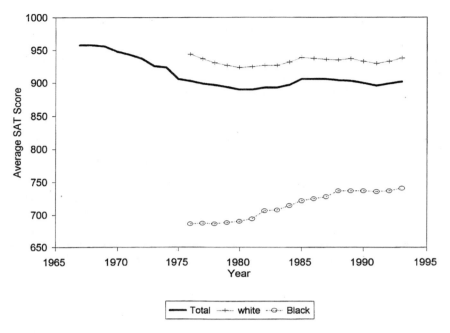

FIGURE 3.3   SAT scores: total and by race, 1966–1993.

SAT performance over two decades. These scores quite convincingly display a disparity that mirrors one also existing on the NAEP tests.[7] During the 1980s, there was a broad-based convergence of black–white score differences, but most recent data suggest that it may have ceased.

The aggregate results, showing that expenditure increases have not been accompanied by improvements in student performance, are confirmed in more detailed studies of schools and classrooms (Hanushek, 1986 and 1989). These more detailed studies document a variety of common policies that increase costs but offer no assurances of commensurate improvements in student performance. The wide range of careful econometric studies reviewed in Hanushek (1989) indicate that key resources—ones that are the subject of much policy attention—are not consistently or systematically related to improved student performance.

---

[7]Although the precise pattern of SAT score changes is obscured by well-known problems of selective test taking, the existence of significant differences over time and by race is beyond question (Congressional Budget Office, 1986). The SAT data are important because they provide the longest continuous time series for student performance and, in the context of racial disparities, because of the significance of the SAT for college attendance.

Perhaps the most dramatic finding of analyses of schools is that smaller class sizes usually have had no general impact on student performance, even though they have obvious implications for school costs. Moreover, the basic econometric evidence is supported by experimental evidence, making it one of the clearest results from an extensively researched topic.[8] Although some specific instruction may be enhanced by smaller classes, student performance in most classes is unaffected by variations in class size in standard operations of, say, 15 to 40 students.[9] Nevertheless, even in the face of high costs that yield no apparent performance benefits, the overall policy of states and local districts has been to reduce class sizes in order to try to increase quality.

A second, almost equally dramatic, example is that obtaining an advanced degree does little to ensure that teachers do a better job in the classroom. It is just as likely that a teacher with a bachelor's degree would elicit high performance from students as would a teacher with a master's degree. Again, since a teacher's salary invariably increases with the completion of a master's degree, this is another example of increased expenditures yielding no gains in student performance.[10] The final major resource category with a direct impact on school spending through salary determination is teacher experience. The evidence on the effectiveness of experienced teachers is more mixed than for the previous categories, but it does not provide convincing support of a strong relationship with performance.

These resource effects are important for two reasons. First, variations in instructional expenditures across classrooms are largely determined by the pupil–teacher ratio and the salary of the teacher, which, in turn, is largely determined by the teacher's degree and experience. If these factors have no systematic influence on student performance—which the evidence shows they do not—expansion of resources in the ways of the past are unlikely to improve performance. Second, either explicitly or implicitly schools have pursued a program of adding these

---

[8]An early review of experimental evidence is found in Glass and Smith (1979). More recently, the state of Tennessee conducted an extensive statewide random-assignment experiment of reduced class size in grades K–3. Except perhaps for kindergarten, no gains in student performance were associated with being in a smaller class (Word et al., 1990). This work and the follow-on studies related to the Tennessee experiment have recently been reviewed in Mosteller (1995). The Mosteller review emphasizes differences in student performance at the end of each grade level in the longitudinal experiment but ignores the fact that adding resources through elementary school has virtually no effect on differences that existed at the end of kindergarten.

[9]There may be special programs, say ones falling outside the range of normal operations, where smaller classes are effective. For example, the Success for All program and the reading tutorial program of the University of Texas at Dallas show that early one-on-one instruction may be beneficial. But these are different from general reductions in overall class sizes or pupil–teacher ratios (Hanushek et al., 1994).

[10]Some states even require that teachers obtain a master's degree in order to be fully certified. While the cost of obtaining the degree falls on the individual teacher, salaries are subsequently adjusted upward to reflect the additional education.

TABLE 3.1   Public School Resources, 1961–1986

Resource	1960–61	1965–66	1970–71	1975–76	1980–81	1985-86	1990-91
Pupil–teacher ratio	25.6	24.1	22.3	20.2	18.8	17.7	17.3
% Teachers with master's degree	23.1	23.2	27.1	37.1	49.3	50.7	52.6
Median years experience of teacher	11	8	8	8	12	15	15
Current expenditure/ADA (1992–1993 dollars)	$1,903	$2,402	$3,269	$3,864	$4,116	$4,919	$5,582

SOURCE: U.S. Department of Education (1994).

specific resources.[11]   Table 3.1 traces these resources over the past several decades. Schools currently have record-low pupil–teacher ratios, record-high numbers for completion of master's degrees, and more experienced teachers than at any time at least since 1960. These factors are the result of many specific programs that have contributed to the rapid growth in per-pupil spending but have not led to improvements in student performance. Schools do not try to ensure that increased student performance flows from increased expenditures.

Interestingly, Marshall Smith's summary of the evidence on schools in this volume concedes that it is common knowledge that variations in resources are unconnected to student performance. Further, he criticizes research aimed at identifying the relationship of resource variations with student performance. Yet, in my view, one objective of public policy ought to be to ensure that public resources devoted to schools are used effectively. Nothing in today's school finance system, save perhaps the ultimate rejection of school budgets, pushes schools to promote efficient use of resources. Unless significant changes occur, there is little reason to believe that additional resources applied in the future will be used any better than resources applied in the past.

Although there is no consensus about which specific factors affect student performance, there is overwhelming evidence that some teachers and schools are significantly better than others. For example, in inner-city schools, the progress of students with a good teacher can exceed that of students with a poor teacher by more than a year of achievement during a single school year.[12] The dramatic differences in performance are simply not determined by the training of teachers,

---

[11]Expansion of these resources is often implicit, resulting, for example, from the introduction of new programs that in turn expand specialized staff. At the same time, it is clear that these resource increases are not the simple result of government mandates to expand school activities such as those for special education (Hanushek and Rivkin, 1994). Instead, they are reflective of a consistent policy to increase the intensity of instruction.

[12]These comparisons provide indications of improvements in standard test performance across classrooms after considering both starting achievement levels and family influences on performance (Hanushek, 1992).

the number of students in the classroom, or the overall level of spending. A primary task of school reform is increasing the likelihood that a student ends up in a high learning environment.

The lack of relationship between resources and performance surprises many people but perhaps should not. The most startling feature of schools, distinguishing them from more successful institutions in our economy, is that rewards are only vaguely associated with performance, if at all. A teacher who produces exceptionally large gains in her students' performance generally sees little difference in compensation, career advancement, job status, or general recognition when compared with a teacher who produces exceptionally small gains. A superintendent who provides similar student achievement to that in the past but at lower cost is unlikely to get rewarded.[13] With few incentives to obtain improved performance, it should not be surprising to find that resources are not systematically used in a fashion that improves performance.

The current inefficiencies of schools, with too much money spent for the student performance obtained, indicate that schools can generally improve their performance at no additional cost. They simply need to use existing resources in more effective ways. These inefficiencies also indicate that continuing the general policies of the past, even if dressed up in new clothing, is unlikely to lead to gains in student performance, even though cost pressures will continue to mount.[14] It may be appropriate to increase spending on schools in the future, but the first priority should be restructuring how existing resources are being used.[15]

WHAT MIGHT BE DONE

One common response to the evidence of pervasive inefficiencies, often linked to appeals for added spending, is that "if we spend money effectively, we can improve student performance." This tautological statement is just the concern. History suggests that spending money on effective programs will not happen naturally or automatically in the current structure of schools. Our panel of economists sees no reason to believe that increases in spending would on

---

[13]As discussed below, the lack of incentives is not restricted to school personnel. A student who gets high grades is not necessarily going to be rewarded by employment over the student with low grades.

[14]These results do not indicate that resources are *never* used effectively. Indeed, there is strong evidence that some schools do use added resources to bring about significant achievement gains. On the other hand, effective uses are counterbalanced by ineffective uses, implying that there is no reason to believe that general increases in funding and resources will yield gains in student performance. See the exchange with Hedges et al. (1994) and Hanushek (1994a).

[15]Statements about overall resource policies are not to be interpreted as rules that are slavishly adhered to at the individual district and school levels. Variations in local circumstances plus requirements for initial expenditure to develop new alternatives may dictate some additional spending. Like the general message below, one size almost surely does not fit all. But, equally, overall increases in spending on average will fit no one, given the current incentives and structure.

average be any more effective than past spending, particularly when they rely on the same people operating with the same basic incentives.

Three key principles, our panel believes, are essential to improving U.S. schools:

- resources devoted to education must be used efficiently;
- improved performance incentives must be introduced in schools; and
- changes must be based on systematic experimentation and evaluations of what does and does not work.

These principles, which appear to be based on common sense and do not seem controversial, are most notable in their virtual absence from today's schools and today's policy setting.

Efficiency

Any reform program must explicitly consider the costs as well as the potential benefits of changes. Efficiency simply relates to the quest to get the largest benefits from any spending. Virtually all past considerations of school reform, on the other hand, have either ignored costs or argued that the benefits are large enough to support any proposed increase in costs. The disregard for costs leads to distorted decisions. Ultimately, this view undoubtedly lowers the likelihood that any proposals will be taken seriously, because policymakers and the public will consider the price tag attached to any major restructuring of schools. As indicated above, however, attention to both costs and benefits should not be restricted to new programs. Many existing programs are inefficient and should be replaced by more cost-efficient ones.

Mention of efficiency is often met by disdain from school personnel, in part because of general misunderstanding of what efficiency means. It is neither a mandate to minimize costs without regard to outcomes nor a narrow view of what schools are expected to accomplish. Instead, it is a recognition of the competition for resources both within schools and elsewhere in society. Moreover, schools are likely to run into greater and greater difficulties in raising funds, especially if they are unable to show results.

Performance Incentives

Incentives based upon student outcomes hold the largest hope for improving schools. Most past policy has been based on a combination of regulations and fixed definitions of inputs to schooling—the resources, organization, and structure of schools and classrooms. Little attention has been focused on the results. Improvement is much more likely if policies are built on what students actually accomplish and if good performance by students gets rewarded. If properly designed, performance incentives will encourage the creativity and effort needed to develop and implement effective programs.

Education is a very complicated task that requires the cooperation and ingenuity of individual teachers, principals, and other school personnel.[16] It is, moreover, virtually hopeless to think of running a high-quality education system without the active involvement of students. Finally, there are many equally effective approaches to learning various subjects and skills, differentiated by how individual teachers and students adapt to specific tactics and techniques. If there is no single-best approach to performing specific educational tasks, it is simply not possible to design policies that are based on full descriptions of what is to be done and how it is to be done in the classroom.

The policy suggestions of our panel of economists differ from most previous school reform documents. We do not recommend a specific program or a major restructuring of schools. Current knowledge does not support a lot of specific prescriptions or broad recommendations. Indeed, we have every reason to believe that many different approaches might be used simultaneously in an effective school system. On the other hand, certain *strategies* for reforms are very clearly more beneficial, and it is these that our panel emphasizes. Strategies involving improved incentives, ongoing evaluation, transmission of performance information, and consistent application of rational decision rules are central to any productive reform path.

As Marshall Smith and his colleagues at the U.S. Department of Education suggest, implementation of performance incentives requires having explicit goals and developing measures of performance that relate to those goals. Improving schools is currently made very difficult by the lack of generally agreed upon measures of performance. And quite clearly, developing incentive systems must include consensus about how good performance is defined and subsequently rewarded. Nonetheless, our panel does not see a test-driven management of schools but instead a reform that incorporates a variety of performance observations. Similarly, as discussed below, we do not see that simply announcing high goals and developing commensurate standards are likely by themselves to lead to accomplishing those goals.

A wide range of incentive structures offer hope for improving schools. These systems are the subject of much heated debate and frequently bring forth emotional responses. The alternatives, along with their pros and cons, are spelled out in detail elsewhere (Hanushek et al., 1994). The essential feature of all of them, however, is that resources and rewards are directed at good student performance and away from bad performance. The commonly discussed plans do this in quite different ways. For example, performance contracting involves developing explicit contracts that base rewards on meeting various performance goals, while merit pay plans take the basic structure of existing schools and attempt to alter the

---

[16]Early statements of the idiosyncratic elements of production in schools and their implications for understanding the effects of school resources can be found in Murnane and Nelson (1984) and Hanushek (1986).

compensation scheme for teachers to conform more with student outcomes. Alternatively, clearer hiring, promotion, and retention policies for teachers on the basis of classroom performance are related to a private school model of the personnel system. Merit school programs build in shared rewards for people in high-performance schools, lessening any tendencies for unhealthy competition among teachers. Going in a different direction, a variety of school choice schemes highlight the potential importance of individual student decisions about which school to attend. Choice systems come in many different forms. Some may leave much of the current structure of school systems intact (such as magnet school programs or intradistrict choice plans), while others may begin to shake the existing foundation of schools (such as interdistrict choice or public–private vouchers). Each of these incentive systems conceptually focuses attention and incentives on student performance, either through school evaluations or parental involvement. As a group, they also differ significantly from the way schools are currently organized.

The most remarkable fact about the range of conceptually appealing performance incentives is that they remain virtually untested. Few examples of their use are available, and, as with the vast majority of new programs instituted in schools, attempts to introduce these various incentive systems are seldom evaluated in any systematic manner. We know neither what forms of incentive systems are best in general or specific circumstances nor precisely what results might be expected from broader use of any specific system. The impotence of current incentives coupled with the observed power of incentives elsewhere in the economy, however, lead our panel to believe that one or more of these alternative incentive schemes could be productively instituted and adapted to virtually every school system in the country. Finding the best set for individual systems will require effort, but the potential for improvement supports undertaking such a quest.

In addition to these incentives directed at schools, it is important to think of incentives directed at students. While the previous discussion emphasized the general lack of performance incentives for teachers and school personnel, the lack of incentives is not limited to them. Students who work hard and perform well in schools typically see only minor differences in rewards when compared with students who do not work hard and who do not perform well. Potential employers, for example, seldom gather any information about the scholastic performance of applicants, and, except for the limited number of highly selective colleges and universities, variations in student performance across a fairly wide range have little impact for postsecondary school attendance. More significant performance incentives for students could reinforce and amplify performance incentives for school personnel.[17]

---

[17]These muted incentives clearly interact with a certain amount of myopia on the part of students. As noted earlier, over their work lives, students with more skills will receive higher incomes. Thus, there are incentives to perform, but they might not be apparent to the high school student.

Evaluation and Experimentation

This lack of knowledge about performance systems calls for a broad program of experimentation and evaluation, the third major component of the decision process proposed here. Improvement on a large scale will be possible only with the development of a knowledge base about effective approaches. Remarkably, evaluation is seldom an integral part of schools today. Any evaluation that is done is much more likely to occur *before* a program is introduced, rather than after.[18] Schools, while recognizing the importance of regular evaluation in the case of their students, avoid evaluation of their own performance.

This is a call for more experimentation and integrated evaluation rather than for more research on schools as they are currently organized. Experimentation would be directed at encouraging wider development and use of new incentive structures. Simply introducing performance incentives is clearly risky because some versions of incentive systems will not work as hoped or predicted.

We must be able to disseminate and build on good results. Evaluation is difficult because it is essential to disentangle the various influences on student performance. Schools and teachers are just one factor that affects student learning. The students and their parents directly influence performance, as do other students and other members of the community. All too often people confuse high absolute levels of performance by students with high performance by schools, not recognizing that schools might be contributing little to students' performance in some situations. Similarly, just the opposite occurs where particular teachers and schools do an exceptional job that goes unrecognized because the overall level of student achievement is low. Both situations lead to poor policies. Evaluation must concentrate on extracting the value added of schools and linking this value added to the programs and organization of the schools.

REFORM PRINCIPLES AND THE CURRENT POLICY DEBATE

The general principles of reform described here have much in common with the current systemic reform movement, but it is easy to overlook essential differences.

Decentralized Decisions—Past and Future

Any improved system will have to harness the energy and imagination of the personnel in the local schools. If incentives are instituted to reward performance,

---

[18]The reforms of the Rochester (N.Y.) City School District are an all-too-common illustration. In 1986, in a policy movement that was widely heralded as a forerunner to future innovations in other schools, a new teachers' contract was negotiated that called for average salary increases in excess of 40 percent over the three-year contract. In exchange, a merit evaluation system was to be developed and introduced. The hopes for reform faded in subsequent contract negotiations. But never during the process was there any serious evaluation of the effects of the reform effort (Marshall and Tucker, 1992).

school personnel must have the freedom to institute the programs and approaches that will best enhance student performance. The specific approaches will almost certainly differ across schools and teachers, even if everybody faces the same reward structure for student performance. This argues for decentralization of decisionmaking. Some form of site-based management is likely to be an important ingredient of new incentive systems.

A current popular approach to site-based management is not fully consistent with the ideas here because it is not directly linked to student performance (Summers and Johnson, chapter 5, this volume). Decentralization of decisionmaking has little general appeal without such linkage and, indeed, could yield worse results with decentralized management pursuing its own objectives not necessarily related closely to student performance. In short, site-based management is not an end in itself but a means for implementing other reforms. Moreover, although the concept of decentralizing decisionmaking is appealing, there is little evidence to suggest that sufficient capacity exists in most schools to make it successful. As with many of the changes suggested here, implementation will require a period of learning and of attracting suitable personnel.

Programs "Known" to Be Successful

Frequently, it is asserted that we do, in fact, know what works. These assertions are often embedded in appeals for new resources because they provide examples of what would be possible with more funds. Some claims point to studies that indicate, for example, that a particular reading program or configuration of resources leads to improved student performance. Other examples, though, go beyond simple appeals for added resources. These include lists of quite convincing ideas such as "performance increases with the amount of time on specific tasks" or "subject matter knowledge by teachers is crucial to higher student performance." These assertions then lead explicitly or implicitly to notions that reproducing these programs or insisting on more time devoted to instruction provides an obvious path to higher student achievement.

When programs that are touted as "proven" to work are not adopted readily, the reason may not be their cost. Many programs described as important reforms require relatively modest expenditures, and some could be accomplished with existing resources. There are three other explanations for the failure of particular reform programs to be adopted. First, as observed earlier, there may not be very strong incentives to introduce such programs even if they are relatively inexpensive. They may be adopted because of idiosyncratic choices in some schools or districts, but nothing compels other districts to follow suit; and simply increasing knowledge about them is unlikely to lead to rapid diffusion. Second, such programs may compete with other programs and other objectives. In other words, they interfere or are perceived to interfere with existing incentives. Third, what is "known" might not be right. When there is limited experience with programs that operate in particular environments with particular people, it is easy to confuse program effectiveness with other elements that make transfer of the program to other locations difficult or impossible. Without wider experimentation *coupled with evaluation and learning*, the list of programs "known" to be good may expand and contract without much relationship to the utility of any given program as a candidate for wider diffusion.

Ideas such as providing more time on core academic subjects or securing teachers with greater knowledge of the subject matter are indeed appealing. At the same time, it is hard to imagine legislating such measures into existence across schools. If their importance is known and if everybody in the schools is working to improve student achievement, we would expect such measures to be in place. When they are not, as is often the case, the prime reason is simply impotent incentives to place a premium on raising student achievement. Knowledge of what will enhance performance in specific circumstances is a minimal requirement for improvement. When such knowledge of what works is available, the need for changes in organization and incentives to ensure quicker and deeper penetration of worthwhile reforms becomes even more evident.

Disadvantaged Students

The educational problems of disadvantaged students are frequently treated differently from more general school reforms, but this is largely inappropriate. The most effective approaches to their education will be based on the same principles outlined here—careful attention to student outcomes, development and institution of performance incentives, evaluation of programs, and attention to both costs and benefits. For example, one of the most promising programs for disadvantaged students, the Accelerated Schools program, emphasizes clear objectives and regular student evaluation. Programs for disadvantaged students must, as with other programs, be driven by performance. Programs for such students may differ from programs for more advantaged students in the details— for example, by devoting more attention to early childhood education and parental involvement—but these elements, too, should be evaluated in the same manner as other school programs.

Goals 2000

The centerpieces of recent federal attention to schooling are the Goals 2000: Educate America Act, signed into law in March 1994, and the reauthorization of the Elementary and Secondary Education Act of 1965, which was signed into law in October 1994.[19] This legislation, which follows from resolutions of the

---

[19]A thorough history of the development of national goals and standards, including Goals 2000, is found in Ravitch (1995).

nation's governors in 1989, has two important features. First, it makes clear that student performance is indeed a national problem that requires serious attention. Second, it begins to lay out consequential goals for students and schools.[20] Both of these represent positive changes from the past.

One underlying assumption of Goals 2000, however, is that developing goals and education standards will itself set in motion steps to bring about their accomplishment. On this premise there is much more controversy.[21] There is little evidence that the development of standards and the associated measurement of achievement *by themselves* will lead to noticeably improved student performance.

Nor is federal and state oversight of local reform plans a substitute for changing incentives. The most controversial goal, of developing opportunity-to-learn standards, or minimum levels of school inputs into the education process, has great appeal—how can we expect schools to meet more demanding academic standards without additional resources?—but also is very much at odds with the proposition that a great deal of inefficiency exists in the provision of schooling. It simply is not possible to specify a reasonable set of "required inputs" into the educational process.

The discussion here is fully consistent with the development of high standards for student performance and with the extension of these standards to better measurement of outcomes.[22] The proposed method of achieving those goals, however, is distinctly different from the traditional approach of adding more resources to the existing incentive structure.

IMPLEMENTING CHANGE

As the current U.S. public school system does not emphasize student performance, it should not be surprising that performance does not meet our expectations. But, worse, the current structure is not on a path to improvement. Most new programs offer little in the way of incentives to improve student achievement and are accompanied by little experimentation and evaluation. Each of

---

[20]At the same time, a number of the proposed goals, while politically understandable, are highly unrealistic. For example, consider "Goal 5: By the year 2000, U.S. students will be first in the world in mathematics and science achievement." Given the significant existing deficits of U.S. students in comparison to students of other countries (U.S. Department of Education, 1994) and the short time until the year 2000, it is inconceivable that this goal could be met through any actions currently being contemplated.

[21]For discussion and evaluation of this proposition, see Education Policy Committee (1994), Porter (1994), McDonnell (1994), and Ravitch (1995). On a related issue, Linn (1994) considers issues of validity in any national testing scheme that might accompany national goals.

[22]The debate about performance standards has become quite confused, with many people using the same language to mean very different things. Moreover, the underlying policies and objectives of different perspectives frequently are quite antithetical. For discussion of various interpretations of the language, see Ravitch (1995) and Manno (1995).

these needs to be changed, but change also implies different roles for the participants in the system. The roles of principals and teachers and others are considered in *Making Schools Work* and receive special emphasis by the Committee for Economic Development (1994).

In many ways, teachers are the most important ingredient of our schooling system, and they must play an active part in the development of improved schools. The teachers who will be best able to work in a new system with enhanced decisionmaking autonomy are probably quite different from many current teachers in terms of experience, training, and aspirations, among other characteristics. Current teachers cannot, however, be ignored in the process. Even though there will be a significant turnover of teachers in the next decade, the current stock of teachers will remain a substantial portion of the total teaching force for many years to come. Implementation of new systems that involve very different responsibilities and rewards must consider transition policies, such as the use of two-tiered employment contracts. New teachers under a two-tiered contract would receive very different contracts from today's standard contract. They would involve altered tenure guarantees, more risks, and greater flexibility and rewards. Existing teachers, on the other hand, would continue under existing employment rules for tenure, pay, and work conditions unless they individually opt for the new teacher contract. Such a structure is one example of an approach designed to recognize the legitimate contractual arrangements with current teachers while establishing radically different structures for the future.

State governments also need to make substantial changes in the role they play in education. The new role of states is to promote and encourage experimentation and implementation of new incentive systems. The long-run future of school reform depends on developing new information, and the states have an essential position in this. They must first work to remove unproductive "input" regulations and certification standards, which unfortunately form the core of most current state education programs. To replace these, states need to work on establishing performance standards and explicit student outcome goals. An important part of this is encouraging experimentation with alternative incentive structures and technologies and providing direct support for the evaluation and dissemination of program information. Clearly, however, local districts do not currently have sufficient capacity to develop, implement, and evaluate their own systems. Moreover, rightly or wrongly, states often mistrust individual districts and undoubtedly will resist permitting complete flexibility within local districts. To deal with local malfeasance, when local systems fail to perform at acceptable levels, states should be prepared to intervene. The form of intervention is important, however. Perhaps the best response involves the assurance to individual students and parents that alternatives will be provided for nonperforming local districts, say through providing extensive choice or voucher opportunities. The opposite approach, pursued now, is either to develop extensive input and process regulations to reduce the range of potentially unacceptable actions by local districts or to threaten to replace existing districts with state personnel. Neither provides the right incentives or any real assurance of improvement.

The role of states should evolve into a policy role and not a direct management role. As highlighted by the Committee for Economic Development (1994), states must retreat from tendencies to micromanage schools—something they cannot do effectively.

The federal government should take on a primary role in enabling standards to be developed, in supporting broad program evaluation, and in disseminating the results of evaluations. It should also be involved in supporting supplemental programs for disadvantaged and minority students. As mentioned, programs for the disadvantaged should follow the same guidelines as above but also may involve expansions of early childhood education, integrated health and nutrition programs, and other interventions to overcome background handicaps. Providing these added programs is the proper role for the federal government, which strives to ensure equality of opportunity for all citizens. The federal roles outlined here are largely consistent with current practice but are extended in directions to complement the performance emphasis proposed for schools.

Local school districts should take new responsibility for curriculum choices, managing personnel, including hiring and firing on a performance basis, and establishing closer links with businesses, particularly for the benefit of students not continuing on to colleges. While none of these departs radically from current roles, they would be significantly different in practice if states removed many of their restrictions on instruction and organization. Moreover, if major decisions devolved to local schools, new emphasis would be placed on management and leadership, and undoubtedly new capacity would have to be developed. Micromanagement by school boards is similarly not the proper focus for their attention, but setting policy is.

Businesses also have new roles. While U.S. businesses have frequently lamented the quality of workers they receive from schools, they have never worked closely with schools to define the skills and abilities they seek in prospective workers. More direct involvement in schools, perhaps coupled with long-term hiring relationships, could help both schools and businesses. Moreover, if businesses insisted that employment candidates demonstrate high scholastic performance, students would have much greater incentives to work hard in school.[23] Businesses could also be helpful in developing systems of performance incentives for school personnel while avoiding unintended adverse consequences.

There is every reason to believe that school performance can be improved. Students can do better, resources devoted to schools can be better used, and society can be better off. But optimism about the chances for improvement should not be confused with optimism that improvement will come quickly or

---

[23]The role of business incentives is emphasized in, among other places, the Committee for Economic Development (1994).

easily. Fundamental changes in perspective, organization, and day-to-day operations are required. There is tremendous enthusiasm and energy for improvement. They must be directed in productive ways.

But here our panel breaks with the tradition of calling for more funding. In fact, reform of schools will best be achieved by holding overall real expenditures constant. Schools must learn to consider trade-offs among programs and operations. They must learn to evaluate performance and eliminate programs that are not working. They must learn to seek out and expand upon incentive structures and organizational approaches that are productive. In short, they must be encouraged to make better use of existing resources. The basic concerns of economics, with its attention to the effectiveness of expenditures and to establishing appropriate incentives, must be used if schooling is to improve.

Marshall Smith observes in this volume that no one really thinks that money per se is important. What really matters is how it is spent. He is not surprised that schools as currently operated are inefficient. But surely the level of spending compared to the outcomes is important to taxpayers and should be important to policymakers. In education it has not been.

Economic discipline cannot be imposed blindly. It is recognized that variations in local circumstances, cases of special need, and start-up costs for new programs may require additional financing. But poor performance is certainly not, as it is often viewed today, an automatically convincing case for more money. Quite the contrary. In the long run, the nation may find it appropriate to increase school expenditures. It is simply hard to tell at this point. But it is clear that expanding resources first and looking for reform second is very unlikely to lead to an improved system—a more expensive system, certainly, but a system with better performance, unlikely.

REFERENCES

Bishop, John. 1989. "Is the test score decline responsible for the productivity growth decline?" *American Economic Review* 79(1):178-197.

Committee for Economic Development. 1994. *Putting Learning First: Governing and Managing the Schools for High Achievement.* New York: Committee for Economic Development.

Congressional Budget Office. 1986. *Trends in Educational Achievement.* Washington, D.C.: Congressional Budget Office.

Education Policy Committee. 1994. *Looking Back, Thinking Ahead: American School Reform, 1993–1995.* Indianapolis, Ind.: Educational Excellence Network, Hudson Institute.

Glass, Gene V., and Mary Lee Smith. 1979. "Meta-analysis of research on class size and achievement." *Educational Evaluation and Policy Analysis* 1(1):2-16.

Hanushek, Eric A. 1986. "The economics of schooling: production and efficiency in public schools." *Journal of Economic Literature* 24(3):1141-1177.

_____. 1989. "The impact of differential expenditures on school performance." *Educational Researcher* 18(4):45-51.

_____. 1992. "The trade-off between child quantity and quality." *Journal of Political Economy* 100(1):84-117.

_____. 1994a. "Money might matter somewhere: a response to Hedges, Laine, and Greenwald." *Educational Researcher* 23(4):5-8.

_____. 1994b. "School Resources and Student Performance." Paper prepared for the Brookings Institution conference, "Do School Resources Matter?"

_____. 1995. "Rationalizing school spending: efficiency, externalities, and equity, and their connection to rising costs." In *Individual and Social Responsibility*, Victor Fuchs, ed. Chicago: University of Chicago Press/NBER.

Hanushek, Eric A., and Steven G. Rivkin. 1994. "Understanding the 20th Century Explosion in U.S. School Costs." Working Paper 388. Rochester Center for Economic Research, Rochester, N.Y.

Hanushek, Eric A., et al. 1994. *Making Schools Work: Improving Performance and Controlling Costs*. Washington, D.C.: Brookings Institution.

Haveman, Robert H., and Barbara L. Wolfe. 1984. "Schooling and economic well-being: the role of nonmarket effects." *Journal of Human Resources* 19(3):377-407.

Hedges, Larry V., Richard D. Laine, and Rob Greenwald. 1994. "Does money matter? A meta–analysis of studies of the effects of differential school inputs on student outcomes." *Educational Researcher* 23(3):5-14.

Jorgenson, Dale W., and Barbara M. Fraumeni. 1992. "Investment in education and U.S. economic growth." *Scandinavian Journal of Economics* 94(Suppl.):51-70.

Kenny, Lawrence W. 1982. "Economies of scale in schooling." *Economics of Education Review* 2(1):1-24.

Kosters, Marvin H. 1991. "Wages and demographics." Pp. 1-32. In *Workers and Their Wages*, Marvin H. Kosters, ed. Washington, D.C.: AEI Press.

Linn, Robert L. 1994. "Evaluating the technical quality of proposed national examination systems." *American Journal of Education* 102(4):565-580.

Lucas, Robert E. 1988. "On the mechanics of economic development." *Journal of Monetary Economics* 22 (July):3-42.

Manno, Bruno V. 1995. "Educational outcomes do matter." *Public Interest* 119(Spring):19-27.

Marshall, Ray, and Marc Tucker. 1992. *Thinking for a Living*. New York: Basic Books.

McDonnell, Lorraine M. 1994. "Assessment policy as persuasion and regulation." *American Journal of Education* 102(4):394-420.

McKnight, Curtis C., F. J. Crosswhite, J. A. Dossey, E. Kifer, J. O. Swafford, Ken J. Travers, and T. J. Cooney. 1989. *The Underachieving Curriculum: Assessing U.S. School Mathematics from an International Perspective*. Champaign, Ill.: Stipes Publishing Co.

McMahon, Walter W. 1991. "Relative returns to human and physical capital in the U.S. and efficient investment strategies." *Economics of Education Review* 10(4):283-296.

Mosteller, Frederick. 1995. "The Tennessee study of class size in the early school grades." *The Future of Children 5*, no. 2 (Summer/Fall 1995):113-27.

Murnane, Richard J., and Richard R. Nelson. 1984. "Production and innovation when techniques are tacit: the case of education." *Journal of Economic Behavior and Organization* 5:353-373.

Murphy, Kevin M., and Finis Welch. 1989. "Wage premiums for college graduates: recent growth and possible explanations." *Educational Researcher* 18(4):17-26.

National Commission on Excellence in Education. 1983. *A nation at risk: the imperative for educational reform*. Washington, D.C.: U.S. Government Printing Office.

National Research Council. 1989. *Everybody Counts: A Report to the Nation on the Future of Mathematics Education*. Washington, D.C.: National Academy Press.

Porter, Andrew C. 1994. "National standards and school improvement in the 1990s: issues and promise." *American Journal of Education* 102(4):421-449.

Ravitch, Diane. 1995. *National Standards in American Education: A Citizen's Guide*. Washington, D.C.: Brookings Institution.

Romer, Paul. 1990. "Endogenous technological change." *Journal of Political Economy* 99(5):S71-S102.

U.S. Department of Education, National Center for Education Statistics. 1994. *The Condition of Education.* Washington, D.C.: U.S. Government Printing Office.

Wolfe, Barbara L., and Sam Zuvekas. 1994. "Nonmarket outcomes of schooling." *PEER Background Paper.* Institute for Research on Poverty, University of Wisconsin. Discussion paper no. 1065-95.

Word, Elizabeth, John Johnston, Helen Pate Bain, B. DeWayne Fulton, Jayne Boyd Zaharies, Martha Nannette Lintz, Charles M. Achilles, John Folger, and Carolyn Breda. 1990. *Student/Teacher Achievement Ratio (STAR), Tennessee's K–3 Class Size Study: Final Summary Report, 1985–1990.* Nashville: Tennessee State Department of Education.

CHAPTER 4

Changes in the Structure of Wages[1]

BROOKS PIERCE
Texas A&M University

FINIS WELCH
Texas A&M University and Unicon Research

How important is schooling to labor market success? In a word, very. In 1992 white men with a college education earned about 50 percent more per week on average than white men with only a high school education. Fifty percent is a large wage premium to command, yet the premium is even greater if we restrict attention to those relatively young people who completed their schooling in the past 10 years. Furthermore, the difference in labor market opportunities for college versus high school graduates translates into differences in employment, hours worked, industries, and occupations as well as to differences in wages. In 1992 the percentage of college-educated men who worked full time year-round was about 10 points higher than for men with only a high school education, and college-educated men worked on average 200 hours more than men with only a high school education. Those with more schooling were also more likely to find higher-paying white collar jobs. But the variations in these averages are large enough that a college degree is no guarantee of success. For example, in 1992 the probability that a randomly chosen high school graduate earned more than a randomly chosen college-educated worker was over 20 percent. Nevertheless, it is clear that the labor market rewards associated with greater schooling are substantial.

This has not always been the case. In fact, the economic returns to education were much lower only 15 years ago. The rapid divergence in labor market outcomes across schooling groups is only one of the dramatic changes in relative

[1]This research was supported by U.S. Department of Health and Human Services grant number R01HD2173-04 to Unicon Research. The opinions expressed here are those of the authors and are not necessarily those of the sponsoring or other governmental agencies.

wages for workers in the United States during the 1980s. In this chapter we summarize what is known about the changing wage structure and some of the more prominent explanations of those changes. The principal findings for the earnings of white men over the past 25 years are that returns to schooling and returns to labor market experience have risen and that wage inequality, both overall and within schooling and experience groups, has risen. The timing and magnitudes of these changes are not always coincident. Inequality increased more or less continually over the same period, but schooling returns actually fell in the 1970s. However, inequality and returns to schooling and experience all rose concurrently in the 1980s. The 1980s were also an interesting period for changing relative wages across gender and racial groups. That period witnessed a pause in the convergence of wages between black and white men as well as the beginnings of rapid wage gains for white women relative to white men.

Validating explanations for these changes has proven difficult, and one would not expect any single factor to account for all of the dimensions of the changing wage structure. However, many of the shifts in relative wages suggest a general rise in the value of what is thought of as generalized ability or "skill." This being the case, researchers have looked to shifts in demand that favor more skilled workers as a possible explanation. Hypotheses about shifts in demand are especially attractive since relative prices and quantities have sometimes moved in the same direction. One possibility is that shifts in product demand—for example, as a result of changing international trade flows—cause some sectors to shrink or grow and result in labor demand shifts in favor of the types of workers employed in the growing sectors. One can assess this theory by determining if expanding industries are the ones that tend to hire more skilled workers. Our impression is that, at least for the education dimension, the data support this version of the demand shift story as a partial explanation. However, most of the change in employment for college graduates is attributable to shifts in industries rather than the changing importance of college-intensive industries.

A second possibility, nonneutral technical change, perhaps linked to the changing availability and power of computers, is often put forward to account for some within-industry employment shifts. This hypothesis is plausible but by its nature difficult to evaluate. One method of accumulating indirect evidence is to determine what types of jobs or occupations are growing. Employment of college-educated workers grew rapidly in the 1970s and 1980s in technical fields such as engineering and computer science and in financial and business-related occupations. In contrast, employment of people with less schooling has shifted toward a different set of occupations, where wages tend to be lower than average. It is not obvious whether this reflects changing labor demand conditions or other factors, such as changing quality of secondary schooling or different raw abilities among those in more recent birth cohorts who do not pursue college degrees. But none of these possibilities suggests that the trends documented below are likely to reverse themselves in the near future.

THE CHANGING WAGE STRUCTURE

This section summarizes some of the salient features of the changing relative wages over the past 25 years. Our particular concern is with relative wages across different education levels, as most would argue that these groupings indicate real skill differences and that changing relative wages reflect changes in skill returns. To complement the trends in relative prices, we also show trends in relative education quantities. We found that, by and large, relative prices move in favor of higher-skilled workers over the period as a whole. Also, relative quantities are frequently seen to move in the same direction. This suggests that the demand for better-educated workers has risen and perhaps that shifts in labor demand in favor of skilled workers can help rationalize observed changes in other relative wages.

Figure 4.1 presents relative wages between college and high school graduates, measured as a percentage differential among white men. We show series for workers who are one to 10 years out of school and for workers of all experience levels. The series track each other, with more dramatic changes in returns to college for younger workers. Among these younger workers, the wage premium earned by college graduates was about 35 percent in the early years of the data. During the 1970s the premium fell substantially, to a low of about 27 percent in 1979. This drop was likely caused by large increases in the number of people attending college about 1970, either because of the Vietnam War or as part of

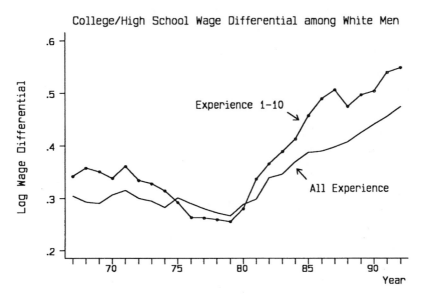

FIGURE 4.1   College wage premium by experience level.

rational educational choices by an unusually large birth cohort. The fall was precipitous enough to induce at least one economist to suggest that Americans might be overinvesting in schooling (Freeman, 1976). Yet the fall in returns to a college degree in the 1970s were dwarfed by the rising returns of the 1980s. By the end of the data the college premium was about 55 percent for recent entrants into the job market and 48 percent over all experience levels. It is not much of an exaggeration to say that the college/high school wage premium has doubled in the past 15 years. The similar timing of the two series suggests that this phenomenon reflects something specific to time rather than something specific to birth cohorts. Although in Figure 4.1 the relative earnings of college and high school graduates are plotted rather than each group's earnings levels separately, we show below that the rising college wage premium apparent in the figure is driven largely by declines in the absolute level of real wages of high school graduates. At least as far as the labor market is concerned, the 1990s have been a bad time to be a young high school graduate.

Figure 4.2 shows much the same trends but uses a different metric. Here we plot, for the two different experience groups, the college graduates' average centile location in the earnings distribution for high school graduates. This is the probability that a randomly chosen high school graduate has lower wages than a randomly chosen college graduate. This metric is useful when the relative wage

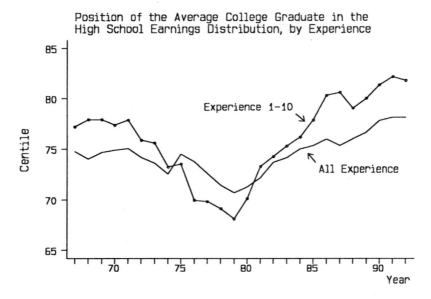

FIGURE 4.2   Relative earnings of college graduates.

dispersion across schooling groups is changing, because it is ordinal in nature.[2] For instance, among workers one to 10 years out of school in 1967, the probability that a randomly chosen college graduate had higher earnings than a randomly chosen high school graduate was approximately 77 percent. For this experience group, the probability fell in the early to mid-1970s and then reversed trend and has risen more or less steadily since. Among workers of all experience levels, education returns by this metric follow the same trends but in a more muted fashion. These location statistics seem small given the benchmark of 50 percent for perfect distributional congruence; there is a lot of overlap in the college and high school wage distributions. Also note that the timing and trends in education returns are roughly consistent across the different metrics in Figures 4.1 and 4.2. This implies that the higher college/high school wage ratios of newer entrants in the 1980s reflect ordinal as well as cardinal wage divergence.

One might wonder whether the trends in Figures 4.1 and 4.2 are attributable to some economy-wide changes in the value of the additional skills embodied in a college degree or merely to a change in the quality of newer cohorts of college and high school graduates. One way to address this question is to follow the same cohort of workers as they age. Table 4.1 presents the college/high school wage differential for different cohorts at different points in time. For example, the last number in the first column indicates that among workers who first entered the labor market in 1970 the college/high school wage differential then was 39.2 percent. Moving across columns in the same row indicates what happened to this wage premium as the cohort aged. In the case of the 1970 entry cohort, the college wage premium fell throughout the 1970s, to a low of 27.1 percent in 1980, and then rose fairly rapidly to 36.9 percent in 1985 and 43.2 percent in 1990. The college premiums for other entry cohorts exhibit this same pattern. When following the same cohort of workers, we are holding fixed the quality of the educational instruction and the underlying raw abilities of the different schooling groups at the time they received their education. For the 1970 entry cohort, and the others as well, there is a pattern similar to those in Figures 4.1 and 4.2, and this leads to the suspicion that there is some real change in the value of skills that the college graduates hold. This does not rule out the possibility that the

---

[2]This metric is constructed as follows. Suppose the earnings of one male college graduate are in the 68th centile of the earnings distribution of male high school graduates of the same age. This number (68) is the probability that a randomly chosen high school graduate will have lower earnings than this particular college graduate. Averaging this number over all college graduates yields the probability that a randomly chosen college graduate will have higher earnings than a randomly chosen high school graduate, or more simply the average centile location of college graduates in the distribution of high school graduates' earnings. For the location statistics we compare annual earnings distributions among full-time, year-round workers. Computations for broad age or experience categories require first calculating location statistics by single year of age or experience and then taking simple averages across the different age experience levels.

TABLE 4.1   College Wage Premium by Labor Market Cohort

Year of Initial Labor Market Entry	Calendar Year				
	1970	1975	1980	1985	1990
1930	21.4				
1935	25.6	26.8			
1940	26.6	25.1	26.1		
1945	28.2	28.0	28.7	31.8	
1950	31.7	30.5	28.8	32.3	37.6
1955	32.0	30.8	31.6	33.6	37.8
1960	33.3	31.1	28.2	37.6	38.2
1965	34.8	32.4	30.0	37.9	40.9
1970	39.2	29.0	27.1	36.9	43.2
1975		26.6	29.2	38.4	45.0
1980			35.8	47.9	51.1
1985				48.9	51.4
1990					51.9

Notes: The college premia given are the difference between average log weekly wages of college graduates and high school graduates, multiplied by 100. Numbers reflect averages within five year periods centered on the stated year; e.g., "1970" is the average over the 1968-1972 year period, etc. Moving left to right within a row shows the changing college premium for a given entry cohort as it ages.

quality of skills of high school graduates has changed across birth cohorts, but it does indicate that the trends in Figures 4.1 and 4.2 are not solely due to such changes in quality.

To this point the concentration has been exclusively on the college/high school wage premium of white males as a measure of returns to schooling. It is useful, of course, to demonstrate that these trends hold for other demographic groups and at other points in the schooling distribution. Table 4.2 presents the college/high school wage premium for different racial and gender groups. Here we average the premia within subperiods of roughly equal length, with the 1973–1979 period capturing most of the declining schooling returns. Most of these demographic groups have higher college/high school wage premiums at the end of the data than in the 1967–1972 period. In all cases the returns to college graduates rose from the 1973–1979 period to the 1980–1986 period, and in all cases returns rise from 1980–1986 to 1987–1992. The data in Table 4.2 suggest

TABLE 4.2   College Wage Premium by Race and Gender

	White Men	White Women	Black Men	Black Women
A. 1-10 Years of Experience				
1967-72	34.8	41.1	36.5	51.9
1973-79	28.2	37.2	37.2	40.4
1980-86	39.0	42.1	44.2	40.8
1987-92	51.2	51.9	44.5	45.3
B. 1-40 Years of Experience				
1967-72	30.2	37.9	27.9	49.4
1973-79	28.4	36.2	30.2	37.6
1980-86	34.6	37.8	36.1	41.3
1987-92	43.4	47.4	43.7	48.4

Notes: Numbers given are the difference between average log weekly wages of college graduates and high school graduates, multiplied by 100. Averages are fixed-weight averages over single years of experience. Within subperiods simple averages are taken over single years.

that the measured phenomenon among white men captures marketwide effects that are also relevant for the other demographic groups.[3]

Table 4.3 gives measured returns to schooling at various points in the schooling distribution. Here the sample is split into four education groups (0–11, 12, 13–15, and 16 or more years of schooling). Each column gives the average wage earned by those in the stated schooling group relative to the average wage in the next schooling group. As before, wage premiums are given in percentages. These statistics would be fairly sensitive to any changes over time in the underlying raw abilities of the people composing each schooling group, perhaps especially at the lower end of the schooling distribution, and so should be interpreted with care. In most cases, however, the returns to education are greater at the end

---

[3]Most of the statistics presented here focus on outcomes for white men, so as to avoid some difficult measurement issues and complicating factors (changes in discrimination, labor force attachment of women, etc.) that do not directly bear on the importance of schooling. The 1980s brought dramatic changes in relative wages across racial and gender boundaries, and these changes are probably related to the returns-to-schooling phenomenon discussed here.

TABLE 4.3   Returns to Schooling among White Men, by Schooling Level

	High School	Some College	College
A. 1-10 Years of Experience			
1967-72	25.3	14.4	20.3
1973-79	26.2	11.3	16.9
1980-86	26.2	16.2	22.9
1987-92	23.4	18.0	33.2
B. 1-40 Years of Experience			
1967-72	21.8	12.3	17.8
1973-79	24.0	10.5	17.9
1980-86	28.5	12.8	21.7
1987-92	30.1	15.9	27.4

Notes: Numbers presented are 100 times the difference in average log wages between the schooling group listed and the next lower schooling group. Fixed weight averages are taken across experience levels. The numbers reported are simple averages of annual statistics within each subperiod.

of the time period than at the beginning. We take this to mean that trends in the college/high school premium are representative of trends in the returns to schooling more broadly defined.

These changes in relative wages would be expected to affect the amount of time spent working, especially if the wage changes are thought to result largely from shifting relative demand in favor of more skilled workers. Table 4.4 gives various employment measures for the broad schooling groups at different points in time. "Percent FTYR" gives the percentage by schooling group that worked full time (at least 35 hours per week) and year-round (at least 50 weeks in the year). The columns "Weeks" and "Annual Hours" give the average number of weeks and hours worked per year. All of these measures are positively related to education, although high school graduates and those with some college are similar. These measures have trended downward for all groups but have fallen much more for the lower schooling groups. For example, annual hours worked by college graduates fell by about 25 hours (a little more than 1 percent), as opposed to about 100 hours (about 4 percent) for those with high school or some college education, and about 350 hours (over 15 percent) for those who did not complete high school.

These statistics, plus the fact that average schooling levels have increased substantially in the past 25 years, indicate that the amount of total employment

TABLE 4.4   Employment Status, by Schooling Level, All Experience Levels

Education Level	1967-1972			1987-1992		
	Percent FTYR	Weeks	Annual Hours	Percent FTYR	Weeks	Annual Hours
0-11 years	68.6	45.4	1978	52.1	38.3	1634
12 years	80.9	48.4	2137	74.8	46.4	2041
13-15 years	80.8	47.9	2122	74.5	45.9	2033
16+ years	89.4	49.9	2274	85.3	48.7	2248

Notes: Columns labelled "Percent FTYR" give the percent of that education group that works full-time, year-round. Columns labelled "Weeks" give the average number of weeks worked per year. Columns labelled "Annual Hours" give average number of hours worked per year. The sample is for white men, experience levels 1-40.

attributable to college graduates has risen over time. Table 4.5 gives the changing distribution of employment across the four broad schooling groups. The purpose of the table is to present changes in relative quantities to complement the results given above on changing relative prices. For example, in the period 1967–1972 only about 16 percent of white male workers had a college degree; 20 years later more than 25 percent did. Since the numbers of hours and weeks

TABLE 4.5   Distribution of Workers and Weeks Worked over Schooling Levels, All Experience Levels

Education Level	1967-1972			1987-1992		
	Workers	Weeks	Annual Hours	Workers	Weeks	Annual Hours
0-11 years	31.7	30.2	29.8	16.7	14.1	13.5
12 years	38.3	38.9	38.8	36.5	37.2	36.8
13-15 years	14.1	14.2	14.2	21.7	21.7	21.8
16+ years	16.0	16.7	17.2	25.1	27.0	27.9
All	100	100	100	100	100	100

Notes: Columns labelled "Workers" give the distribution of people across education groups. Columns labelled "Weeks" and "Annual Hours" give the weeks worked- and annual hours worked-weighted distributions, respectively, of people across education groups. The samples are for white men, experience levels 1-40.

worked are lower for the lower schooling groups, and because hours and weeks worked fell much more over time for the lower schooling groups, the distributions of weeks and hours worked show greater shifts toward the college educated. The changes would be even more dramatic if the labor supplied were measured by earnings. The fact that relative quantities shifted toward the higher education groups is important because it adds support to the idea that the changes in returns to schooling over the period as a whole were driven mainly by demand-side phenomena. College-educated workers command a higher wage premium than they once did despite the fact that this group of workers supplies so much more labor now. It is reasonable to interpret much of the observed changes in relative quantities as a supply response to these changing demand conditions.

INDUSTRY-BASED COMPOSITION EFFECTS

The fact that the relative price of college-educated labor increased during a period when its relative quantity rose implies growth in the demand for college graduates that has outpaced any growth in supply. At the same time, other parts of the wage structure have changed in ways consistent with increased demand for skilled workers. Experience returns rose in the 1980s. In addition, the wage premiums enjoyed by males at the top end of the wage distribution rose throughout the 1970s and 1980s. It might be said that the 1980s wage convergence between males and females partly reflected greater returns to cognitive skills, as males disproportionately relied on or worked in jobs that required physical skills.

Identifying the sources of wage structure changes has proven difficult. Given that relative wages and quantities have frequently moved together, some prominent explanations are based on industry-related shifts in demand. For example, changing demands for goods produced domestically, induced by changing trade flows or different income elasticities of demand, could change relative factor demands in favor of those types of workers disproportionately employed in the expanding sectors. Similarly, expansion of certain industries as a result of factor-neutral technical changes could change factor demands. These explanations have some plausibility given the large industrial shifts in the United States in recent years and can, in principle, be verified by analyzing the labor composition of expanding and shrinking sectors. Specifically, with respect to the increased demand for college graduates, growth can be accounted for in one of two ways— either by growth of industries that have greater-than-average demands for college graduates or by individual industries increasing the number of college graduates in the face of a rising relative price for them. The first of these effects entails significant growth in college-intensive industries; the second corresponds to shifts in labor demand in favor of college graduates in individual industries.

To address these possible effects, Table 4.6 shows which industries have expanded and contracted as well as which are college intensive. The first three columns give the share of aggregate workers employed in each of 11 industry

TABLE 4.6   Employment Shares and Percentage College Labor by Industry, 1968–1991

Industry	Employment Shares			Percentage College Labor		
	(1) 1968	(2) 1991	(3) Change 1968-91	(4) 1968	(5) 1991	(6) Change 1968-91
Agriculture and Mining	5.7	3.9	-1.8	8.9	24.6	15.7
Construction	6.6	6.6	0.0	9.1	19.0	9.9
Durables Mfg.	18.5	11.1	-7.4	14.6	28.9	14.3
Non-Durables Mfg.	11.7	7.8	-3.9	14.2	26.9	12.7
Transportation and Utilities	7.4	7.2	-0.2	11.5	29.0	17.6
Wholesale Trade	3.8	4.4	0.6	20.6	34.7	14.1
Retail Trade	13.0	13.9	0.9	11.2	23.5	12.3
Professional and Financial	11.5	18.9	7.4	34.3	51.4	17.0
Education and Welfare	8.3	10.5	2.2	67.1	68.2	1.0
Government	6.4	6.2	-0.2	24.0	44.5	20.5
Other Services	7.2	9.6	2.4	14.0	30.9	16.9
All Industries	100.0	100.0	0.0	20.6	37.0	16.3

Notes: All quantities refer to fixed-wage weighted aggregates of annual hours across experience, sex, and education. Employment shares refer to the percentage of aggregate fixed-wage weighted labor hours employed in the industry. The percentage college labor refers to the percent of the fixed wage weighted labor accounted for by the college wage aggregate. See text.

groups in 1968 and 1988 and the percentage change in these shares between those years.[4]   The final three columns give the fraction of aggregate workers in an industry accounted for by the college educated.[5]   The shrinking sectors—agriculture, mining, and the manufacturing industries—tend to be less college intensive than average. For example, 14.6 percent of the employment in durables manufacturing industries during the period 1967 to 1969 was college-educated labor, and

---

[4]In table 4.6, all quantities refer to fixed-wage weighted aggregates of annual hours across experience, gender, and education cells. For aggregation across education levels, those with less than a high school diploma are assigned a weight of 0.82 for aggregation with high school graduates, and

that sector shrank by 40 percent over the 20-year period. Expanding industries, especially professional and financial ones, tend to be relatively college intensive. In 1968 over 30 percent of the employment in the professional and financial services industry aggregate involved college-educated workers, and employment in that sector grew by about as much as durables manufacturing shrank. The last column in the table also suggests that the within-industry changes in education levels have been extraordinary; the fraction of college labor increased in all industries.

A simple employment change decomposition can help us understand the relative importance of these effects. If the fraction of overall labor employed in industry i in year t is K_{it}, and the share of college labor in the industry is R_{it}, the aggregate fraction college, R_t, can be expressed as

$$R_t = \sum_i K_{it} R_{it}$$

and the change in this fraction from year τ to year t may be written as

$$R_t - R_\tau = \sum_i (K_{it} - K_{i\tau})(R_{i\tau} - R_\tau) + \sum_i K_{it}(R_{it} - R_{i\tau})$$

The first term in this expression captures what might be called a "between" effect of changing industrial composition. It is the change in industry share times the difference between the college-educated fraction in the industry and the college-educated fraction in the economy as a whole. If expanding industries are more college intensive than average, this term will be positive. The second term is the "within"-industry effect, measured as a weighted average of changing college intensities, where weights are the fixed industry employment shares. Therefore, changing industry composition cannot contribute to the within-industry effect, which holds industry composition fixed by construction. If explanations based on industry-related demand shifts are correct, the between component of the change in R_t must be substantial and positive. As implemented here, the industry index i ranges over 49 separate industries, the time index t refers to the 1987–1989 period, and the time index τ refers to the 1967–1969 period.

Table 4.7 gives results from this decomposition, with the industry classification aggregated up to the industry groups corresponding to Table 4.6. The columns correspond to the between, within, and total effects, respectively. The employment effects listed in column one for particular industries are positive for

---

those with 13 to 15 years of schooling are assigned a weight of 0.696 for aggregation with high school graduates and a weight of 0.296 for aggregation with college graduates. Employment shares are calculated as a percentage of the aggregate fixed-wage weighted labor hours employed in the industry. Tables 4.6 and 4.7 present data for three-year windows: 1968 refers to a simple average for the years 1967–1969, and 1988 refers to a simple average for the years 1987–1989. See Murphy and Welch (1993) for further details.

[5]The percentage college labor refers to the percent of the fixed-wage weighted labor accounted for by the college wage aggregate.

TABLE 4.7   Decomposition of Growth in College Employment, 1968–1991

Industry	(1) Between Effect	(2) Within Effect	(3) Total Effect
Agriculture and Mining	0.27	0.73	1.00
Construction	0.00	0.67	0.67
Durables Manufacturing	0.67	2.08	2.75
Non-Durables Manufacturing	0.52	1.13	1.65
Transportation and Utilities	0.04	1.30	1.34
Wholesale Trade	-0.00	0.59	0.59
Retail Trade	-0.17	1.86	1.69
Professional and Finance	1.32	2.44	3.76
Education and Welfare	0.79	0.15	0.94
Government	0.07	1.25	1.32
Other Services	0.24	1.06	1.30
All Industries	3.75	13.26	17.01

Notes: Quantities are computed as noted in table 4.1. Columns (1)-(3) give the within- and between-decomposition as described in the text.

the most part, implying that employment has expanded most in the sectors that hire more college graduates than average and contracted most in the sectors that hire disproportionately more high school graduates. For instance, the contractions in the agriculture/mining and manufacturing industries contributed 1.46 percentage points of the 3.75-percentage-point increase in the share of college labor. Expansions in professional/finance and education/welfare, industries that typically have more educated workers, account for another 2.11-percentage-point increase in the between-industry component.

Although these industry composition changes help explain the increased relative demand for college graduates, they by no means explain the majority of the total effect. The last row of Table 4.7 shows that, for all industries aggregated, 3.75 percentage points of the 17.01-percentage-point increase in the college share of aggregate employment is attributable to the between-industry component. The rest of the growth in college labor over this period is attributable to growth in the college-educated fraction within industries. Since the college-educated fraction of workers increased in each industry group, the within-industry effects in column two are all positive. The demand in growth for better-educated workers in each of these industries was great enough to offset the incentive to substitute away from college labor that is caused by its increased relative cost.[6]

It is clear from Tables 4.6 and 4.7 that explanations based on industry composition effects can account for only a portion of the demand shift toward college graduates. What, then, can be made of the within-industry changes? One possible explanation is that of a nonfactor-neutral technical change at the level of individual industries. Perhaps a more or less pervasive computer and information revolution has shifted factor demands in favor of better-educated, better-skilled workers. This explanation may strike some as plausible, others as merely a relabeling of our ignorance. In any case, the explanation is difficult to verify or reject given the available data. One approach is to identify the occupations where employment of various education groups rose the most. For instance, do college graduates increasingly go into higher-paying occupations while high school graduates increasingly go into lower-paying ones? Or perhaps there are common themes describing the types of occupations that are growing or shrinking. The next section investigates the possibilities.

Occupational Shifts

The U.S. labor market has become increasingly segmented by schooling levels in the sense that wages and hours-worked differentials have expanded, especially in the 1980s. Some portion of these changes is plausibly related to industry shifts caused by changing product demands. Yet the industrial composition of the U.S. work force does not necessarily reveal much about the tasks performed by workers with different levels of schooling. Examining the occupational composition of various schooling groups gives additional insight into workers' functions.

It would be interesting to know if the schooling-related segmentation observed in wages and employment applies to occupations as well. The types of occupations that high school and college graduates enter and their associated wages also have the potential to reflect any changes in the "quality" of the graduates. For example, what types of jobs do high school graduates typically get? A simple way to approach these issues is to treat the wages of a given schooling group as a weighted average of the wages prevalent in the occupations where that group works. Then, the changing wages of, say, high school graduates can be thought of as deriving from a change in occupations (for given occupational wages) or from a change in the wages of high school graduates in given

---

[6]Similar but more direct attempts at mapping trade flows to changing labor demands via changes in industrial composition also give results that go in the right direction but are again relatively weak. See Murphy and Welch (1992).

occupations holding the occupational distribution fixed. If we let w_{sot} represent average log wages of schooling group s in occupation o at time t, and f_{sot} represents the fraction of schooling group s at date t that are in occupation o, the average log wage of schooling group s at date t (w_{st}) is given by

$$w_{st} = \sum_{0} f_{sot} w_{sot},$$

That is, wages are a weighted average (across occupations, with weights given by f_{sot}) of occupation-specific wages for that schooling group. Equivalently,

$$w_{st} = \sum_{o} f_{sot} w_o^* + \sum_{o} f_{sot}(w_{sot} - w_o^*).$$

where w_o^* is the average wage in occupation o that by construction does not vary with time or schooling group. The first term captures changes through time in occupational distributions, f_{sot}, holding fixed the occupational wage premium w_o^*. Because this term reflects only movements across occupations, it is a "between-occupation" effect. The second term, however, captures changing wages within occupations ($w_{sot} - w_o^*$), and can therefore be thought of as including changing wages "within occupation." This partitioning of wage changes is useful because it separately identifies the component of wage changes due only to changing jobs.

Table 4.8 gives the within/between-occupation schooling premium decomposition for high school and college graduates. Newer entrants (those with one to 10 years of experience) are considered, as well as all experience levels. Two subperiods, 1970–1981 and 1982–1990, must be considered separately because of changes in the occupational classification scheme used in the data. For the purposes of presentation, the wages of each schooling group, and the between-occupation component are normed relative to average wages over each subperiod. For example, the number –5.7 in the first row under "Total" for high school workers indicates that in 1970–1972 young high school workers earned 5.7 percent less than all new entrants in the 1970–1981 subperiod. Of that deficit, 3.3 percentage points can be attributed to high school workers in that time period being in occupations with lower-than-average wages; the remainder of 2.3 percent is attributed to a within-occupation differential. Wages of young high school graduates fell by about 3.1 percent between 1970–1972 and 1979–1981. About four-fifths of the decline can be attributed to a shifting occupational distribution, with young high school graduates increasingly entering occupations with lower-than-average wages. The 1980s saw an even greater erosion in this group's wages, with most but not all of the change attributable to effects within occupational categories.

Compare this to the experience of young college graduates. Wages for this group fell enough in the 1970s that the college/high school wage premium fell during this period (recall Figure 4.1). Most of the decline in the 1970s can be

TABLE 4.8   Between- and Within-Occupation Wage Effects, by Schooling Level

	High School			College		
	Total	Between	Within	Total	Between	Within
A. Experience 1-10						
1970s						
1970-72	-5.7	-3.3	-2.3	31.1	19.3	11.8
1973-75	-4.8	-4.0	-0.8	27.4	18.2	9.3
1976-78	-5.9	-6.1	0.1	21.6	15.7	5.8
1979-81	-8.8	-5.9	-2.8	21.2	17.4	3.8
1980s						
1982-84	-9.6	-8.8	-0.8	31.0	23.3	7.7
1985-87	-14.8	-9.3	-5.5	34.4	24.8	9.6
1988-90	-17.3	-9.2	-8.0	32.7	23.8	9.0
B. Experience 1-40						
1970s						
1970-72	-3.1	-2.3	-0.8	31.1	18.9	12.2
1973-75	-1.7	-3.0	1.3	30.4	18.9	11.5
1976-78	-3.4	-4.1	0.7	27.5	18.0	9.5
1979-81	-5.0	-4.3	-0.7	26.2	19.2	7.0
1980s						
1982-84	-6.9	-7.3	0.4	30.6	20.4	10.2
1985-87	-9.6	-8.1	-1.5	31.7	20.4	11.3
1988-90	-13.7	-8.5	-5.3	31.1	20.0	11.1

Notes: Columns marked "Total" give the wage differential, in percentage terms, between the indicated schooling group and the overall average wage in the relevant decade. The "Total" figures are partitioned into one component due to the occupational distribution of the schooling group ("Between") and a remainder ("Within"). See text for details. The 1970s and 1980s are considered separately because of a change in occupational classification systems in 1982; within subperiods we take simple averages over three year bands.

attributed to within-occupation effects. Wages for this group went up slightly in the 1980s, with about one-third of the change attributable to across-occupation shifts and the remainder to a within-occupation phenomenon. The contrast across the college and high school groups in the importance of occupational shifts is interesting; clearly, a portion of the increasing college/high school wage premium between 1970 and 1990 was due to the fact that there was an occupational downgrading among high school graduates. The panel for all experience levels reveals similar patterns—a convergence in the wages of college and high school graduates during the 1970s along with a divergence in the 1980s and a steady erosion in the types of occupations that high school graduates occupy. The college educated experienced no such erosion.

Table 4.9 uses this between/within-occupation methodology to compare the wages of college graduates with those of high school graduates and those with some college (13 to 15 years of schooling). The first four columns compare college graduates and high school graduates. The columns labeled "College Between" and "High School Between" are repeated from Table 4.8, and the columns labeled "Wage Differences" and "Within Differences" are simple differences (across schooling groups) of the "Total" and "Within" columns, respectively, of Table 4.8. Most of the changing college/high school wage differential can be attributed to within-occupation changes. Yet there is clearly a movement of high school graduates into lower-wage occupations. For example, the wages of these two schooling groups converged by about 3 percentage points during the 1970s for the sample of workers with one to 40 years of experience, even though changing occupational distributions alone indicate a *divergence* of 2.3 percentage points [(4.3 − 2.3) + (19.2 − 18.9)].

The last four columns of Table 4.9 show the same analysis for the college/some-college comparison. There is not quite as much wage convergence in the 1970s or wage divergence in the 1980s in the college/some-college comparisons, but workers with some college education have typically moved into less lucrative occupations over time. For example, among new workers in the 1970s, the wage premium to college versus some college fell by about 2.1 percentage points (20.6 − 18.5), whereas the movement of the some-college group into lower-paying occupations alone would have resulted in a wage *divergence* of 5.7 percentage points.

In short, then, the increasing segmentation by schooling level observed in wages and employment does seem to extend to occupations. Table 4.10 identifies the occupations that gained or lost the most employment of given schooling classes along with each occupation's wage premium.[7] For example, in the 1970s the occupational category "Managers, Not Classified Elsewhere" exhibited the

---

[7]The occupational wage premium is the w^*_o discussed in the between/within decomposition above, minus the average wage of all workers in this period. The calculations in Table 4.10 are for workers with 1 to 40 years of experience.

Improving America's Schools: The Role of Incentives

TABLE 4.9   Relative Wage Decompositions

	College vs. High School				College vs. Some College			
	Wage Diff	College Between	HS Between	Within Diff	Wage Diff	College Between	Some Col Between	Within Diff
A. Experience 1-10								
1970s								
1970-72	36.8	19.3	-3.3	14.1	20.6	19.3	6.8	8.1
1973-75	32.2	18.2	-4.0	10.0	20.9	18.2	3.9	6.7
1976-78	27.5	15.8	-6.1	5.7	16.0	15.8	2.8	3.0
1979-81	30.0	17.4	-5.9	6.6	18.5	17.4	1.1	2.2
1980s								
1982-84	40.6	23.3	-8.8	8.5	22.7	23.3	2.9	2.3
1985-87	49.1	24.8	-9.3	15.1	29.1	24.8	2.5	6.8
1988-90	50.0	23.8	-9.2	17.0	30.8	23.8	2.1	9.1
B. Experience 1-40								
1970s								
1970-72	34.2	18.9	-2.3	13.0	19.1	18.9	8.2	8.4
1973-75	32.1	18.9	-3.0	10.2	19.3	18.9	7.0	7.5
1976-78	30.9	18.0	-4.1	8.8	20.3	18.0	5.0	7.4
1979-81	31.2	19.2	-4.3	7.7	20.3	19.2	5.1	6.2
1980s								
1982-84	37.5	20.4	-7.3	9.8	25.6	20.4	3.9	9.1
1985-87	41.4	20.4	-8.1	12.9	26.8	20.4	3.4	9.8
1988-90	44.9	20.0	-8.5	16.4	28.0	20.0	2.6	10.6

Notes: Columns labelled "Wage Diff" are wage differentials across the indicated schooling groups, in percentage terms. Columns labelled "Between" are analogous to the "Between" calculations in table 4.8. Columns labelled "Within Diff" are differences in the "Within" columns of table 4.8 across the relevant schooling groups. See notes to table 4.8 and the text for details.

greatest absolute increase in employment of college graduates, and workers in that occupation earned wages that were 18.8 percent higher than those of the average worker. The occupation that experienced the greatest decrease in college-educated employment was "dentists," which was associated with an 84.6 percent wage premium during the period examined. Many of the occupations with the largest growth in employment of college graduates in both the 1970s and 1980s are business or finance related. The categories with employment losses are not as clear, although we would note the shrinking elementary and secondary

TABLE 4.10   Occupations with Largest Employment Gains and Losses, by Schooling Level

		Employment Gains		Employment Losses	
		Occupation	Premium	Occupation	Premium
A. College					
1970s	1.	Managers, NEC	18.8	Dentists	84.6
	2.	Bank Officers/Financial Mgrs	34.5	Mechanical Engineers	42.5
	3.	Physicians	52.3	Sales Engineers	42.6
	4.	Accountants	30.5	Sales Representatives, Mfg	23.5
	5.	Sales Representatives, Whse	14.9	Bookkeepers	-6.9
1980s	1.	Managers, NEC	23.3	Teachers, Secondary School	5.4
	2.	Computer Systems Analysts	44.8	Physicians	60.9
	3.	Supervisors, Sales	-2.4	Supervisors, Production	12.4
	4.	Other Financial Officers	35.5	Administrators, Education	30.7
	5.	Postsecondary Teachers, NEC	18.8	Teachers, Elementary School	5.0
B. Some College					
1970s	1.	Managers, NEC	18.8	Accountants	30.5
	2.	Blue Collar Worker Super.	8.0	Sales Representatives Mfg.	23.5
	3.	Truck Drivers	-14.7	Personnel and Labor Relations	29.4
	4.	Auto Mechanics	-17.9	Draftsmen	11.7
	5.	Restaurant Managers	-22.2	Bank Officers/Financial Mgrs.	34.5
1980s	1.	Managers, NEC	22.3	Sales Representatives, Mining	17.7
	2.	Correctional Inst. Officer	-6.7	Insurance Sales	16.9
	3.	Electricians	12.7	Accountants	33.7
	4.	Truck Drivers, Light	-26.0	Supervisors, NEC	15.1
	5.	Specified Mechanics	-10.5	Computer Operators	5.0

continued

school occupations in the 1980s. The wage premiums associated with the employment growth occupations in panel A of Table 4.10 are, on average, similar to those of the employment loss occupations.

Panels B through D of Table 4.10 show the same analyses for the other schooling groups. A striking characteristic of these panels is that the occupations with college-educated employment growth have low wages relative to college-educated employment losses. In panel B the workers losing the most labor with 13 to 15 years of schooling are white-collar, high-wage-premium occupations. Large negative wage premiums are especially apparent in the occupations with large employment gains in panels C and D. There is some educational "upgrading" going on within occupations. For example, accountants experienced large

TABLE 4.10   *Continued*

	Employment Gains		Employment Losses	
	Occupation	Premium	Occupation	Premium
C. High School				
1970s	1. Carpenters	-7.2	Managers NEC	18.8
	2. Truck Drivers	-14.7	Stock Clerks	-10.0
	3. Auto Mechanics	-17.9	Sales Mgrs., exc. Retail Trade	39.1
	4. Heavy Equipment Mechanics	-1.0	Not Specified Laborers	-32.6
	5. Welders	-5.9	Sales Representatives, Mfg.	23.5
1980s	1. Truck Drivers, Heavy	-22.7	Sales Representatives, Mining	17.7
	2. Managers, NEC	22.3	Telephone Installers	27.3
	3. Truck Drivers, Light	-26.0	Heavy Equipment Mechanics	5.3
	4. Janitors	-44.8	Supervisors, Mechanics	18.4
	5. Groundskeepers	-56.6	Drillers, Oil Well	-14.2
D. HS Dropouts				
1970s	1. Cooks	-48.1	Truck Drivers	-14.7
	2. Waiters' Assistants	-82.0	Managers, NEC	18.8
	3. Shoe Repairers	-64.4	Machine Operatives	-11.0
	4. Mine Operatives, NEC	-4.2	Delivery Workers	-18.6
	5. Drywall Installers	-4.0	Janitors	-38.0
1980s	1. Cooks	-61.3	Truck Drivers, Heavy	-22.7
	2. Groundskeepers	-56.6	Supervisors, Production	12.4
	3. Misc. Food Preparation	-83.7	Indust. Machinery Repair	0.9
	4. Cashiers	-57.3	Supervisors, Sales	-2.4
	5. Packaging Operators	-33.3	Indust. Truck Drivers	-15.9

Notes: This table gives, for each time period and schooling group, the occupations experiencing the greatest increases and decreases in employment of that schooling group. Columns marked "Premium" give the difference in percentage terms between average wages in that occupation and average wages among all workers.

college-educated employment gains but large some-college-educated losses. Similarly, truck drivers experienced large employment gains for high school graduates and large losses for high school dropouts. Although it is difficult to make generalizations based on only a few occupations, the growth in employment for high school graduates in such occupations as "janitors" and "groundskeepers" in the 1980s and the clear movement of those with some college education out of some white-collar and financial services occupations are striking.

There are several possible explanations for the declining occupational placements of workers those with less than 16 years of schooling. One is simply that the economy produces different goods and requires different tasks of its workers than previously, and workers without the cognitive knowledge-based skills acquired with or implied by a college education can no longer fall back on skilled and semiskilled trades. This is consistent with the shifting industrial composition outlined earlier. An alternative possibility is that the "quality" of high school graduates and those with some college education is not what it used to be. It is likely that with more people going to college the person not continuing beyond high school in 1990 is much different from the person who did not continue beyond high school in 1970. Perhaps even the quality of the instruction received in high school has changed for the worse. Data do not easily permit an evaluation of these possibilities, especially those related to the changing "quality" of high school graduates across different birth cohorts. It is clear that today, for one reason or another, young people without a college education are entering the labor force at an ever-increasing disadvantage.

SUMMARY

Education has become a more important determinant of labor market outcomes in the recent past. This is at least partly the result of economy-wide factors that have acted to increase the demand for relatively skilled workers. It is difficult to imagine that this phenomenon will reverse itself in the immediate future. Indeed, all indications are that it will continue. We are not able to make education policy recommendations based on the broad trends laid out here, but it is clear that now, more than at any time in the past 25 years, improvements in the delivery of education in this country would have large benefits. Increasingly, it appears that secondary-level schooling is successful only insofar as it prepares students for college. The prospects that those who drop out of high school or stop with a high school degree will fare well in the labor market are poor.

REFERENCES

Freeman, Richard. 1976. *The Overeducated American*. New York: Academic Press.
Murphy, K. M., and F. Welch. 1992. "The role of international trade in wage differentials." Pp. 101–132. In *Workers and Their Wages: Changing Patterns in the United States,* Marvin H. Kosters, ed. Washington, D.C.: AEI Press, 1994.
Murphy, K. M., and F. Welch. 1991. "Industrial change and the rising importance of skill." Pp. 39–69. In *Uneven Tides: Rising Inequality in America,* S. Danziger and P. Gottschalk, eds. New York: Russell Sage Foundation, 1993.

CHAPTER 5

The Effects of School-Based Management Plans

Anita A. Summers
*The Wharton School, and Graduate School of Education,
University of Pennsylvania*

Amy W. Johnson
*The Institute for Research on Higher Education,
University of Pennsylvania*

Virtually every school district in the United States is actively reviewing the concept of increasing the decision-making autonomy of individual schools—developing school-based management (SBM) plans. The objective of this chapter is to review the evidence produced by reasonably systematic studies on the impact of increased autonomy on the performance of schools, particularly on the achievement performance of the children in these schools.

Questions about the effectiveness of SBM are part of a long-standing debate about the best paradigm for the organizational structure for the delivery of primary and secondary education. One paradigm, not currently in favor, is to increase centralization by expanding the scope of governance. The arguments for increasing centralization run along several lines: (1) the legal boundaries of political jurisdictions, determined by a set of historical factors, are irrelevant to the determination of appropriate educational standards that are for the good of the whole; (2) there are economies of scale; (3) there are substantial externality and public good characteristics in K-12 education, and these require governance over a large number of districts to ensure consistency in the delivery of standards that are for the good of the whole; (4) the equal educational opportunity clauses of state constitutions require more equality in service levels, and this can only be achieved through large-area governance mechanisms.

An alternative paradigm, now being widely embraced, and which is consistent with the view of public choice theorists, is that a larger number of smaller units is the preferred governance structure. There are a number of arguments for decentralization: (1) there are many diseconomies of scale—many negative externalities of a very heterogeneous student body and substantial inefficiencies in uniform regulations for different communities; (2) the larger the unit of governance, the less able citizens are to express their individual preferences, which the education system's organization ought to satisfy insofar as possible; (3) the smaller the unit of governance, the more parents will participate, contributing to higher student achievement; and (4) if parental choice of schools is added to the plan for decentralization, competition will improve the service quality per dollar.

The next section of this chapter develops a taxonomy for grouping the very wide range of characteristics and objectives of the SBM plans that have been introduced in recent years. It is important to observe that the enthusiasm for SBM, expressed in hundreds of articles and papers, does not, on the whole, stem from positive student achievement results. The third section describes our search for all available systematic studies of SBM, the complete results of which are available from us directly.

Section four describes the findings of the 20 systematic studies we found, concentrating particularly on those that used as an outcome measure actual student achievement, in contrast to teacher, principal, or parent perceptions. The conclusion of this review is that there is no collective evidence of positive effects because the methodologies of the studies are inadequate, and because even the few results based on some empirical data have not, on the whole, been positive.

The last section suggests what the characteristics of an adequate evaluation of SBM reform should be. Experimentation with new governance structures is essential, but to do so without adequate evaluation is to repeat the errors of the past. Trade-offs are required, but dropping ineffective methods and adding effective ones require serious assessments of effectiveness. The country is not now doing this for the most widespread educational reform currently being considered.

MEANING OF SCHOOL-BASED MANAGEMENT

While there are many ways in which school-based management can be practiced, all forms are based on the premise that the school site becomes the central locus of control in decision making. The rationale behind SBM is that those who are closest to the primary business of schools will make the best-informed decisions. The essential purpose of redistributing decision-making authority to increase the autonomy of the critical stakeholders is to improve the instructional process and, although rarely stated, student outcomes. SBM is frequently advocated on the grounds that it increases the accountability of school-site personnel. Schools are forced to become more responsive to local needs through the inclusion of parents and community members on decision-making committees. In exchange for increased autonomy, schools are usually required to report the results of SBM efforts to the central administration.

The term "school-based management" has many variations—school-site management, school-site autonomy, shared decision making, shared governance, school improvement program (or project or process), school-based budgeting, and administrative decentralization. In part because school-based management is intended to enable schools to respond to local needs, it can vary greatly from school to school in three fundamental characteristics: the authority that has been delegated, the resources (inputs) devoted to implementation of SBM, and the stated objectives in introducing SBM.

Authority Delegated

The cornerstone of school-based management is delegating greater authority to the local school site. The nature of this increased authority is defined by three elements: the areas of decision making to which the increased authority applies, the constraints limiting exercise of that authority, and the collection of individuals who receive the new authority.

Areas of Authority

Clune and White (1988) define the areas of authority as curriculum, budget, and personnel; Malen et al. (1990) refer to budget, personnel, and program. Here, delegation of authority refers to areas of curriculum, budget, personnel, and strategic planning. Strategic planning, of course, frequently involves decision making in all of the other three areas, but it is often a distinct function of school committees. Some schools may be given authority in all of these domains. Others may be given more limited authority. A school may be charged with outlining its strategic long-term plan, for example, without acquiring any increased budget authority. Another school might be allowed to make recommendations for selection of a principal but have little voice in curriculum restructuring.

Constraints to Authority

Most of the increased autonomy or decision-making authority is constrained by "the web of rules embedded in the broader system" (Malen et al., 1990, p. 301). The extent of these constraints or the existence of procedures designed to exempt certain decisions or processes from constraint varies widely by school. Some superintendents have made great efforts to reduce the constraints imposed by central administration standards or state mandates. Some unions have cooperated in allowing procedural deviations from preexisting contract stipulations. In some cases, however, state mandates or district regulations preclude any possibility of substantive or autonomous decision making. Thus, for certain schools, increased authority consists solely of being permitted to make recommendations to the central administration; for others, significant discretion and flexibility are the norm.

The extent of the constraints imposed determines whether school-site personnel have planning responsibility or actual decision-making authority, an important but subtle distinction (Malen et al., 1990). Developing school improvement plans without significant authority for curriculum, budget, and personnel decisions, merely making recommendations to the central administration; or merely designing disciplinary policies and instructional strategies does not mean that the traditional governance structure has been altered. And the risk may be even greater. Once the initial excitement that accompanies this anticipated change wears off, school-site personnel may lose interest if only a marginal increase in authority is granted.

Recipients of Increased Authority

A third question about governance reform is who will exercise the increased authority. Most schools with some form of SBM have what is commonly referred to as a "school-site council." Sometimes council members are elected; sometimes they participate voluntarily. Most councils comprise some combination of teachers, parents, principal, community members, and, in secondary schools, students. But councils are conducted in different ways. The principal, for example, may or may not chair the group and in the former case may or may not involve others. Which members develop meeting agendas varies across schools, as do the types of involvement afforded parents and community members. In some cases, decision-making authority clearly rests with the principal; in others it is held by a representative group in which the principal retains no particular advantage. Council composition is very relevant in determining which traditional power or influence relationships are maintained or altered.

Inputs to School-Based Management

A second characteristic that contributes to the final shape and scope of SBM in a given school or district is the allocation of resources for program implementation. Very little specificity is given in the individual SBM descriptions of these resources. Dollar resource estimates are mostly absent and, where given, anecdotal. Three kinds of resources are referred to in establishing SBM—training of school personnel, government or foundation funding, and new positions within the central administration or at the local school site. In some cases, no such resources are provided; in others two are used; occasionally, allocations are made in all three areas. There is simply no evidence in the published literature on which to base cost estimates. Many school personnel indicate that lack of adequate time, funding, and training are impediments to successful implementation, but the data available on both inputs and outputs make it impossible to render a judgment on the efficiency of the current allocation of resources.

Objectives

The variety of objectives attributed to SBM efforts suggests that this restructuring movement is designed to address a wide range of issues and problems at the local school site. In one school the emphasis might be on teacher empowerment and increased professionalism; in another it might be school climate. Most project descriptions mention such objectives as increased involvement, ownership, empowerment, professionalism, and leadership of personnel. Many mention efficiency, accountability, and improved educational programs. Some mention student achievement. Although rarely mentioned from project descriptions explicitly, it can be inferred that schools often believe that SBM will create a chain reaction, improving the morale and planning efforts of school personnel, which in turn will improve student achievement. Few schools, however, use concrete measurement criteria of student outcomes in their efforts to assess whether restructuring efforts are effective. The lack of quantitative evidence, and the overwhelming portion of SBM descriptions devoted to discussing stakeholder empowerment, underscore the absence of focus on student achievement.

SOURCES

Background information on school-based management and evaluations of individual schools and districts was collected from a variety of sources. We conducted a computer search of the Educational Research Information Clearinghouse (ERIC) files, focusing primarily on files from 1983 through 1993. The initial general search, using such ERIC descriptors as "school-based management," "school-site management," and "participative decision making," uncovered over 800 documents. The great majority of these consisted of general discussions on the topic or were brief descriptions. These are not included in the bibliography in this chapter. A more targeted search located 70 sources that purported to be project evaluations. Most of the literature, however, offered cursory descriptions of the implementation process and relied heavily on impressionistic reports regarding restructuring outcomes. Of the 70 sources, only 20 exhibited a systematic approach to evaluation, and only seven included a measurable assessment of student outcomes based on actual student performance.

At the same time, selected superintendents, researchers in the field, and educational organizations were contacted in an effort to identify other SBM evaluations that specifically included student achievement indicators. Some of this outreach yielded additional useful information. Most of the individuals contacted, however, confirmed the results of the ERIC searches; very few systematic investigations of the impact of SBM on student achievement have been done.

The 20 systematic evaluations we found were summarized in terms of five broad characteristics: the form of SBM (how and to whom authority is delegated), the inputs to SBM (resources made available specifically for SBM implementation), the stated objectives of SBM and the associated measurement instruments, impediments to successful implementation, and outcomes of SBM and the qualitative and quantitative techniques used to derive them. The process of forcing the content of the studies into some sort of uniform format was laborious because the studies tended to be either diffuse descriptions or produced every permutation and combination of data arrayed into dozens of tables. Brief summaries of a number of characteristics of each study, including the statistical measurements and techniques used and results with respect to student achievement outcomes, are given in Table 5.1.

SCHOOL-BASED MANAGEMENT AND STUDENT OUTCOMES

Our review of the literature, as indicated earlier, revealed the general characteristics of SBM efforts. The studies, and therefore their evaluations, concentrated on changing methods of governance and changing relationships among the stakeholders as governance structures change. There is an implicit assumption that, if the processes of decision making change, schools will be more effective instruments for educating children. The studies were designed, however, to look at the effects of SBM on governance processes, not educational outcomes, just as SBM efforts are designed to alter stakeholder relationships via governance changes, not to change student performance.

Essentially, the large literature on the effectiveness of SBM ignored the effects on student achievement, either because the SBM advocates do not regard achievement as an important output measure or because there is faith that increased school discretion will increase student learning. As a result, there is little evidence to support the notion that SBM is effective in increasing student performance. There are very few quantitative studies, the studies are not statistically rigorous, and the evidence of positive results is either weak or nonexistent.

Summary of 20 Studies

What did the 20 relatively systematic studies reveal about the authority delegated under a specific SBM program, the inputs to the program, the explicitly stated objectives, and, most importantly, the outcomes?

Authority Delegated

The four major areas where schools introduced greater discretionary power were curriculum, budget, personnel, and strategic planning. Eleven of the plans delegated increased authority to all four areas, six of the plans to three areas, and three of the plans to two areas. With a few exceptions (strategic planning in Hammond, Indiana; Chicago; New York City; Dade County, Florida; and Monroe County, Florida; budgetary functions in Chicago and Monroe County; and curriculum and personnel in Chicago), the authority delegation, when given, was partial. In these exceptions it was complete. A dominant characteristic, then, in the systematically reviewed plans is that there was an increase in the delegation of authority in most of the major administrative areas. But partial delegation—an advisory, rather than decision-making role—was the norm.

Inputs

All but two of the 20 SBM plans involved additional fiscal resources in the form of increased budgets to facilitate new activities and training programs for the participants. In most cases, new administrative positions were created to administer SBM. In the Canadian (Brown, 1987) and Riverside, California (Wissler, 1984) programs, more discretion was given to the schools, but not more dollars. Despite several years of SBM experimentation, reflected in more than 800 published reports on the initiatives, it is not possible to estimate the costs of SBM. The omission of this information from the hundreds of descriptions and evaluations suggests that little emphasis has been placed on the financial resources required, and none on the opportunity costs.

Objectives

All of the programs were intended to empower teachers and give principals more independent decision-making authority. Most sought greater involvement of parents and/or the community. Although most stated in very general terms that improved student achievement or learning was an objective, five did not— Edmonton, Canada (Brown, 1987); Chesterfield, Missouri (Burns and Howes, 1988); Cleveland, Ohio (Dentler et al., 1987); Memphis, Tennessee (Smith et al., 1991); and Riverside, California (Wissler, 1984). Only three—New York City (Kelley, 1988; New York City Board of Education, 1992); Chicago (Consortium on Chicago School Research, 1993); and Philadelphia (Winfield and Hawkins, 1993)—specified achievement targets in quantitative terms.

In terms of space allocated in the statements of objectives, the prime target of SBM was organizational—changed governance, changed decision-making processes, and changed stakeholder relationships. Even in the 20 studies where it was mentioned, improved student achievement received relatively little attention.

Outcomes

Six of the studies reported decisively that there was enhanced teacher and principal empowerment and other stakeholder involvement, seven reported evidence of some increase in autonomy, and the remaining seven had either no significant results or negative ones in terms of these criteria. The results of SBM on the ultimately important outcome, student achievement, were not reassuring. Of the 20 studies,

- nine reported no results;
- three asserted positive results but gave no achievement data;
- one asserted no results or negative ones but gave no achievement data;
- two included achievement data and showed positive results; and
- five included achievement data and showed no results or negative results.

The results of SBM, then, appear to be some greater sense of empowerment and involvement of the stakeholders, although not uniformly so, but there is virtually no evidence that such changes produce improvements in student performance. Of particular concern is that the four evaluations using hard data on student achievement as outcomes and adequate controls in the evaluation[1] showed negative results or no significant benefits from SBM (Table 5.1).

Summary of Four Evaluations Using Student Scores and Controls

Four studies warrant individual attention because student achievement was regarded as an important objective and received relatively careful evaluation.[2] In these evaluations hard data were used to measure student performance, and some control factors other than SBM were introduced to isolate the effects of SBM.

Dade County, Florida (Collins and Hanson, 1991)

The Dade County Office of Educational Accountability mounted a three-year evaluation of its SBM program. The first two years of evaluation focused on process characteristics, such as how principals and teachers thought the implementation was proceeding and the attitudes of the stakeholders. The third year of evaluation continued addressing the process but focused on the impact of SBM on a wide variety of performance indicators, including student achievement and attendance.

In the 33 pilot schools selected to test an SBM program, a 5- to 12-person faculty council (consisting of the principal, other administrators, and faculty members) was set up as the decision-making body. The councils were supported by a number of faculty subcommittees. The faculty councils were given partial

---

[1]These are marked with an asterisk and without a "C" in the "Statistical Problems" column of Table 5.1.

[2]Subsequent to submission of this article for publication, we reviewed the literature on school-based management for 1994 and 1995. One additional study is worthy of note. It evaluates the restructuring efforts in the Chicago public schools. Student achievement is the primary measurable objective; no input controls were used (Walberg and Niemiec, 1994). The results of this study were: between 1989 and 1991, student achievement scores in reading and math declined in the elementary and high schools; student attendance rates did not change noticeably; and student graduation rates declined.

authority for curriculum, budget, and personnel and virtually full authority for strategic planning. More teacher empowerment was a stated objective. Other objectives included increased discretionary resources to schools, increased evaluation of instruction, and increased community and parental involvement. Only late in the project was improved student achievement—measured by the Stanford Achievement and Florida State Student Assessment test scores, days attended, the number of disciplinary referrals, and the number of dropouts—made an explicit objective. The 33 schools were selected on the basis of a call for proposals from the 259 schools in Dade County. Student performance was not included as an objective of the experiment. Fifty-three schools applied; 33 were selected on the basis of "most likely to succeed." Changes in the results of the 33 SBM schools were assessed in relation to changes in the performance of all non-SBM schools by simple comparisons of results, with tests of significance applied to some of the differences. No other controls were used.

The results showed no significant change in test scores at any level of schooling—elementary, middle, and senior high schools—or for reading or math separately. Student attendance appeared to improve slightly in SBM schools but not decisively so. Suspension rates were significantly lower in SBM middle and senior high schools in comparison to non-SBM schools, as were dropout rates.

Dade County's evaluation offers some support for the proposition that increased school-site discretion may improve student performance. Although no improvement in test scores was observed, improvements in attendance and dropout rates might reasonably be expected to translate into higher achievement in the long run, since they suggest that the learning environment is more attractive to students. The positive results were small, however, and no effort was made to identify the characteristics of the SBM schools, other than having an SBM program, that might explain even these small differences. The policy force of this evaluation, therefore, is weak.

Dade County, Florida (Taylor and Bogotch, 1992)

Taylor and Bogotch conducted an independent evaluation of Dade County's restructuring efforts. They looked at 33 schools in the county, 16 of which were restructured and 17 of which were used as comparison schools. Their analysis of the delegation of curriculum, budget, personnel, and strategic planning authority matched that of the study by Collins and Hanson (1991). Their analysis of the SBM objectives for teachers and students was the same, although there were differences in the objectives of the two Dade County studies for other stakeholders. Taylor and Bogotch's evaluation showed no significant correlations between student achievement and teacher participation in deciding what and how to teach, or subject and grade assignment. Their study is one of the most sophisticated of the SBM evaluations, and it found no positive effects of this restructuring. This study adds an important dimension to the SBM evaluation by examining the

TABLE 5.1   Summaries of Effects of SBM on Student Outcomes in
20 Systematic Evaluations

Study	State	Unit of Observation	Authority Delegated[a]				Inputs to SBM
			Curriculum	Budget	Personnel	Plan	
B-1	CA	197 elementary and secondary schools in 46 districts	1	1	1	1	State funding Training

Student Outcomes
Student achievement according to direct survey results of teachers: 8% responded substantially higher achievement, 26% somewhat higher, 31% slightly higher, 24% no change, 6% lower achievement. Student achievement, according to regressions on survey data, is significantly affected by several SBM characteristics.

| **B-2** | | Schools in 2 districts: Edmonton schools in Alberta and Langley school district in British Columbia | 0 | 1 | 1 | 0 | Increased principals' discretion |

Student Outcomes
Some increase in junior and senior high school students' satisfaction in learning was reported. Evidence on learning outcomes was not available.

| **B-3** | MO | Parkway school district | 1 | 1 | 1 | 1 | Additional staff Local funding Training |

Student Outcomes
None stated.

| **C-1** | NY | 29 schools in New York City | 1 | 0 | 0 | 1 | Additional staff Chapter 1 funding Foundation funding Stipends for meetings Training |

Student Outcomes
Student discipline and attendance improved (no data available). Test scores increased in some schools (no data available).

| **C-2** | IN | Hammond school district | 1 | 1 | 1 | 2 | Additional staff Foundation funding Local funding Released time Training |

Student Outcomes
Achievement improved, failures decreased, and attendance increased (no data presented, although article indicates that district scores show steady improvement since 1984; Hammond High School showed "remarkable turnaround" in 2 years in these measures.)

| **C-3*** | FL | 33 pilot schools in Dade County: 16 restructured schools and 17 comparison schools | 1 | 1 | 1 | 2- | Additional staff Consultants Financial awards State funding Training |

Student Outcomes
Compared with all Dade County public school students, SBM students performed no differently on Stanford and state student tests, maintained slightly higher attendance over pilot period, had significantly better suspension figures, and showed a significant decline in dropouts.

Objectives for Students	Measurement Instrument	Statistical Techniques	Statistical Problems[b]
Improved achievement	Student interviews Test scores Teacher surveys	Ethnographic procedures Survey percentages Regression analysis	C, D
Greater educational focus Programs responsive to students' needs	Student surveys	Data reduction techniques Survey percentages	B, C, D
Increased participation Improved educational quality	Superintendent's perceptions	None	A, C, D
Improved achievement Concentration on basic skills	SBM committee surveys	Survey scores	B, C, D
Improved achievement Improved attendance	Committee perceptions	None	A, C, D
Improved achievement More evaluation of instruction	Test scores Student data	Tests of significance Comparison of SBM schools with non-SBM schools	D

continued

TABLE 5.1 *Continued*

Study	State	Unit of Observation	Authority Delegated[a]				Inputs to SBM
			Curriculum	Budget	Personnel	Plan	
C-4*	IL	Over 400 elementary schools in Chicago	2-	2	2	2	Option to remove staff Reallocation of funds Regulatory relief

Student Outcomes
No changes in attendance rates at the 6 schools studied in depth (which had high rates to begin with). 5 of the 6 showed declines in mobility rates from 1989-1992; 3 of the 6 showed increases in enrollment; all showed reduced numbers of retained students. Little indication that student achievement is yet the primary target of reform. Evaluator does not regard achievement goals to be realistic.

Study	State	Unit of Observation	Curriculum	Budget	Personnel	Plan	Inputs to SBM
D-1	WA	Bellevue school district	1	1	1	1	Training

Student Outcomes
School-centered decision making (SCDM) has helped schools gain ground in helping all students become successful learners: the average rating scale score in 1991-1992 over all stakeholders surveyed was 2.0. Parents felt that their children are sufficiently challenged academically: 1 of 3 stakeholders had stronger agreement with this statement in 1991-1992 than in 1989-1990; the average rating scale score in 1991-1992 over all stakeholders surveyed was 2.4.

Study	State	Unit of Observation	Curriculum	Budget	Personnel	Plan	Inputs to SBM
D-2	OH	Cleveland public schools	1	1	1	1	Additional staff Increased length of paid service for principals Training

Student Outcomes
None stated.

Study	State	Unit of Observation	Curriculum	Budget	Personnel	Plan	Inputs to SBM
K-1*	NY	7 elementary schools in New York City	1	1	0	1	Additional staff Foundation funding Local funding Stipends for meetings Training

Student Outcomes
Participating schools had mean gain of 1 percentage point in number of students at or above grade-level, compared to 2.4 percentage points citywide. On the reading test, 8% attained a 5% increase in grade level performance, while 11% did in other mandated schools. In math, 24% met gain standards, compared to 28% in other mandated schools. In other reading test, 39% met goal, compared with 35%. 1 of 7 increased attendance over 3 years.

Study	State	Unit of Observation	Curriculum	Budget	Personnel	Plan	Inputs to SBM
L-1	NY	12 schools in New York City	1	0	0	2	Training

Student Outcomes
Restructuring efforts created better learning environments for students and resulted in changes in curriculum and teaching strategies.

Study	State	Unit of Observation	Curriculum	Budget	Personnel	Plan	Inputs to SBM
N-1*	NY	32 secondary schools in New York City	1	1	0	1	Chapter 1 funding Local funding Technical assistance Training

Student Outcomes
34% of schools with 9th graders met the first-year attendance objective. 62% of schools with 10th graders met the first-year attendance objective. 81% of schools met the first-year dropout objective. 41% of schools met the first-year reading objective. 59% of schools met the first-year writing objective. 16% of schools met the first-year mathematics objective. 62% of schools with 9th graders met the first-year credit accumulation objective. 47% of schools with 10th graders met the first-year credit accumulation objective.

Objectives for Students	Measurement Instrument	Statistical Techniques	Statistical Problems[b]
Specific benchmarks for student achievement Improved attendance Improved graduation rates	Student interviews Student data	Survey percentages	C, D
Improved performance	Administrator, parent, and staff surveys	Survey scores	B, C, D
None stated	None	Correlation matrix Averages and standard deviations of questionnaire results	B, C, D
Specific benchmarks for student gains in reading, and math, and attendance	Test scores	Summary of test results	C, D
Improved learning Program change to meet needs Change in discipline procedures	SBM committee interviews	None	A, C, D
Improved attendance Improved retention Improved credit accumulation Improved achievement	Student data Student interviews	Summary of data results	C, D

continued

TABLE 5.1 *Continued*

Study	State	Unit of Observation	Authority Delegated[a]				Inputs to SBM
			Curriculum	Budget	Personnel	Plan	
P-1	OR	70 schools	1	1	1	1	State funding Technical assistance

Student Outcomes
Staff members perceived the greatest amount of progress in student achievement,
followed by student attitudes and student behaviors. 8% thought there had been "a lot"
of improvement in achievement by fall 1988 and 16% by spring 1989; 39% thought there
has been a "moderate" amount of improvement in achievement by fall 1988 and 50% by
spring 1989; 38% thought there had been "slight" improvement in achievement by fall
1988 and 27% by spring 1989; 15% thought there had been no improvement in
achievement by fall 1988, and 7% by spring 1989.

Study	State	Unit of Observation	Curriculum	Budget	Personnel	Plan	Inputs to SBM
P-2	CA	53 schools in LA	1	1	0	1	Regulatory relief Stipends for meetings Training

Student Outcomes
30% of certified staff, 41% of classified staff, and 65% of parents felt SBM gave
students more input into how the school is run. 71% of parents felt SBM increased
students' sense of self-esteem (staff were not asked about this). 26% of certified
staff, 39% of classified staff, and 61% of parents felt shared decision making (SDM)
gave students more input into how the school is run. 69% of parents felt SDM increased
students' sense of self-esteem.

Study	State	Unit of Observation	Curriculum	Budget	Personnel	Plan	Inputs to SBM
S-1	TN	7 schools in Memphis	1	1	1	1	Regulatory relief Technical assistance Training

Student Outcomes
In 1991/1992, school-based decision making (SBDM) resulted in improved attitudes toward school
(49%/22%); student involvement in decision making (32%/39%); improved attendance
(40%/36%); improved behavior (40%/36%); and higher expectations for student
achievement (77%/9%). 82.8% of principals noted student achievement as an
SBDM-related school improvement in 1991; in 1992 no principals noted this outcome.

Study	State	Unit of Observation	Curriculum	Budget	Personnel	Plan	Inputs to SBM
S-2*	FL	Monroe County school district	1	2-	1	2	Additional staff Consultants Increased pay for principal Local funding State funding Substantial training

Student Outcomes
Reading: county 3rd grade scores showed no change while state scores improved slightly, equal
improvement for 5th grade, greater improvement in 8th grade, and less decline than
state in 10th grade. Math: county outperformed state in 5th, 8th, and 10th grades, while 3rd
grade showed equal improvement. Writing: county 3rd grade declined while state
increased, 5th grade showed same increase, county increased and state declined for 8th
grade, and county declined less than state in 10th grade. SAT math scores show relative
decline when compared with nation in recent years, and no change in verbal scores.

Study	State	Unit of Observation	Curriculum	Budget	Personnel	Plan	Inputs to SBM
T-1*	FL	33 schools in Dade County: 16 restructured schools; 17 comparison schools	1	1	1	2-	Training

Student Outcomes
There is a significant correlation between teacher participation in what to teach, how to teach,
subject/grade assignment, and student attendance (r=.43, p<.05). No significant correlations
appeared between student achievement and teacher participation in what to teach, how to teach,
subject/grade assignment, or teacher participation in decisions on instructional materials. (r refers
to the correlation coefficient; p refers to the statistical probability.)

Objectives for Students	Measurement Instrument	Statistical Techniques	Statistical Problems[b]
Improved learning	Staff surveys	Means and standard deviations over time Regression analysis for nonachievement outcomes Survey scores	B, C, D
Improved achievement Increased participation	Staff and parent surveys	Survey percentages	B, C, D
Improved attitudes Improved attendance Improved behavior Increased collaboration	Staff surveys	Survey percentages	B, C, D
Improved achievement	Student data Test data	Specific evaluation instruments Tables on student performance Comparison of SBM schools with non-SBM schools	D
Improved achievement Improved attendance Improved behavior	Student data Test data	Principal component analysis Correlation matrix Multivariate analysis of variance Comparison of SBM schools with non-SBM schools	D

continued

TABLE 5.1   *Continued*

Study	State	Unit of Observation	Authority Delegated[a] Curriculum	Budget	Personnel	Plan	Inputs to SBM
W-1	WA	State-legislated program; summaries from 34 projects	1	1	0	1	State funding Training

Student Outcomes
A greater sense of empowerment was reported.

Study	State	Unit of Observation	Curriculum	Budget	Personnel	Plan	Inputs to SBM
W-2*	PA	60 elementary schools in Phila.: 40 restructured schools; 20 comparison schools	1	1	1	0	Chapter 1 funding Training

Student Outcomes
The effect of schoolwide projects on students' reading achievement, as compared to students in schools without schoolwide projects, was as follows: 1st grade, no effect; 2nd grade, positive significant effect; 3rd grade, negative significant effect; 4th grade, positive but not significant effect; 5th grade, positive but not significant effect.

Study	State	Unit of Observation	Curriculum	Budget	Personnel	Plan	Inputs to SBM
W-3	CA	Riverside Unified school district	1	1	1	0	Increased principal and teacher involvement

Student Outcomes
Greater opportunities for individualized instruction were reported. There was a generalized impression of increased test scores.

*Document included adequate student achievement indicator(s).

[a]The degree of authority delegated is coded as follows: '0' indicates no authority; '1' indicates partial authority (e.g., decisions subject to board approval); and '2' indicates complete authority (a '2-' indicates virtually complete authority). For full details, see complete study summaries.

[b]Key to coding of statistical problems: A, qualitative type evaluation only; B, survey data only; C, inadequate controls; and D, no random assignment.

relationship between the "voices" of teachers with increased authority and their effects on student achievement—but finds no linkage.

Monroe County, Florida (South, 1991)

SBM was introduced in Monroe County schools in the mid-1970s. By 1979 some evaluation studies had been commissioned to evaluate the effects on process changes in the schools. Great emphasis was put on ongoing data collection and evaluation from the beginning of the discussions on SBM. School planning teams had complete control over developing a strategic plan, substantial control over allocating resources within an overall budget, partial control over personnel (with considerable stress on the importance of performance measures), partial control over curriculum, and complete autonomy over implementation of the curriculum. Teacher and principal empowerment was a major objective. In-

Objectives for Students	Measurement Instrument	Statistical Techniques	Statistical Problems[b]
Improved achievement (9 schools) Improved self-esteem (1 school) Improved discipline (1 school)	Principal progress reports	None	A, C, D
Improved achievement in reading	Test scores in reading	Regression analysis	D
More educational opportunities Development of potential	Teacher surveys	Survey percentages	B, C, D

creased student achievement was a specific objective, and test data were regarded as the appropriate measurement instrument.

The student achievement results are presented more systematically in this study than in the other three. Monroe County student performance was compared with that of Florida students generally and, in the case of scores on the Scholastic Assessment Test (SAT), with the national performance. The major conclusions to be drawn from the statewide data comparing 1985-1986 with 1988-1989 are as follows: (1) reading scores increased slightly more in the state than in Monroe County for third-grade students, showed the same level of increase for fifth-grade students, were less for eighth-grade students, and declined less in Monroe County than in the state for tenth-grade students; (2) writing scores increased for third graders in the state, although in the county they declined; for fifth graders they stayed virtually unchanged for both; scores for county eighth graders increased, while state scores declined; and for tenth graders, county scores declined less than scores for the state overall; (3) in math, changes in the county were about the same for third graders, increased slightly more for fifth graders, and were higher in Monroe County for eighth and tenth graders.

With respect to SAT scores in 1984-1985 and 1988-1989, (1) the national averages for verbal scores declined four points, in Florida declined one point, and in Monroe County went up two points; (2) in math scores, national averages increased one point, in Florida increased four points, and Monroe County declined four points.

All in all, comparisons on K-12 statewide testing showed no clear evidence of higher student performance in Monroe County than in the rest of the state. The comparisons of SAT scores suggest that Monroe County students did somewhat better than students elsewhere in the state on the verbal test and somewhat worse on the math test.

Philadelphia, Pennsylvania (Winfield and Hawkins, 1993)

Winfield and Hawkins undertook a longitudinal evaluation of the effects on student achievement of increased collaboration within a school under the auspices of the Center for Research on Effective Schooling for Disadvantaged Students at Johns Hopkins University. Site-based facilitation of collaboration in 40 elementary schools in Philadelphia was the major characteristic of the plan for increased autonomy. Twenty other schools constituted a comparison group.

Increased collaboration and empowerment were major objectives of the Philadelphia SBM plan, and surveys of principals indicated some success, largely with respect to selecting basic materials and purchasing instructional hardware. Another major objective was getting Chapter 1-eligible students to make the same average gain in reading scores as other students in the school district. Only for second graders was there empirical evidence that increased collaboration translated into comparably improved reading scores. For first, third, fourth, and fifth graders, no significant effect was found.

The study also examined the impact of seven components of the collaborative efforts on reading achievement. In only two out of the seven was a consistent positive effect found—teacher involvement in the deployment of human resources (for all grades except the fourth), and a school's use of district-wide programs (for all grades except the third). Chapter 1 funds, amounting to $900 per pupil, were used to implement the program. This expenditure appears to have teachers given more voice but did not yield consistent improvements in student reading achievement.

Conclusions

A review of the SBM literature, including a close look at four studies using controls and specific information about student performance under SBM, yields two major conclusions. First, there are overwhelming obstacles in the way of evaluating the impact of SBM on student achievement. There is virtually no empirical or statistical evidence in the literature. SBM programs exhibit many different designs, and few identify student achievement as a major objective. The focus is on organizational processes, with virtually no attention to how process changes may affect student performance.

Second, the handful of studies with some controls and statistical data provide no significant support for the proposition that school-based management will increase student achievement. But, this is not a conclusion to act on. The data are inadequate, statistical controls are largely nonexistent, no repeated effort has been made to classify various types of SBM designs in a uniform way, and the time period may be too short to yield results.

WHAT'S NEXT?

To merit support, the concept of decentralizing authority in America's public schools needs to be fully evaluated, especially for its effects on student performance. A major impetus behind the current reform movement in education is the evidence of declining student performance. The long-standing pattern in educational evaluation of setting up many objectives, most of which cannot be measured, also applies to our reviews of SBM efforts. School-based management may contribute to a number of good results, but if it does not result in improved educational performance by students, it cannot be judged a success.

A large-scale, cross-sectional study or several cross-sectional studies in states that have been experimenting with SBM for some time is needed. Florida, Minnesota, New York, and California are examples. This would eliminate many of the problems of controlling for interstate differences in data, funding, and political organization. An important component of such a study would be the development of a taxonomy of incentive schemes associated with various SBM designs, drawing on principal-agent theory to classify the nature of the "contracts" among the educational stakeholders. Such a study should focus on educational achievement as a major output measure. There is clearly increased acceptance of this standard. Some of the most recent SBM studies, although they concentrate on implementation processes, analyze SBMs effects on student achievement scores. Reports by the Committee for Economic Development (1994) and by Eric A. Hanushek et al. (1994) emphasize the importance of basic skill performance measures as prime criteria of success. If investments in education decentralization are regarded as means of improving society's human capital, we must set up an adequate measure of the returns.

REFERENCES

Brown, D. J. 1987. *A Preliminary Inquiry into School-Based Management.* Social Sciences and Humanities Research Council. Ottawa, Ontario.

Burns, L. T., and J. Howes. 1988. "Handing control to local schools; site-based management sweeps the country." *The School Administrator* 45(7):8-10.

Clune, W. H., and P. White. 1988. *School-Based Management—Institutional Variation, Implementation, and Issues for Further Research.* Center for Policy Research in Education, State University of New Jersey, Rutgers.

Collins, R. A., and M.K. Hanson. 1991. *Summative Evaluation Report: School-Based Management/ Shared Decision-Making Project 1987-88 Through 1989-90.* Office of Educational Accountability. Dade County Public Schools, Miami, Fla.

Consortium on Chicago School Research, Steering Committee. 1993. *A View from the Elementary Schools: The State of Reform in Chicago.* Consortium on Chicago School Research, Chicago.

Dentler, R. A., C. Flowers, and K. Mulvey. 1987. "Decentralization in the Cleveland public schools: an evaluation." *Equity & Excellence* 23(1-2):37-60.

Kelley, T. 1988. *Small Change: The Comprehensive School Improvement Program.* Educational Priorities Panel, New York, NY.

Malen, B., R. T. Ogawa, and J. Kranz. 1990. What Do We Know About School-Based Management? A Case Study of the Literature—A Call for Research. In *Choice and Control in American Education, Vol. 2. The Practice of Choice, Decentralization, and School Restructuring,* W. Clune and J. Witte, Eds. Philadelphia: The Falmer Press.

New York City Board of Education, Office of Research, Evaluation, and Assessment. 1992. *Project Achieve. 1990-1991. Parts I and II.* Board of Education, Brooklyn.

Smith, D. L., T. C. Valesky, and D. D. Horgan. 1991. *Impact of school-based decision making on school climate.* Paper presented at the annual meeting of the American Educational Research Association, Chicago.

South, O. 1991. *From Compliance to Continuous Improvement—Leading and Managing School-Based Management.* Monroe County, Fla.

Taylor, D. L., and I. E. Bogotch. 1992. *School-level effects of teachers' participation in decision-making.* Unpublished paper, Louisiana State University, Baton Rouge.

Winfield, L., and R. Hawkins. 1993. *Longitudinal Effects of Chapter 1 Schoolwide Projects on the Achievement of Disadvantaged Students.* Report no. 46. Center for Research on Effective Schooling for Disadvantaged Students, John Hopkins University, Baltimore, Md.

Wissler, D. F. 1984. *Decentralization of decision-making in Riverside Unified School District: an historical analysis.* Unpublished doctoral dissertation, University of California, Riverside, Ca.

BIBLIOGRAPHY

Beers, D. E. 1984. School based management. Paper presented at the national convention of the National Association of Elementary School Principals, New Orleans.

Berman, P., and T. Gjelten. 1984. *Improving School Improvement; A Policy Evaluation of the California School Improvement Program Volume 2: Findings.* Berman, Weiler Associates, Berkeley, Calif.

Burton, N., et al. 1982. School-Based Planning Manual. Part II: Supplementary Materials. Department of Planning, Research, and Evaluation. Seattle Public Schools, Seattle, Washington.

Canner, J., et al. 1985. *School Improvement Project: 1983-84. Fifth Annual Process Assessment.* New York City Board of Education, Office of Educational Assessment.

Carr, R. A. 1988. "Second-wave reforms crest at local initiative." *The School Administrator* 45(7):16-18.

Casner-Lotto, J. 1988. "Expanding the teacher's role: Hammond's school improvement process." *Phi Delta Kappan* 69(5):349-353.

Cistone, P. J., J. A. Fernandez, and P. L. Tornillo, Jr. 1989. "School-based management/shared decision making in Dade County (Miami)." *Education and Urban Society* 21(4):393-402.

DeLacy, J. 1992. *The Bellevue Evaluation Study (Second Report). Studying the Effects of School Renewal.* Institute for Study of Educational Policy, University of Washington, Seattle.

Dreyfuss, G. 1988. "Dade County opens doors to site decisions." *The School Administrator* 45(7):12-15.

Gomez, J. J. 1989. The path to school-based management isn't smooth, but we're scaling the obstacles one by one." *American School Board Journal* 176(10):20-22.

Harrision, C. R., J. P. Killim, and J. Mitchell. 1989. "Site-based management: the realities of implementation." *Educational Leadership* 46(9):55-58.

Lieberman, A. 1988. "Expanding the leadership team. *Educational Leadership* 45(5):4-8.

Malen, B., and R. T. Ogawa. 1985. *The Implementation of the Salt Lake City School District's Shared Governance Policy: A Study of School Site Councils.* City School District, Salt Lake City, Utah.

Morgan, J. M. 1983. The Cincinnati school-based management information system. Paper presented at the annual meeting of the American Educational Research Association, Montreal, Quebec, Canada.

Paule, L., B. Faddis, and W. Savard. 1989. *Oregon School Improvement and Professional Development Project. Final Report.* Northwest Regional Laboratory, Portland.

Pike, D. W. 1993. *The Survey of Instructional Programs, Spring 1991.* Program Evaluation and Assessment Branch, Unified School District. Los Angeles.

Robinson, C. 1987. *School-Based Budgeting Survey Study of Pilot Schools.* Albuquerque Public Schools, Albuquerque, N. Mex.

Walberg, H. J., and R. P. Niemiec. 1994. "Is Chicago school reform working?" *Phi Delta Kappan* 75(9):713–715.

Washington Office of the State Superintendent of Public Instruction. 1988. *Report to the Legislature on the School Based Management Program.* Washington Office of the State Superintendent of Public Instruction, Olympia.

Watts, G. D., and R. M. McClure. 1990. "Expanding the contract to revolutionize school renewal." *Phi Delta Kappan* 71(10):765-774.

Background Articles on School-Based Management

Applegate, T. P., and W. K. Evans. 1990. *Preliminary Items from the Statewide Evaluation of Outcome-Based Education in Utah.* Research and Development Consultants. Salt Lake City, Utah.

Briggs, G., and S. Lawton. 1989. Efficiency, effectiveness, and the decentralization of local school systems. Paper presented at the annual meeting of the American Education Finance Association, San Antonio, Tex.

Burton, N., et al. 1982. *School-Based Planning Manual. Part II: Supplementary Materials.* Department of Planning, Research, and Evaluation, Seattle Public Schools, Seattle, Wash.

Citywide Educational Coalition. *School-Based Management/Shared Decision-Making: The First Full Year.* Citywide Education Coalition, Boston.

Cohen, M. 1988. *Restructuring the Education System: Agenda for the 1990s.* Center for Policy Research, National Governors' Association, Washington, D.C.

Committee for Economic Development. Forthcoming. *Putting Learning First: Governing and Managing the Schools for High Achievement.* Committee for Economic Development. New York.

Consortium on Chicago School Research. *Achieving School Reform in Chicago: What We Need to Know. A Research Agenda.* Consortium on Chicago School Research, Chicago.

David, J. L., and S. M. Peterson. 1984. *Can Schools Improve Themselves? A Study of School-Based Improvement Programs.* Bay Area Research Group, Palo Alto, Calif.

David, J. L., with S. Purkey and P. White. 1989. *Restructuring in Progress: Lessons from Pioneering Districts.* Center for Policy Research, National Governors' Association, Washington, D.C.

David, J. L. 1989. "Synthesis of research on school-based management." *Educational Leadership* 46(8):45-53.

Dean, P., A. Bryk, and J. Q. Easton. 1992. Studying school improvement in Chicago: a construction of post-reform school index measures. Paper presented at the annual meeting of the American Educational Research Association, San Francisco.

DeLacy, J. 1990. *Addendum to Assuring Equity and Excellence: The Bellevue Evaluation Study.* Institute for Study of Educational Policy, University of Washington.

Finn, C. 1990. "The biggest reform of all." *Phi Delta Kappan* 71(8):585-592.

Futrell, M. H. 1989. "Mission not accomplished: education reform in retrospect." *Phi Delta Kappan* 71(1):9-14.

Glasser, W. 1990. "The Quality School." *Phi Delta Kappan* 71(6):425-435.

Hanushek, E. 1994. *Making Schools Work: Improving Performance and Controlling Costs.* Washington, D.C.: The Brookings Institution.

Levin, H. M. 1988. *Accelerated Schools for At-Risk Students.* Center for Policy Research in Education, State University of New Jersey, Rutgers.

Lindelow, J., and J. Heyndericks. 1989. "School-based management." In *School Leadership Handbook for Excellence*, S. C. Smith and P. K. Piele, eds. Eric Clearinghouse on Educational Management, College of Education, University of Oregon, Corvalis.

Lindquist, K. M., and J. J. Mauriel. 1989. "School-based management: doomed to failure?" *Education and Urban Society* 21(4):403-416.

McDaniel, T. R. 1989. "Demilitarizing public education: school reform in the era of George Bush." *Phi Delta Kappan* 71(1):15-18.

Moore, D. R. 1991. *Chicago School Reform: The Nature and Origin of Basic Assumptions.* Research & Policy Analysis Series No. 7, Chicago.

Murphy J. T. 1989. "The paradox of decentralizing schools: lessons from business, government, and the Catholic church." *Phi Delta Kappan* 70(10):808-812.

Murphy, M. J. *A Prospectus for a Study of the Site-Based, Collaborative Decision-Making Reform in the Denver Public Schools.* University of Colorado, Boulder.

Olson, L. 1988. "The 'restructuring' puzzle." *Education Week*, pp. 7-8+.

Purkey, S. C., and M. S. Smith. 1983. "Effective schools: a review." *The Elementary School Journal* 83(4):427-452.

Shanker, A. 1990. "The end of the traditional model of school—and a proposal for using incentives to restructure our public schools." *Phi Delta Kappan* 71(5):345-357.

Sirotnik, K. A., and R. W. Clark. 1988. "School-centered decision making and renewal." *Phi Delta Kappan* 69(9):660-664.

Strusinski, M. 1989. "The provision of technical support for school-based evaluation: the researcher's perspective." Paper presented at the annual meeting of the American Educational Research Association, San Francisco.

Timar, T. 1989. "The politics of school restructuring." *Phi Delta Kappan* 71(4):265-275.

Tucker, M. S. 1988. "Peter Drucker, knowledge work, and the structure of schools." *Educational Leadership* 45(5):44-46.

White, P. A. 1988. *Resource Materials on School-Based Management.* Center for Policy Research in Education, State University of New Jersey, Rutgers.

_____. 1989. "An overview of school-based management: what does the research say?" *NASSP Bulletin* 73(518):1-8.

Wissler, D. F., and F. I. Ortiz. 1986. "The decentralization process of school systems." *Urban Education* 21(3):280-294.

Wohlstetter, P., and R. Smyer. 1983. New boundaries for school-based management: the high involvement model. Paper presented at the Fifteenth Annual Research Conference of the Association for Public Policy Analysis and Management, Washington, D.C.

CHAPTER 6

Management Decentralization and Performance-Based Incentives: Theoretical Consideration for Schools

JANE HANNAWAY
The Urban Institute and Stanford University

The conventional wisdom is that schools in the United States are in trouble. Student performance overall is stagnant, at best, and performance disparities among students are large and persistent. Compared to other industrialized countries, student performance levels in the United States do not look good. Simple solutions—for example, increasing teacher salaries, reducing class size—have not yielded promising results, and most analysts agree that the problems of educational productivity require more complex remedies than simply increasing expenditure-related inputs. The system itself, they argue, must be changed: better-managed resources will yield better returns. Governance reforms such as school-based management, charter schools, and choice schemes are at the center of education policy discussions in the 1990s. They promise better managed resources. But how effective are governance of reforms in education? Are they the key to improved student performance?

This chapter complements the one by Summers and Johnson in this volume, who report on the results of a comprehensive review of published and unpublished studies on the most common type of governance reform—school-based management (SBM). After an exhaustive examination of the evidence, they conclude that it simply is not known whether SBM is worthwhile. Advocacy for increasing school-site discretion has been vigorous, and school districts across the country have embraced it in various forms, but research on its effects on student performance is remarkably sparse. Moreover, the little valid empirical evidence that is available suggests that at least this governance reform is not likely to lead to significantly higher levels of student achievement.

Too often we shy away from asking the hard questions about the effect of

97

education reforms on student achievement, sometimes for good reasons[1] and sometimes not. But clearly the value of any education reform effort is determined ultimately by its contribution to student learning. As Shanker (1994) recently wrote:

> Is student learning better in schools where there are democratic school councils or in schools where the principal runs the show? . . . The whole point of school reform is to have students learn more. If this doesn't happen, the experiment is a failure, no matter how happy the children, the parents and teachers—and the reformers are.

Establishing the link between school-based management and student achievement is not, however, just an empirical problem; it is also a theoretical one. We need to ask why school-based management might be expected to promote student achievement? A long series of connections must be realized for SBM to affect student achievement. Only when we have some understanding of what it is about decentralization that affects or does not affect student learning can we develop appropriate models to estimate the effects of governance reforms on student achievement, and only then can we come to reasonable interpretations of results that are useful for policy making.

This chapter reviews common claims made about the presumed intermediate effects of school decentralization in terms of the available evidence. My anaylsis suggests that we should not be surprised by the findings of Summers and Johnson. There is little reason to expect decentralization alone to have significant beneficial effects on student performance. Indeed, there is reason to suspect that it might have negative consequences by increasing disparities (Hannaway, 1995). Others agree with the analysis here suggesting that the problem in education is not just who makes decisions. The problem, they claim, is the lack of incentives that tie decisions to performance (Hanushek, 1994). So, also reviewed are the likely consequences of instituting performance-based incentives. I claim its prospects alone, too, are problematic. But performance-based incentives, *in tandem with* decentralization, may have significant benefits, partly because the advantages of one reform may help balance the limitations of the other, as explained below. Reviewed first is the evidence on decentralization, followed by a discussion of the limitations of incentives.

Decentralization is Insufficient

Many claims have been made that decentralized governance arrangements have important efficiency advantages primarily because local actors are presumed to have better information about the problems and production possibilities of the system. These advantages are especially pronounced in situations where

---

[1]See, for example, Koretz et. al. (1992), Koretz (in this volume), and Haertel (1986) for a discussion of some of the problematic issues involved in testing and assessment.

the work is complex, nonroutine, and not easily monitored by centralized mechanisms. On the surface, education appears to be an area where decentralized management arrangements are likely to be particularly advantageous.

Consider the following, however. First, education is inherently a highly decentralized operation. Teachers work relatively independently in their classrooms. In fact, many observers use the term "isolated" to describe how teachers function in the education system. Evidence of wide variations from classroom to classroom in what gets taught and how it is taught provides fairly clear *prima facie* support for already high levels of teacher discretion.[2] Claims that teachers are overly constrained by central policies and that freedom from these constraints would unleash creative energies and more productive teacher behavior are, at best, overstated.[3] Indeed, from the perspective of individual teachers, SBM centralizes decision making in the school and rests operating and performance responsibility with agents who are closer to teachers. So any positive benefits of SBM may actually come from *decreasing* rather than *increasing* the discretion of individual teachers! Recognizing this possibility is important not only for the effective design of SBM efforts, but also because it allows us to then compare the relative merits of SBM with other means of influencing teaching efforts.

Second, SBM proponents presume that locating more decision-making authority at the school level would involve actors with interests or information different from actors at the center. As a consequence, different and presumably better decisions will flow from the process. Case studies of decentralization efforts, however, question this effect. Malen and Ogawa (1988), for example, found that even when local school councils were given considerable authority and training, teachers and parents exercised little influence on significant decision-making areas. Weiss and Cambone (1994) found that while SBM opened opportunities for teacher involvement in decision making, relatively few teachers became engaged. Similarly, Easton and Storey (1994) examined rates of participation in the local school councils (LSCs) that were established as part of the Chicago School Reform Act of 1988 and found that while principals participated in council deliberations at high rates, teachers, parents, and community representatives were much less active. Teachers tended to become more involved over time, though their focus on improving instruction remained weak (Hess, 1993).

A related and centrally important issue is the presumption in many decentralization reforms, including SBM, that the skills and knowledge necessary to improve student performance already exist at the school level and need only be

---

[2]See, for example, Porter (1989).

[3]Many centrally determined policies, with regard to mainstreaming, textbook selection, and some categorical programs, for example, undeniably have significant effects on teachers' classroom behavior; but they are a consequence of state and federal program regulations or court rulings and are unlikely to change significantly under most school-based management schema. For the most part, these regulations focus on social issues; that is, local discretion is constrained by policies determined by wider social values.

released. Studies of SBM suggest this assumption is a risky one to make. It is unclear that school-level actors have any better idea of how to improve teaching and learning in schools than central actors. A common problem identified in the studies of SBM, for example, is lack of training, suggesting that school-level councils, albeit empowered, are unsure how to proceed and are looking for direction. Although it is too early to judge the effect of Chicago's complex reform effort, preliminary reports suggest that the LSCs focus much of their effort on noninstructional areas such as facilities improvement and student discipline. Some of these efforts may contribute to an environment in which learning is more likely to take place, but observers claim that less than a quarter of the schools have developed plans that are likely to have any significant direct effect on instruction (Hess, 1993).[4] No doubt part of the reason for a lack of focus on teaching and learning is that it is far from obvious how to proceed. If certain knowledge about how to increase student performance were readily available, it would have been put into practice long ago.

Teachers themselves appear to be an unlikely source of instructionally oriented reform in schools. In the Chicago experiment, teachers see little need for changes in classroom practice. In a recent survey, teachers reported that they felt they were already performing competently in the classroom and that change on the part of the students, not teachers, is necessary for school performance to improve (Hess, 1993). Findings by Weiss and Cambone also suggest that teachers are unlikely to generate instructional reform. She found that teachers in the SBM schools she observed tended to focus their energies on areas not directly related to teaching and learning, such as hall behavior or management of the copying machine. Overall, Weiss and Cambone found little difference in the types of decisions reported in schools with and without SBM.

This is not to suggest that allowing schools to determine their own priorities has no value, but experience to date suggests that the changes that take place are likely to be minor and, for the most part, not directly focused on teaching and learning. In short, there is no assurance that schools, left to their own devices, will direct their efforts to a much greater extent than they already do to matters that contribute to higher student achievement.

Local accountability is a third issue. One of the premises of SBM is that the local actors—principals, teachers, and, particularly, parents—precisely because they are local will be able to hold school operations more accountable than would a remote authority. They are supposedly a source of close-up quality control. It is known, however, from both survey and ethnographic studies that some schools, primarily higher-socioeconomic-status (SES) suburban schools, operate with high

---

[4]Although instructionally relevant change was introduced in only a minority of schools, generating any changes that better daily life in these schools should still be considered an important accomplishment.

levels of parental control, even when it is neither explicitly encouraged or formally constituted, than schools in lower-SES areas.

Higher-SES parents, for example, are far more likely to actively monitor academic assignments, placement decisions, classroom practices, and their child's progress. They are more likely than lower-SES parents to think that getting involved in core academic issues is both their right and their responsibility (Lareau, 1987, 1989). In short, higher-SES parents are already behaving in ways that effectively constitute an important management role in schools. Differences in family-school relations by social class are long standing and well known. Indeed, every study of the intersection of families and schools over the past two decades has underscored significant and important differences by social class (e.g., Ogbu, 1974; Stevenson and Baker, 1987; Heyns, 1978; Lareau, 1987, 1989). Higher levels of education, confidence, knowledge, and status facilitate the involvement of higher-SES parents. Recent survey results paint a similar picture of the differential involvement of higher- and lower-SES parents in their children's schooling. According to the National Education Household Survey, only 7 percent of parents with less than a high school education reported high levels of involvement in school matters, while 42 percent of parents with at least a college degree were highly involved (Zill and Nort, 1994).

The existing patterns of parental involvement suggest that decentralization reforms might have one of three results. First, nothing may change. That is, higher- and lower-SES parents might involve themselves at about the same rates as they have in the past despite new opportunities for participation. As it is now, higher-SES parents apparently see few limitations on their involvement in school matters, so the provision of formal mechanisms may have little effect on their behavior. And even with more formal participatory mechanisms, lower-SES parents may still be reluctant to participate for some of the same reasons their participation is low now.

A second plausible scenario is that participation rates of higher- and lower-SES parents might converge. That is, while the participation rates of higher-SES parents may already be near their limit, the establishment of formal structures might encourage greater participation by lower-SES parents. The granting of formal "participation rights" may overcome whatever hesitation lower-SES parents otherwise have about getting involved in school affairs. Of course, the involvement of lower-SES parents may or may not be effective in managing school operations and influencing policy decisions in ways that make the schools more productive.

A third possibility is that the "take-up rate" on new opportunities for involvement may be greater for parents in higher-SES schools than it is for parents in lower-SES schools. Higher-SES parents already exhibit a greater propensity to get involved, and opening more channels may encourage further participation. In addition, if higher-SES parents also possess the skills, knowledge, and confidence to be involved more effectively than lower-SES parents, decentralization reforms may lead to greater inequalities in schooling, as parents with different backgrounds make different levels and types of demands on schools. It is not difficult to imagine SBM schools in low-income neighborhoods functioning pretty much on their own, only weakly managed by parents, and SBM schools in more advantaged neighborhoods operating with parents exercising high levels of quality control. Differences in the focus of demands might also vary by school. Of course, the discretion to identify different objectives is one of the major advantages of decentralization. But one result may be that schools in some neighborhoods focus more heavily and more directly on academic excellence because parents have a better understanding of its long-term benefits, while schools in other neighborhoods are diverted to other objectives.

Consistent with the last scenario, preliminary results from the Chicago reform effort suggest that the effect on student performance of shifting governance to the school level is critically linked to the characteristics of a school's students. In particular, schools with large numbers of low-income children (i.e., students eligible for subsidized school lunches) appear to be the least likely to improve student performance as a consequence of decentralization (Downes and Horowitz, 1994).[5]

Negative distributional consequences may result from decentralization not only because of differences in the types and levels of parental demands on schools, but also because decentralization may result in a less-than-optimal allocation of teacher effort. School-based management, by definition, increases teacher involvement in management tasks, and there is some indication that involvement in management diverts time from teaching and classroom-related activities (Weiss and Cambone, 1994; Hannaway, 1993). A critical question for productivity in education is how teachers should allocate their time among the three basic activities—classroom teaching, management, and professional development—that consume most of their time. The trade-offs may be important for student achievement. It is probably reasonable to expect greater complementarities between instructionally oriented professional development activities and classroom instruction than between management and instruction. And there is evidence that these complementarities may be particularly important for teachers of at-risk students, who typically encounter severe instructional problems in the classroom (Hannaway and Chaplin, 1994). The clear implication, at least for teachers of at-risk students, is that teachers'nonteaching time might be better spent in professional development and support activities directly related to their teaching responsibilities than in management duties that relate only indirectly to student learning.

---

[5]Changes in district policies in retention and inclusion of students with limited English proficiency in the testing program, however, may affect patterns of student performance results in the Chicago experiment (Bryk et. al., 1994a).

In summary, the traditional arguments for why SBM increases productivity in education are, at best, suspect. A careful look at what actually goes on in the education process suggests that teachers may wind up with less discretion, new high-quality information and influence channels may not open, and teacher attention may be diverted from the classroom. But decentralized management is not the only reform whose benefits have likely been overstated; this is also true of performance-based incentives.

Incentives: A Solution and a Problem

The Panel on the Economics of Educational Reform's[6] proposal for education reform persuasively argues that, without performance-based incentives, decentralization is unlikely to yield expected improvements in performance. The above discussion and review of evidence support this view; decentralization alone is not likely to be sufficient to promote higher performance in education. Indeed, decentralization alone may do more harm than good by increasing disparities in performance more than it increases average performance. Lack of performance incentives is no doubt part of the problem. The difficulty of solving the incentives problem in any comprehensive way, however, should not be underestimated. Performance incentives create their own problems that are significant enough to call into question the easy efficacy of performance-based reforms in education.

Performance-based incentives pose three major problems in education. First, to reward performance, the desired output must be articulated. This is not a trivial task. Education has numerous valid goals, some of which may not even be complementary. Parents, for example, expect schools to not only promote the academic performance of students but also foster creativity, curiosity, self-esteem, tolerance, good citizenship, athletic performance, and a host of other objectives. Even if we limit our discussion to academic objectives, there are still problems. Most Americans support higher academic standards in schools, but there is little agreement about what those standards should be (Ravitch, 1994). Efforts, for example, to develop national standards in history have been particularly contentious, but there have also been skirmishes surrounding math, science, and English standards.

Second, there are measurement problems. Defining and agreeing on goals in education is one problem; measuring progress toward those goals is even more difficult, even if we again limit ourselves to only the academic ones.[7] Although student performance in such basic skills as math and reading can be measured with reasonable and recognized standards, measuring performance in other aca-

---

[6]See Hanushek (1994).
[7]See, for example, Koretz in this volume.

demic areas, such as those associated with higher-order skills, still pose serious problems despite considerable recent development efforts. Establishing value-added measures in these areas greatly compounds the difficulty.

A third problem is distortion. The most serious distortion problem is that incentives focus effort on those objectives most amenable to measurement. Whatever is not measured and not rewarded is likely to get less serious attention than it might otherwise merit. Objectives associated with the development of students' problem-solving and higher-order skills, which present difficult measurement problems, are likely to suffer.

History suggests that a second important distortion also might result: the performance contracting experiments of the 1970s showed that teachers tended to focus their efforts on students in the middle of the performance distribution, ignoring both high achievers and low achievers, because it was middle students who were most likely to make the biggest performance gains and, therefore, reap the biggest rewards for the teachers (Gramlich and Koshel, 1975). Similar results were reported from attempts in England in the nineteenth century to build performance incentives into education (Rapple, 1990).

Drawing on basic research by Holmstrom and Milgrom (1992), using a principal-agent model, I have suggested elsewhere that one solution to the distortion problem created by incentives in situations where there are multiple goals may be in structuring tasks according to different objectives (Hannaway, 1993). For example, the teaching force might be divided into basic skills specialists and higher-order skills specialists, or the school day might be so divided. Incentives could be applied to those personnel or to those tasks for which they are more appropriate, and the structural boundaries around the other tasks would provide protection from distortion. Such a solution, however, would not be easy to implement and might create other problems (Hannaway, 1993). For example, a better-crafted incentives scheme might reduce the likelihood that teachers would devote their efforts disproportionately to some students at the expense of others, but it would also likely complicate its design and implementation.

The advantages and distortions associated with performance-based incentives in education have been well known for some time, and, perhaps not surprisingly, experiments with them have generally been short lived (Cohen and Murnane, 1985; Martin et al., 1976). Indeed, in the face of likely distortions it is unclear that such incentives, on balance, are beneficial. That is, in situations where agents (teachers) pursue multiple objectives and where supervision and monitoring systems designed to ensure that all objectives are being adequately pursued are imperfect or costly, the overall system may perform better without explicit performance incentives (Holmstrom and Milgrom, 1992).

At a minimum, incentives alone–like decentralization alone–may do more harm than good in education. Incentives alone are likely to lead to unacceptable distortions; decentralization alone is likely, at best, to have little effect and, at worst, to lead to unacceptable levels of disparities. Below it is suggested that there may be real advantages to a system that combines a performance incentive scheme with a decentralized governance arrangement.

Incentives and Decentralization

Although this chapter has emphasized the limitations and problems associated with both decentralization and incentives, each has important potential to improve student performance, and this potential should not be easily dismissed. Moreover, the advantages of one may at least partially offset the drawbacks of the other. In fact, it could be argued that if a well-designed incentives scheme could be developed, there would be little need for decentralized management arrangements.

The primary advantage of incentives is that they direct behavior. One of the major criticisms of education in the United States in recent years is that it has lost its central focus. What goes on across schools and classrooms, even in the same school district, is often highly variable and too little directed at challenging academic objectives. If incentives are developed to reward school-level actors for promoting defined areas of student achievement, almost certainly school-level actors will focus more heavily on student achievement, at least in those areas that count in the incentives scheme. Performance incentives are particularly appropriate because of the complexity of the work of teaching; standard rules and regulations governing the process are largely inappropriate.

The behavior-directing power of incentives addresses a central weakness of decentralization. A primary drawback of decentralization policies is that many local schools, especially those in disadvantaged areas, may not have the capacity to guide school behavior effectively. Incentives, in contrast, can be counted on to direct some significant fraction of school behavior to valued educational objectives even if the objectives are limited. In effect, incentives ensure some base level of effort to some areas of student achievement and, as a consequence, schools with low capacity will not be left to flounder on their own.

The major drawback of incentives is distortion. An advantage of decentralization is that it provides a way to tune the system relatively easily when it becomes distorted. It allows close-up monitoring and adjustments unencumbered by bureaucratic red tape, procedures, and hierarchy. If parents observe, for example, that teachers are overly concentrating on basic skills, they are able to move with little hindrance to correct the behavior, perhaps with the structural remedies described above. Local school actors would not be starting from scratch because the incentives system would have part of the school's work already under control. The job of local actors would be more narrowly defined—to monitor, adjust, and fine-tune the allocation of effort at school. Parents have natural incentives with respect to the operation of schools—the welfare of their children. They simply need a system that makes their job realistically manageable and limits the risk of poor management.

Incentives provide a check on decentralization where the risk is that local actors may not direct the school's instructional program well. Decentralization provides a check on the distortions likely to emerge in an incentives-only system. The major hitch is that local monitors, usually parents, must be able to detect distortions and be able to make judgments about both the seriousness of the distortions and ways to correct them. This is largely an information problem. Ultimately, for an SBM system with incentives to work most effectively, central authorities should provide information and technical assistance to school-level actors. The content of the information and the way it is provided are consequential. The information contained in "report cards" on schools, for example, has some of the same problems that incentives do, albeit less severe ones. It can divert attention to those things easily measured.

A second type of information, though more costly to provide, is likely to be more valuable. This is information to enhance local actors' understanding of the range of production possibilities in education. It might be acquired by visiting other schools to learn what they are doing; joining a network of schools where technical advice is shared, or bringing in consultants on particular issues. This type of information would help local school actors identify possible shortcomings in their school's instructional program as well as likely solutions.

In short, performance incentive schemes in education and decentralized management arrangements each have advantages and disadvantages. To some extent, however, they balance each other out. Decentralized management systems are important because local monitoring can correct some of the distortions created by imperfect incentive systems and incentives are important because of the weaknesses in the management capacity of many local schools. Even with both decentralization and performance incentives, quality performance and process information is needed to ensure success.

Research Considerations

As Summers and Johnson observe in their chapter in this volume, information on the contribution of SBM and other education reforms to student performance is meager. But we should not be overly critical of education research for the lack of good evaluations. A number of research problems make it a difficult area in which to obtain clear results.

One problem noted earlier is the absence of agreed-upon goals. The extent to which all schools are pursuing the same objectives is unclear. Even if a common set of agreed-upon objectives could be defined, there would still be serious measurement issues. If it were easy to identify and measure value-added in education, it would be easy to design incentive schemes to elicit the desired behavior; management issues would be of little concern. Management in education is important, but difficult to evaluate and prescribe precisely, because identifying and measuring agreed-upon value-added is so difficult.

Second, any analysis of the value of governance reforms on student achievement has to deal with problems of endogeneity. To a large extent management approaches are shaped by the context in which they operate, as a large literature in organization theory attests. In education the degree to which authority is distributed to lower levels is significantly shaped by the social and political environment in which a school district operates. The more conflicting pressure in the political environment of the district, the more likely it is that the school system will be run in a centralized way. External political pressures, for example, as measured by union strength, urban location, or share of revenue received from federal and state sources, have been shown to be negatively correlated, on average, with student performance (Hannaway, 1993). Evidence in the general organization literature also shows that poor performance itself leads to more centralized operations. The implication of this is that simple correlations between governance and performance can be misleading.

A third issue is the implicit assumption in much of the reform discussion of a tight connection between management and education productivity. While reformers are likely to overstate the tightness of the connection, some causal link between the management of education organizations and the academic achievement of students is reasonable. We should not, however, underestimate the difficulty of establishing the connection with empirical research. Earlier research has consistently shown that out-of-school factors, especially family background characteristics, are the dominant determinants of student performance. If management has an effect on student performance, it is not likely to be large and therefore requires careful research and precise measurement to capture. Unfortunately, accurate measures of output and process are difficult in education. The small differences in the performance of public and private school students, where management differences are large, support the likely difficulty of capturing clear links between management changes and performance in education.

Fourth, decentralization may have different effects in different settings. If it is not explicitly taken into account that SBM may have a greater beneficial effect in some schools than in others, there is a risk of lumping all schools together and coming to faulty conclusions about effects. In some school districts, for example, otherwise alienated families and schools might be bound together in ways that reduce dropout rates later, even though they might have little effect on measured student learning in the short run. The interaction of technical assistance and decentralization also might vary by setting. For example, technical assistance might be an especially critical catalyst for effective decentralized management in disadvantaged areas.

Realizing there are limitations to what we can learn from systematic evaluations of governance reforms, however, is no excuse for not attempting them. Indeed, the field is in dire need of more careful analyses of effects in order to guide policy.

Finally, with organizational reforms of any kind the "devil is in the details." And in the case of governance reforms in education, we are not sure what the critical details are. We need more than simple models, for example, of the ways in which the various elements of governance reforms, such as SBM with incentives, interact with different contexts to affect student performance. There are, indeed, too many studies that focus only on process when the goal is to affect output; but to have any confidence that reforms are having an effect, we have to understand the process. Furthermore, with a better understanding of process we may be able to design alternative, perhaps more efficient, reforms that produce the same process. In short, along with systematic evaluations on the effects of governance reform efforts on student performance, more studies are needed on the nature of education governance itself.

REFERENCES

Bryk, A. S., P. E. Deabster, J. Q. Easton, S. Luppescu, and Y. M. Thum. 1994a."Measuring achievement gains in the Chicago public schools." *Education and Urban Society* 26:306–319.

Downes, T., and J. L. Horowitz. 1994. An analysis of the effect of Chicago reform on student performance. Mimeo, Tufts University, Medford, Mass.

Easton, J. Q., and S. L. Storey. 1994. "The development of local schools councils." *Education and Urban Society* 26:220–237.

Haertel, E. 1986. "The valid use of student performance measures for teacher evaluation." *Educational Research and Evaluation* 8:45–60.

Hannaway, J. 1993. "Decentralizing in two districts: challenging the standard paradigm." Pp. 135–162 in *Decentralization and School Improvement: Can We Fulfill the Promise?* J. Hannaway and M. Carnou, eds. San Francisco: Jossey-Bass.

Hannaway, J. 1995. "Decentralization and school reform: a demand perspective." Pp. 203-232 in *Advances in Research and Theories of School Management and Educational Policy.* R. Ogawa, Ed. Greenwich, Conn.: JAI Press.

Hannaway, J., and D. Chaplin. 1994. *Breaking the Cycle: Instructional Efficacy and Teachers of "At-Risk" Students.* Washington, D.C.:The Urban Institute.

Hanushek, Eric. 1994. *Making Schools Work: Improving Performance and Controlling Costs.* Washington, D.C.: The Brookings Institution.

Hess, G. A., Jr. 1993. "Race and the liberal perspective in Chicago school reform." In *The New Politics of Race and Gender*, C. Marshall, ed. New York: The Falmer Press.

Holmstrom, B., and P. Milgrom. 1992. "Multi-task principal-agent analyses: incentive contracts, asset ownership, and job design." *Journal of Law, Economics and Organization.*

Koretz, D. M., G. E. Madaus, E. Haertel, and A. E. Beaton. 1992. *National Standards and Testing: A Response to the Recommendations of the National Council on Education Standards and Testing.* Washington, D.C.: Rand Corp.

Lareau, A. 1987. "Social class and family-school relationships: the importance of cultural capital." *Sociology of Education* 56:73–85.

Lareau, A. 1989. *Home Advantage.* New York: The Falmer Press.

Malen, B., and R. Ogawa. 1988. "Professional-patron influences on site-based governance councils: a confounding case study." *Educational Evaluation and Policy Analysis* 10:251–270.

Martin, D. T., G. E. Overholt, and W. J. Urban. 1976. *Accountability in American Education: A Critique.* Princeton, N.J.: Princeton Book Co.

Ogbu, J. 1974. *The Next Generation.* New York.

Porter, A. 1989. "A curriculum out of balance: elementary school mathematics." *Educational Researcher* 18:9–15.

Rapple, B. 1990. *Payment by Educational Results: An Idea Whose Time Has Gone?* The MacArthur/ Spender Special Series on Illinois School Finance. Normal: Illinois State University.

Shanker, A. 1994. "Where we stand: the Chicago reform." *New York Times*, Jan. 3, p. E7.

Stevenson, D. L., and D. P. Baker. 1987. "The family-school relation and the child's school performance." *Child Development* 58:1348–1357.

Weiss, C., and J. Cambone. 1994. "Principals, shared decision making, and school reform." *Educational Evaluation and Policy Analysis* 16:287–301.

Zill, N., and C. Windquist Nort. 1994. *Running in Place: How American Families are Faring in a Changing Economy and an Individualistic Society.* Washington, D.C.: Child Trends. Inc.

CHAPTER 7

Signaling, Incentives, and School Organization in France, the Netherlands, Britain, and the United States

JOHN H. BISHOP
Cornell University

Despite similar standards of living, the secondary education systems of France, the Netherlands, Britain, and the United States produce very different levels and patterns of achievement. In primary school, Americans do not trail their European counterparts. Reading ability varies little across these four countries. When 14 year olds were compared at the beginning of the 1980s, however, the French and Dutch were about 1.3 to 1.5 grade-level equivalents ahead of the Americans in math and science. At the end of secondary school, performance differentials were even larger.

What causes differences in secondary school achievement across these four nations? The first section of this chapter describes these achievement differences. Seven hypothesized proximate causes are evaluated in the second section. Four hypotheses can be rejected. The rest cannot: teacher quality, priority given to academics, student engagement, and time on task.

The third section addresses a more fundamental question: Why do American students, teachers, parents, and school administrators place a lower priority on academic achievement than their counterparts abroad? Why, for example, is student engagement in learning higher in France and the Netherlands? Some people blame American culture, antiintellectualism, or historical tradition. Such

[1]Preparation of this paper was funded by grants from the German Marshall Fund of the United States, the Pew Charitable Trust, and the Center on the Educational Quality of the Workforce (agreement number R117Q00011-91, as administered by the Office of Educational Research and Improvement, U.S. Department of Education). The findings and opinions expressed here do not reflect the position or policies of the Office of Educational Research and Improvement or the U.S. Department of Education.

ad hoc explanations cannot be ruled out, or in, by the analysis that follows. The purpose here, instead, is to propose an alternative explanation derived from economic theory and a few observations regarding the contrasting ways in which learning achievement is measured and then signaled to parents, school administrators, colleges, and employers in the five countries. The third section also shows how signaling theory, game theory, and agency theory provide a robust explanation of the learning deficits in American upper secondary schools.

According to the economic theory developed below, the fundamental cause is the structure of incentives for learning and high-quality teaching of demanding material. American employers reward credentials, but they fail to recognize and reward what is actually learned in school. Admission to the best colleges depends on measures of relative performance—rank in class and grades—and aptitude tests that do not assess what is taught in school, not external assessments of competence in particular subjects. Only one of the 50 states has a system of subject-specific external exams similar to the Baccalaureat (Bac), the General Certificate of Secondary Education (GCSE), and the Dutch exams. The result has been grade inflation and students selecting undemanding courses where it is easy to get a high grade. Students pressure each other not to study, in part because they are being graded on a curve. Teachers are pressured to keep failure rates low, so passing standards are effectively forced down by peer pressure against studying. The final section of this chapter summarizes the analysis and comments on the implications for economic analysis of education policy.

DIFFERENTIALS IN ACADEMIC ACHIEVEMENT

The differences in achievement levels at ages 13, 14, and 15 are summarized in Table 7.1. The table presents data from studies conducted in the 1980s and 1990s comparing France, the Netherlands, England, Scotland, and the United States. The International Association for the Evaluation of Educational Achievements (IAEEA) studies sampled students at particular grade levels, not at particular ages. Consequently, age-adjusted scores on its tests are reported where possible and information on the age of the sample is provided in the footnotes of the table.

Reading. In the 1990–1991 IAEEA study of reading, age-adjusted scores indicated that American 9 year olds (see column 1 of Table 7.1) were reading about 58 percent of a U.S standard deviation (SD) better than Dutch 9 year olds and about .20 SDs better than French 9 year olds. However, by age 14, differences between the countries (column 2) were tiny.

Mathematics. In the 1981–1982 study of mathematics achievement of 13 to 14 year olds conducted by the IAEEA, Dutch and French 13 to 14 year olds ranked second and third, respectively, behind only Japan. Of the 17 industrialized nations participating in the study of 13 to 14 year olds, Americans were

TABLE 7.1   Achievement in Lower Secondary School

	1991 IEA Reading Age Adjusted			1982 IEA Math	1983 IEA Science			1991 IAEP Mathematics			1991 IAEP Science		
					Ages 14-15 (not adjusted for age)			Level Age 13			Level Age 13		
	Age 9	Age 14		Ages 13-14			Adjusted for			Gain			Gain
	Mean	Mean	(SD)	% Correct	Mean	(SD)	Age Difference	% Correct	(SD)	Age 9 to Age 13	% Correct	(SD)	Age 9 to Age 13
France	526	533	(68)	53.9	—	—	—	64.2	(20.3)	—	68.6	(17.1)	—
Netherlands	494	523	(76)	57.1	63.7	(16.1)	62.2	—	—	—	—	—	—
England	—	—	—	47.1	55.9	(15.7)	62.2	60.6	(21.4)	29.8	68.7	(17.5)	18.7
Scotland	—	—	—	48.4	—	—	—	60.6	(20.3)	26.5	67.9	(16.5)	20.8
United States	543	528	(85)	46.4	53.7	(16.7)	53.7	55.3	(20.9)	25.4	67.0	(16.4)	17.2

Columns 1, 2, and 3 are the age-adjusted means and standard deviations of the overall reading score in the IAEEA reading study (Elley 1992).

Column 4 is a weighted mean percent correct for students in the grade where the majority have attained 13:00 to 13:11 years by the middle of the school year from the Second International Mathematics Study (McKnight et al., 1987). The French, English, and American students all had the same mean age, 14.1. Mean age was 14.0 for Scotland and 14.4 for the Netherlands. Adjusting for the greater age of the Dutch students would have lowered their percent correct by about 2 points.

Columns 5 and 6 are the percent correct and standard deviation for ninth graders on the full 50-item IAEEA science test (Postlethwaite and Wiley, 1992). An estimate of how U.S. students would have performed on the full test was made by subtracting 1.1 percentage points (the average difference between core and full test scores for England and the Netherlands) from the U.S. core test score. The mean age of students differed a great deal. Mean age was 14:2 for England, 15.3 for the United States, and 15:6 for the Netherlands.

Column 7 is an estimate of scores for the full 50-item IAEEA science test for students who are 15.3 years old, the mean age of U.S. students. The age gradient used was the average for Sweden (4.3) and Italy (7.4), the two countries for which it was available.

Columns 8, 9, 11, and 12 are the mean percent correct and standard deviation from the 1991 IAEP study of mathematics and science achievement of 13 year olds (IAEP, 1992a, b).

Columns 10 and 13 are the increase in the percent correct on items common to the tests given to 9 and 13 year olds.

ranked twelfth, English eleventh, and Scots tenth (McKnight et al., 1987). After adjusting for small differences in mean age, American 14 year olds scored 10.7 points below Dutch students, and 7.5 points below French students, of comparable age (see column 4). The 1991 International Assessment of Educational Progress (IAEP) mathematics study obtained similar results (columns 8–10). The gap between French and American 13 year olds was 42.6 percent of a U.S. standard deviation (about 1.3 U.S. grade-level equivalents).[2] British students were about halfway between the French and the Americans (IAEP, 1992a). The gap remained roughly constant even though the math achievement of 13-year-old Americans improved by .20 SDs between 1982 and 1992 (NCES, 1994).

The performance gap between the American and European students grows even larger during upper-secondary school (see Table 7.2). The Americans who participated in the Second International Math Study were high school seniors in college preparatory math courses, such as trigonometry, precalculus, and calculus. This very select group, representing 13 percent of American 17 to 18 year olds, got 39.8 percent of the questions correct. The 6 percent of English students studying mathematics at A-level got 59.8 percent correct (McKnight et al., 1987). Substantial proportions of French and Dutch secondary students specialize in mathematics and science; 20 percent of French youth are in the mathematics and science lines known as C, D, or E of the *lycee general*. The questions asked on their final examinations suggest that these students achieve at a very high level.

Science. In the 1983 IAEEA study of science achievement of 14 to 15 year olds, the Netherlands ranked third and the United States ranked last among 17 industrialized countries. After a rough adjustment for age differences, American students lagged slightly more than half a standard deviation (about 1.4 U.S. grade-level equivalents) behind English and Dutch students (see column 5, Table 7.2).

The 1991 IAEP science study found that at age 9 American students were ahead of students in Scotland, England, and most other European countries. Data for France and the Netherlands are not available for this age. By age 13, English, Scotch, and French students were ahead, although the differences were small and not statistically significant (IAEP, 1992b). The gap is smaller in the more recent study in part because overall science achievement of 13 year old Americans rose by .21 SDs between 1982 and 1992 (NCES, 1994).

---

[2]If mean differences in achievement are to be given a grade-level equivalent (GLE) interpretation, an assumption must be made about the relationship between grade-level equivalents and the sample standard deviation for the test. This relationship varies across tests and across societies, depending on the age of the students tested, the character of the test, and the pace of instruction. The approximate number of GLEs per SD for 13 year olds is about four for NAEP assessments, three for the Iowa Test of Basic Skills (eighth graders), and 2.85 for the IEA science test. Where an estimate for the specific test is not available, I assume an SD on a test taken by 14 year olds equals 3 U.S. GLEs.

TABLE 7.2   Achievement at the End of Upper Secondary School

| | 1982 IEA Mathematics Final Year of Secondary School | | | 1983 IEA Science--Final Year of Upper Secondary School | | | | | | | | | |
| | | | | Physics | | | Chemistry | | | Biology | | | |
	% Correct	% Age Group	% Time Math	% Correct	% Age Group	Hr. Per Week	% Correct	% Age Group	Hr. Per Week	% Correct	% Age Group	Hr. Per Week	Total Science Homework
France	—	—	—	—	—	—	—	—	—	—	—	—	—
Netherlands	—	—	—	—	—	—	—	—	—	—	—	—	—
Belgium	50.0	10	20	—	—	—	—	—	—	—	—	—	—
Finland	60.6	15	14	37.9	14	2.0	35.9	16	1.0	50.2	41	2.0	3.1
Norway	—	—	—	54.1	10	5.0	44.3	6	5.0	55.4	4	5.0	—
England	59.8	6	21	62.4	6	5.1	69.3	5	5.2	62.4	4	5.2	7.2
Scotland	42.8	18	17	—	—	—	—	—	—	—	—	—	—
United States	39.8	12	14	45.3	1	5.0	37.7	2	5.0	38.1	12	5.0	2.8

Column 1 is a weighted mean percent correct for students in the final year of secondary school from the Second International Mathematics Study (McKnight et al., 1987). The mean age was 17:8 for the U.S., 18:1 for England, 16:9 for Scotland, 18:6 for Finland, 19:2 for Sweden, and 18:3 for Belgium.

Column 2 is the share of the age cohort in advanced mathematics courses included in the study.

Column 3 is the share of school time spent in mathematics classes.

Columns 4, 7, and 10 give the percent correct for students studying each science subject in the final year of secondary school.

Columns 5, 8, and 11 are the proportions of the age cohort taking each science subject in the final year of secondary school (for the U.S. it is the share of students taking their second year of the subject).

Columns 6, 9, and 12 are the number of hours per week spent in classes in each science subject (Postlethwaite and Wiley, 1992). The mean age was 17:5 to 17:10 for the U.S., 18:0 for England, 18:7 for Finland, and 18:11 for Norway.

Few American upper secondary school students study science in depth (see Table 7.2). Only 1 or 2 percent of this age cohort takes two years of physics or chemistry. Despite the highly selected nature of this group, many of whom were taking the subject for advanced placement college credit, only 47.5 percent of the questions were answered correctly on the IAEEA physics exam and only 37.7 percent were correct on the IAEEA chemistry exam. The 4 or 5 percent of this age cohort of English youth who in their thirteenth year of schooling were studying these subjects for their A-level exams got 62.4 and 69.3 percent correct, respectively (Postlethwaite and Wiley, 1992).

TEACHER QUALITY, TIME, AND ENGAGEMENT: THE PROXIMATE CAUSES OF ACHIEVEMENT DIFFERENTIALS

American elementary school students do not lag their counterparts in Europe. Indeed, in reading they are substantially ahead and in science slightly ahead (see rows 1 and 13 of Table 7.1). What, then, caused the large deficits in achievement in mathematics and science at the end of secondary school? Why does achievement lag in math and science but not in reading? Let us start by looking at seven proposed proximate causes of achievement differentials across countries:

- Diversity
- Restricted access to secondary education
- Teacher quality and salaries
- Overall spending per pupil
- Priority given to academic achievement
- Time devoted to instruction and study
- Engagement or effort per unit of scheduled time

The purpose here is not to select a single most important explanation for U.S. students lagging their French and Dutch counterparts. Rather, the objective is the more modest one of narrowing the list of possible causes.

Diversity

Non-Hispanic whites score about .45 GLEs higher than the overall U.S. average on NAEP reading tests, about .56 GLEs higher on NAEP mathematics tests, and .98 GLEs higher on NAEP science tests. If all French and Dutch students are compared to the 77 percent of American students who are neither black nor Hispanic, the European advantage is smaller. For mathematics at age 13, the gap would be about 0.9 GLEs in both 1982 and 1991. In 1983 white U.S. 13 year olds were about 0.5 GLEs behind the Dutch in science and in 1991 about .6 GLEs ahead of French 13 year olds.

But is it really fair to compare the non-Hispanic white population of the

United States to the total population of France and the Netherlands? The United States is not the only country with a diverse student population. The Netherlands accepted 120,000 immigrants in 1990—twice the rate of immigration into the United States. In both France and the United States the share of students who are taught in a language different from their mother tongue is 6 percent; it is 5 percent in Scotland, 12 percent in Canada, 15 percent in Northern Italy, and 20 percent in Switzerland (IAEP, 1992a). If scores are adjusted for the demographic and socioeconomic backgrounds of students, why not hold parent's education constant as well? If this were done, the French/Dutch lead over the United States would increase.

Access—Numbers of Students and Graduates

It is sometimes said that low achievement is the price that must be paid for greater access. However, only the United Kingdom exhibits the expected trade-off between achievement levels and enrollment ratios (see Table 7.3). Only 43

TABLE 7.3   1991 Enrollment and Completion Rates

	France	Netherlands	United Kingdom	United States
Percent enrolled full time in secondary school				
Age 16	92.0	97.2	62.4	90.2
Age 17	86.4	90.0	43.1	74.7
Age 18	57.2	67.4	12.3	21.1
Age 19	31.6	41.5	3.4	5.0
FTE enrollment in tertiary education				
Age 18	19.1	12.7	24.4	33.1
Ages 18–21	26.6	19.5	16.0	33.4
Ages 22–25	12.7	14.0	4.8	13.5
Ages 26–29	4.0	4.0	2.2	6.2
FTE years in school between ages 16 and 29[a]	4.6	4.9	2.3	4.1
School enrollment rate, Ages 5–29	57.7	55.2	52.7	55.2
Secondary diplomas awarded / population of theoretical completion age[b]	75.8	82.2	74.4	75.5
First-degree graduates from universities / population of theoretical completion age	16.3	8.3	18.4	29.6

SOURCES: OECD (1993), NCES (1992), and Government Statistical Office (1992).

   a Calculated by summing the ratios of FTE enrollment to population for one-year age groups from ages 16 to 29.

   b The U.S. data do not include GED certificates. The labor market does not view the GED as equivalent to a high school diploma. GED-certified high school equivalents are paid 6 percent more than high school dropouts but 8 to 11 percent less than high school graduates. The graduation rate for the United Kingdom is spuriously high because it counts regular GCSE exams taken at the end of the eleventh year of schooling as graduation. If one or more A-level exams had been the definition of secondary school graduation, the graduation rate would have been 28 percent.

percent of British 17 year olds and 12 percent of 18 year olds were attending secondary school full time in 1991. Students preparing for A-level exams achieve at high levels, but they represent a decided minority of their age cohorts. By contrast, French and Dutch youth have higher enrollment rates than American youth. For example, 86.4 percent of French and 90 percent of Dutch 17 year olds were in secondary school in 1991, but only 74.7 percent of American 17 year olds were. At age 18 enrollment in either secondary or tertiary education was 76 percent in France, 80 percent in the Netherlands, and 54 percent in the United States. Despite lower college attendance rates in France and the Netherlands, larger shares of 18 to 21 year olds in France (52.2 percent on a full-time equivalent [FTE] basis) and the Netherlands (56.4 percent) are enrolled in school (either secondary or tertiary) than in the United States (40.4 percent). Between ages 16 and 29, the average American spends 4.1 FTE years in school, British youth 2.3 years, French youth 4.6 years, and Dutch youth 4.9 years (OECD, 1993). These statistics contradict the widely held belief that the American education system, despite all its faults, at least achieves higher levels of participation than the European systems.

Not only are secondary school graduation standards higher eslewhere than in the United States, graduation rates are higher as well. In 1991 the graduation rate was 82.2 percent in the Netherlands, 75.8 percent in France, and 75.5 percent in the United States. The large proportions of 18 to 19 year olds attending secondary school in France and the Netherlands indicate how high graduation standards are made compatible with high graduation rates. Students having difficulty with the fast-paced curriculum do not drop out; rather, they repeat grades and thus gain extra time to prepare for the demanding external exams. Many participate in vocational programs and apprenticeships, which currently account for 54 percent of French and 70 percent of Dutch upper secondary students (OECD, 1993).

The benefit of earlier completion of secondary school in the United States is that large numbers of students enter tertiary education at a young age. However, some of the material covered during the first two years of college in the United States is covered in upper secondary school in France and the Netherlands. More bachelor's degrees are awarded in the United States, but some doubt that the B.A.s awarded by America's second-rank universities represent the same standard of achievement as comparable European degrees. Hard evidence on this issue is not available.

Teacher Quality and Compensation

The quality of the people recruited to teach is very important. A teacher's general academic ability and subject knowledge are the characteristics that most consistently predict student learning (Hanushek, 1971; Strauss and Sawyer, 1986; Ferguson, 1990; Ehrenberg and Brewer, 1993; Monk, 1992).

Secondary school teaching is not a prestige occupation in the United States, and it apparently does not attract the same level of talent as in France and the Netherlands. Since university admission standards are higher in Europe, the university graduate pool from which European secondary school teachers are recruited is better educated on average than the college graduate pool out of which American teachers are recruited. Furthermore, American teachers are generally not the most talented members of the pool of college graduates. In 1977–1978 the mathematics Scholastic Aptitude Test (SAT) score of intended education majors was .38 standard deviations (SDs) below the overall average, 1 SD below engineering majors, and 1.2 SDs below physical sciences majors. The verbal SAT scores of intended education majors were .30 SDs below the overall average (NCES, 1992). In this respect, Britain is similar; entrants into programs to prepare primary school teachers have significantly lower A-level grades than average for university entrants (O'Leary, 1993).

In France, by contrast, secondary school teachers must do a double major in the two subjects for which they seek certification and then pass rigorous subject matter examinations. In 1991 only 31.3 percent of those who took the written exam for the *Certificat d'Aptitude au Professorat de l'Enseignement du Secondaire*, the most common of these examinations, passed. The best teaching jobs go to those who pass an even more rigorous examination, the *Agregation Externe*, which in 1991 had a pass rate of 17.7 percent (Ministere de l'Education Nationale et de la Culture, 1992a and 1992b). French and Dutch secondary school teachers tend to be recruited from the middle of a pool of graduates of tertiary education, which in turn is a more selected sample of the nation's population.

Furthermore, American teachers are often not expert in the fields they teach. Recent college graduates recruited into math or science teaching jobs spent only 30 percent of their college career taking science and mathematics courses. Since 46 percent had not taken a single calculus course, the prerequisite for most advanced mathematics courses, it appears that most of the math taken in college consisted of reviewing high school mathematics (NCES, 1993). The graduates of the best American universities typically do not become secondary school teachers because the pay and work conditions are relatively poor.

Compensation. The high academic standards for entry into upper secondary school teaching in France and the Netherlands are sustainable only if wages and work conditions are attractive. Data on the relative compensation of secondary school teachers are presented in rows 1 and 2 of Table 7.4. American upper secondary school teachers start at a wage that is 14 percent below that of the average worker, and after 15 years of experience they earn only 33 percent more. Starting salaries are equally low in England. However, the starting salaries in France are 6 percent above the average for all workers and in the Netherlands they are 39 percent higher. In France, England, and Scotland, upper secondary school teachers with 15 years of experience are paid 61 to 63 percent more than the average worker, and in the Netherlands they are paid 132 percent more than

TABLE 7.4   Teacher Compensation and Conditions of Work

	France	Netherlands	England	Scotland	United States
Compensation–Teacher/All Employees[c]					
Upper secondary school teacher–starting	1.06	1.39	.87	91	.86
Mid-career (15 yr)	1.61	2.32	1.63	1.61	1.33
Lower secondary school teacher–starting	.95	1.12	.87	.91	.86
Mid-career (15 yr)	1.44	1.58	1.63	1.61	1.33
Primary school teacher–starting	.93	.97	.87	.91	.84
Mid-career (15 yr)	1.34	1.39	1.57	1.61	1.30
Teacher Class Contact Hours/Year[d]					
Upper secondary school	532	943	776	887	825
Lower secondary school	706	943	776	887	748
Primary School	875	1014	1013	950	1098
Class Size[e]					
Upper secondary school	29	24	16	15	25.6
Lower secondary school	24	28	16	20	26.8
Primary school	23	25	25	20	24.0
Secondary School Students/Teachers[f]	14.0	15.9	14.7	14.7	15.5
Secondary School expenditure/student relative to GDP per capita	28.1	24.7	28.0	28.0	29.4
Share of staff not classroom teachers[g]	36%	20%	—	—	47%

SOURCES: Nelson and O'Brien (1993), OECD (1993), Ministere de l'Education Nationale et de la Culture (1992a and b), and NCES (1992).

a Compensation of secondary school teachers was calculated by multiplying their salary by the ratio of compensation to wages for manufacturing workers. This estimate of teacher compensation was then divided by the average compensation of all workers. The figure for French upper secondary school teachers is a weighted average of salaries for Agregé (20%) and others (80%).

b Mean number of hours teaching a class per week times the mean number of weeks in the school year. Time devoted to preparation, in-service training, and to nonteaching activities is not included in this total.

c Mean number of students in each class.

d The ratio of the number of FTE pupils enrolled in public and private secondary schools to the number of FTE secondary school teachers.

e Share of all staff employed in publicly funded elementary and secondary schools and ministries of education that are not classroom teachers. The nonteaching staff includes administrators at all levels, teachers aides, guidance counselors, librarians, nurses, custodial staff, food service workers, bus drivers, and clerical workers. The Dutch figure is for all three levels of schooling. The French figure is for secondary education only. The U.S. figure is for public elementary and secondary schools and does not include people working for state departments of education. In the U.S. teachers aides account for 8.8 percent of school staff.

the average worker. For primary school teachers, by contrast, American pay levels are comparable to their Dutch and French counterparts (see row 6).

The lower pay in the United States is not compensation for more attractive work conditions (see rows 7–13 of Table 7.4). French upper secondary school teachers are in front of a classroom only 532 hours per year. Their American counterparts teach 825 hours per year. Teaching hours in England and Scotland are similar to U.S. levels, 776 and 886, respectively, but class sizes are substantially smaller. Dutch upper secondary school teachers are the only group that clearly have heavier teaching loads than American teachers (Nelson and O'Brien, 1993).

When the salaries of college graduates are compared, those who enter teaching come out at the bottom. The starting salaries of U.S. mathematics and physical science majors who entered teaching were 42 percent below the salaries of those who obtained computer programming and system analyst jobs and 35 percent below the starting salaries of those obtaining jobs in mathematics or the physical sciences (NCES, 1993). University graduates who majored in a physical science earned 78 percent more and economics majors earned 92 percent more than education majors over the course of their working lives (Kominski and Sutterlin, 1992). Since Americans with university training in mathematics and science can earn much more outside teaching, those with talent in these areas are difficult to recruit into high school teaching. The result is that most American teachers of mathematics and science are less well prepared than their Northern European counterparts. This may help explain why American students lag French and Dutch students in mathematics and science but not reading. The fact that American primary school teachers are paid almost as much as French and Dutch teachers may also help explain why American 9 to 10 year olds compare favorably to their counterparts abroad.

There is a deeper question, however. Why are the academic standards for entry into upper secondary school teaching in the United States set so low? Why are salaries so low? These questions will be addressed later.

Overall Spending per Pupil

Data on pupil-teacher ratios and spending per pupil are presented in rows 13 and 14 of Table 7.4. Pupil-teacher ratios are quite similar in the five countries, as are the ratios of spending per pupil to per-capita gross domestic produce (GDP). Consequently, "low" overall levels of spending on K–12 education are not the cause of the lag in U.S. student achievement.

Priority Given to Academics

If American spending per pupil is comparable to that in our four comparison countries, why are salary levels lower? What happens to the money saved by paying lower teacher salaries? It is used to hire additional nonteaching staff. Nonteachers account for nearly one-half of the employees in public education in the United States but only one-fifth in the Netherlands and 36 percent of secondary education employees in France (see bottom row of Table 7.4). These staff members perform services (such as bus transportation, sports activities, before- and after-school day care, counseling, and occupational training) that are provided by other governmental organizations or the private sector in some other nations. The money also pays for the more attractive buildings, sports facilities, large school libraries, numerous computers, and colorful texts that are typical of American secondary schools. In part, this reflects the fact that in the United States books, computers, and buildings are cheaper relative to teachers of constant quality. U.S. spending patterns also reflect different goals. Academic achievement is the overarching—some would say the only—goal of French and Dutch secondary schools. In the United States, academic achievement must compete with other goals. American schools are also expected to foster self-esteem and provide counseling, supervised extracurricular activities, musical training, health services, community entertainment (such as interscholastic sports), and drivers' education—and do so in a racially integrated setting. These other goals require additional and different kinds of staff members. They may not be served by hiring teachers with a strong background in calculus or chemistry, so resources get diverted from paying the high salaries necessary to recruit teachers who are thoroughly educated in chemistry. Unlike France, selection into teaching is not based almost solely on competence in the subject matter.

The question remains, however, of why American school administrators give academic achievement lower priority than French and Dutch administrators do. This question will be taken up later.

Time Devoted to Instruction

Many studies have found learning to be strongly related to time on task (Wiley, 1976; Walberg, 1992). How do the five countries differ in the time that students spend in classrooms and doing homework? Table 7.5 reports the results of a variety of studies that compare time devoted to instruction. While estimates vary across studies, the pattern for secondary school students in the 1980s and 1990s is that French, Dutch, and Scottish students spent 5 to 15 percent more time in school than U.S. students. English students, by contrast, spent 6 to 9 percent less time in school than U.S. secondary school students.[3]

Differences in instruction time may explain some achievement differentials between countries, but they do not explain the generally poor showing of U.S. secondary school students in mathematics and science. While American students spend less total time in school, they get more mathematics and science instruction time than do French, Dutch, and Scottish students. Heavy European time commitments to foreign language study tend to crowd out mathematics and science instruction. In lower secondary school, British students study one foreign language and French and Dutch students generally study two. In America, by

---

[3]Estimates of total time students in a country spend in school seem to depend on who is asked and how the question is worded. The data quality problem was dealt with by calculating an average across studies. The total instruction per year for each country was first expressed as a ratio to the U.S. level. Then a mean ratio was calculated by averaging the ratios from the studies that provided a comparison with the United States. Sources are given in the notes to Table 7.5.

TABLE 7.5   Student Time—Instruction and Homework

	France	Netherlands	England	Scotland	United States
Total hours of instruction/year					
Primary school—1971	918	1040	900	1040	900
Grade 5 in 1982	—	—	984	—	1070
Grade 4 in 1991	840	975	—	—	954
Secondary School—1971	775	1120	900	1080	900
Grade 9 in 1982	—	1007	1025	—	1141
Grade 8 in 1982	1187	1000	896	1067	1008
Grade 9 in 1991	1030	1092	—	—	792
Age 13 in 1991	1073	—	960	1031	1003
Hours of Homework in All Subjects					
Hours/week—grade 9 in 1982	—	8.4	6.0	—	9.6
Hours/week—grade 8 in 1982	8	5	5	3	5
Hours/week—grade 12 math in 1982	—	—	—	—	9
Hours/week—grade 12 science in 1982	—	—	11.5	—	9.8
Hours/week—grade 4 in 1991	0.53	0.13	—	—	1.89
Homework GT 2 hours/day, age 13 in 1991	55%	—	30%	15%	30%
Hours worked on language arts—grade 4	9	7	—	—	11
No. language arts homework assignment/week, grade 9 in 1991	1.6	.4	—	—	2.3
Time Devoted to Mathematics					
Math share—grade 8 in 1982	12%	10%	13%	14%	14%
Hours/week math instruction—age 13 in 1991	3.83	—	3.17	3.50	3.80
Hours/week math homework—age 13 in 1991	1.93	—	1.27	1.00	1.52
Hours/week math homework—grade 8 in 1982	4.0	2.0	1.0	2.0	3.0
Time Devoted to Science					
Grade 5 in 1971	8%	2%	3%	3%	7%
Grade 5 in 1982	—	—	4%	—	10%
Grade 9 in 1971	8%	7%	8%	5%	10%
Grade 9 in 1982	—	25%	10%	—	20%
Hours/week science instruction, age 13 in 1991	2.90	—	3.23	3.00	3.88
Hours/week science homework, age 13 in 1991	0.68	—	0.97	0.65	1.06

SOURCES: Passow et al. (1976), Postlethwaite and Wiley (1992), Robitaille and Garden (1989), IAEP (1992a, b), Lundberg and Linnakyla (1993).

contrast, few lower secondary school students study a foreign language and, by high school graduation, students have taken an average of only 1.46 years of a foreign language (NCES, 1992).

European students learn mathematics and science more thoroughly than American students do even when they spend less time on it. For example, in the IAEP study, mathematics instruction time was the same in France and the United States, yet French students knew about 1.47 U.S. grade-level equivalents more than American students. In science, by contrast, instruction time was one hour per week less in France, yet Americans still trailed French students by about one-third of a U.S. grade-level equivalent. Why does an hour of instruction in French and Dutch classrooms produce more learning than in American classrooms? Could heavier homework assignments be the explanation?

Cooper's (1989) meta-analysis of randomized experimental studies found that students assigned homework scored about one-half of a standard deviation higher on posttests than students not receiving homework assignments. The impact of homework on the rate at which middle school students learn also was significant, although somewhat smaller. Non-experimental studies using IAEEA and IAEP data come to similar conclusions.

French lower secondary school students spent more time doing mathematics homework and homework of all types (see Table 7.6). For example, 55 percent of their 13-year-olds reported doing over two hours of homework a night, compared to 30 percent in the United States and England and only 15 percent in Scotland.[4] This is consistent with their lead in mathematics achievement. In science, however, there is no evidence that Dutch and French students had more homework than American students. Furthermore, English and Scottish lower secondary school students do less homework and have less instruction time in mathematics and science than American students but still outperform them.

Engagement—Effort per Unit of Scheduled Time

Classroom observation studies reveal that American students actively engage in learning activities for only about half the time they are scheduled to be in a classroom. A study of schools in Chicago found that public schools with high-achieving students averaged about 75 percent of class time for actual instruction; for schools with low-achieving students, the average was 51 percent of class time (Frederick, 1977). Overall, Frederick et al. (1979) estimated 46.5 percent of potential learning time is lost due to absences, lateness, and inattention.

Just as important as the amount of time spent participating in a learning activity is the intensity of the student's involvement in the process. At the completion of his study of American high schools, Sizer (1984) characterized students as "all too often docile, compliant, and without initiative" (p. 54). Goodlad (1983) describes "a general picture of considerable passivity among students" (p. 113). The high school teachers surveyed by Goodlad ranked "lack of student interest" as the most important problem in education. In a Longitudi-

---

[4]The educational excellence movement in the United States caused a substantial increase in homework assignments and the time spent on homework between 1980 and 1990. In 1982, 27 percent of 13 year olds and 30 percent of 17 years olds reported not being assigned any homework. Another 11.5 percent of 17 year olds and 6 percent of 13 year olds reported not doing it. By 1990 only 5 to 6 percent of 13 and 17 year olds reported getting no homework and only 4 to 8 percent reported not doing what was assigned (NCES, 1993).

nal Survey of American Youth (1989) 62 percent of 10th graders agreed with the statement "I don't like to do any more school work than I have to."

Formal studies comparing ratios of on-task time to scheduled time are not available for European countries. Nevertheless, people who have visited classrooms in France or the Netherlands and the United States report that European teachers are less likely to talk about extraneous matters and that European students are more likely to pay attention and do their assignments. My own school visits in France and the Netherlands generated similar impressions.

Summary

Four of the seven proposed explanations for American students trailing French, British, and Dutch students in math and science can be ruled out: diversity, restricted access, spending per pupil, and time for instruction. Three hypotheses survive the first round of tests: lower-quality teachers, lower priority attached to academic goals, and lower levels of student engagement. With only five data points, no further narrowing of the list of hypothesized proximate causes is possible. Now let us look behind these proximate causes for ultimate causes. Why does an hour of instruction and homework time apparently have larger learning effects in England, France, and the Netherlands than in America? Why do French and Dutch secondary school mathematics and science teachers apparently expect more of their students than American teachers do? The next section of this chapter proposes some tentative system-level answers to these questions. The purpose is to show that a very simple application of economic theory can provide a plausible explanation for the large system-level differences in goals and learning efficiency cited above.

SIGNALING AS THE ULTIMATE CAUSE: EXTERNAL EXAMINATIONS AS STANDARD SETTERS

In a 1990 paper I proposed the following answer to these questions:

The fundamental cause of the low effort level of American students, parents, and voters in school elections is the absence of good signals of effort and learning in high school and a consequent lack of rewards for effort and learning. . . . In most other advanced countries mastery of the curriculum taught in high school is assessed by . . . examinations which are set and graded at the national or regional level. Grades on these exams signal the student's achievement to colleges and employers and influence the jobs that graduates get and the universities and programs to which they are admitted. How well the graduating seniors do on these exams influences the reputation of the school and in some countries the number of students applying for admission to the school. In the United States, by contrast, students take aptitude tests that are not intended to assess the learning that has occurred in most of the classes taken in high school.

The primary signals of academic achievement are grades and rank in class—criteria which assess achievement relative to other students in the school or classroom, not relative to an external standard. (Bishop, 1990, p. 3.)

Costrell (1994a, b) formally modeled the setting of educational standards and concluded that decentralized standards setting (i.e., teacher grading or school graduation requirements) results in lower standards, lower achievement, and lower social welfare than does more centralized standards setting (state or national achievement exams). He also concluded that "the case for perfect information [making scores on external examinations available rather than just whether an individual passed or failed] would appear to be strong, if not airtight: for most plausible degrees of heterogeneity, egalitarianism, and pooling under decentralization, perfect information not only raises GDP, but also social welfare" (1994a, p. 970).

Of the 50 states, only New York has a system of curriculum-based achievement exams that affect individual student grades and are taken by large shares, about one-half, of high school students. This or something else unique to New York state appears to have raised achievement levels. Graham and Husted (1993) discovered this fact when they examined the determinants of mean SAT test scores in the 37 states with reasonably large test-taking populations. Controlling for the proportion of high school seniors taking the SAT and the race, gender, parental income, and parental education of the test takers, they found that New York state had the highest adjusted mean SAT scores. They did not, however, test the statistical significance of the New York state effect and used an unusual log-log specification.

Are their findings robust to changes in specification? How large is the difference between New York and the rest of the nation? Is the differential statistically significant? Table 7.6 presents the results of a regression predicting 1991 mean SAT math and verbal scores for the 37 states for which data are available. With the exception of the dummy variable for New York state, all right-hand-side variables are proportions—generally the share of the test-taking population with the characteristic described. Clearly, New Yorkers do significantly better on the SAT, particularly the math portion, than do students of the same race and social background living in other states.[5] For individuals the

---

[5]When this model is estimated without the New York state dummy variable, New York has the largest positive residual in the sample. The next largest (Wisconsin) positive residual is 87 percent of New York's residual. Illinois and Nevada have positive residuals that are about 58 percent of New York's value. Arizona, California, Colorado, Florida, New Mexico, Ohio, Rhode Island, Texas, and Washington have negative residuals greater than 10 points. Many of these states have large populations of Hispanics and recent immigrants, a trait not controlled for in the analysis. This makes New York's achievement all the more remarkable since Hispanics and recent immigrants make up a very large share of the state's school children. Adding the pupil-teacher ratio and spending per pupil to the model reduces the New York state coefficient by 25 percent. It remains significantly greater than zero, however. This suggests that Regents exams may be one of the reasons that New York is a high-expenditure state and that greater spending and smaller classes may mediate some of the effects of a curriculum-based examination system.

TABLE 7.6 Determinants of Mean SAT Scores for States

	New York State	Participation Rate	Parents AA-BA+	Private School	Proportion Black	Large School	3 + Math Courses	3 + English Courses	$\overline{R2}$ RMSE
Total SAT	46[a] (2.7)	68[a] (2.6)	370[b] (6.4)	60 (1.6)	-135[b] (3.2)	-44[a] (1.8)	85 (1.3)	-36 (.3)	.93 14.8
Mean	.027	.414	.581	.207	.078	.129	.617	.797	Tot SAT 55
StanDev	.164	.240	.097	.082	.064	.113	.067	.038	925

[a]significant at 5% level.
[b]significant at 1% level.

summed SAT verbal and math scores have a standard deviation of approximately 200 points. Consequently, New York state's SAT mean is about 0.2 SDs or about 0.75 grade-level equivalents higher than the regression's prediction.

This occurred despite that fact that Regents exams involve very modest stakes. Exam grades account for less than one-half of final course grades and influence only the type of diploma received. A passing score on a Regents exam is not necessary for admission to community colleges and employers often ignore exam results when they make hiring decisions.

How do the examination systems of our four comparison countries work? In 1992, 71 percent of French youth took a Baccalaureat (Bac) exam. Fifty-one percent of the age group passed. Thirty-eight percent of the baccalaureates awarded were Bac Technologique or, in vocational lines, the Bac Professionel (Ministere de L'Education Nationale, 1992a and b). This was a major accomplishment, for Bac exams are set to a very high standard. The three-year lycee programs that prepare 43 percent of the age cohort for the Bac General are quite rigorous. Bac exams in mathematics, history/geography, and French are set and marked by 23 regional academies. School-based assessments are used for other subjects (Madeus and Kellaghan, 1991). The Bac exams taken in any one area of concentration are comparable to the advanced placement exams taken by American students seeking college credit for high school work. Cornell University, for example, generally awards advanced placement credit to recipients of the Baccalaureat General.

In France the payoff to higher education is high, so access to a university is highly prized. A Bac is necessary for university admission and the line pursued and the mentions obtained on the exam influence which university program a student can enter.[6] About 10 percent of those obtaining a Bac General enter special programs that prepare them for the exam regulating admission to the elite Grandes Ecoles. The job market also rewards young people who have passed the Bac. There are alternative lower-level qualifications for employment such as the Brevet d'Enseignment Professionnel (BEP) and the Certificat d'Aptitude Professionelle (CAP), but the Baccalaureat confers greater access to preferred jobs. In 1987, unemployment rates for 15 to 24 year olds were in France 37 percent for those without a diploma, 22 percent for those with CAPs or BEPs, 18 percent for those with a Bac, and 10 percent for university graduates (Ministere de l'Education Nationale, 1992b).

Dutch university graduates ages 45 to 64 earn 65 percent more than secondary school graduates (OECD, 1992, 1993), so access to higher education is highly prized in the Netherlands as well. Examinations set by the Ministry of Education influence access to postsecondary education, so the high achievement of Dutch

---

[6]While the Bac is a necessary first step to getting a university education in France, it is not a guarantee of success because failure rates at universities are quite high.

students in mathematics and science can be explained in the same way.[7] In both France and the Netherlands, questions and answers are published in newspapers and available on video text. The published exams signal the standards that students and teachers must aim for.

Nine-tenths of English youth now take the General Certificate of Secondary Education (GCSE) exam at the end of eleventh grade, and an increasing number take A-level exams two years later. Scotland also has a system of external examinations. For the United Kingdom as a whole, the ratio of the number of school leavers passing at least one A-level exam (or the Scottish equivalent) to the number of 19 year olds was 23 percent in 1991 (Government Statistical Service, 1993). Completing an A-level qualification lowers unemployment rates for 25 to 34 year olds from 16.9 to 6.9 percent and graduating from university lowers it further to 4.3 percent. University graduates earn 66 percent more than secondary school graduates at ages 45 to 64 (OECD, 1992). Performance on the GCSE and A-level exams and the equivalent Scottish exams determines whether a student can continue his or her schooling and which university and program he or she can enter. Grades on the GCSE and A-level exams are included on resumes and requested on job applications, so employment opportunities depend on school results as well (Raffe, 1984).

In the United States, by contrast, admission to the best colleges depends on teacher assessments of relative performance—rank in class and grades—and aptitude tests that are *not* keyed to the courses taken in secondary school.

External assessments of achievement that directly affect access to preferred educational and job outcomes clearly increase students' rewards for studying. They also change the structure of rewards for learning and, therefore, the incentive environment of students, teachers, and administrators. I will argue that the structure of rewards for study is at least as important as their size. These issues will be discussed under seven headings:

- Peer group norms
- Teacher incentives
- Administrator incentives
- Competition among upper secondary schools
- Standards of the external exams
- *Redoublement* as mastery learning and an incentive to study
- Choice of specialization as goal setting

---

[7]The Ministry of Education sets an exam that has both essay and multiple-choice components. The multiple choice component, which represents half the written paper, is graded centrally. The essay component is marked by the student's own teacher and by a teacher from another school with the aid of a marking scheme supplied by the ministry. Oral components of the test are administered by the student's teacher.

Peer Group Norms

In the United States peer groups often try to discourage academic effort. No adolescent wants to be considered a "nerd, geek, or grade grubber." Nor do blacks want to be accused of "acting white." That, however, is what happens in most classrooms to students who study hard. Because the school's signals of achievement assess performance relative to fellow students through grades and class rank, not relative to an external standard, students have a personal stake in persuading each other not to study.

An important reason for peer pressure against studying is that pursuing academic success forces students into a zero-sum competition with their classmates. Their achievement is not being measured against an absolute external standard. In contrast to scout merit badges, for example, where recognition is given for achieving a fixed standard of competence, the school's measures of achievement assess performance relative to fellow students through grades and class rank. A student who does well on exams makes it more difficult for other members of the class to get an A or to be ranked at the top of the graduating class. Since devoting time to studying for an exam is costly, the welfare of an entire class is maximized if no one studies for exams that are graded on a curve. The cooperative solution is "no one studies more than the minimum." Participants are generally able to tell who has broken the "minimize studying" code and reward those who conform and punish those who do not. Side payments and punishments are made in a currency of friendship, respect, and ridicule that is not limited in supply. For most black students the benefits that might result from studying are less important than the very certain costs of being considered a "geek" or "acting white," so most students abide by the "minimize studying," "don't raise your hand too much" norm.

The peer norms that result are: "It's OK to be smart. You can't help that. But it is definitely not OK to study hard to get a good grade." This is illustrated by the following story related by a Cornell undergraduate:

> Erroneously I was lumped into the brains genus by others at [high] school just because of the classes I was in. This really irked me; not only was I not an athlete but I was also thought of as one of those "brain geeks." Being a brain really did have a stigma attached to it. Sometimes during a free period I would sit and listen to all the brains talk about how much they hated school work and how they never studied and I had to bite my lip to keep from laughing out loud. I knew they were lying, and they knew they were lying too. I think that a lot of brains hung around together only because their fear of social isolation was greater than their petty rivalries. I think that my two friends who were brains liked me because I was almost on their level but I was not competitive.

Note how those who broke the "minimize studying" norm tried to hide that fact from their classmates. They did not espouse an alternative "learning is fun and important" norm.

The costs and benefits of studying vary across students because interest in any given subject varies, ability varies, parental pressure varies, and rewards vary. This heterogeneity means that some students break the "minimize studying" norm. When they are a small minority, they cannot avoid feeling denigrated by classmates. In the top track and at schools where many students aspire to attend competitive colleges, they are numerous enough to create a subculture of their own, with its own norms denigrating those who do poorly on tests or who disrupt classroom activities. This is the structural basis of the "brains" and "preppie" cliques found in most American high schools. Most high school students, however, are in cliques that denigrate studying. At some school awards ceremonies, some in the crowd jeer as students are called to come up to receive awards (Suskind, 1994).

Peer pressure was discussed in my interviews of school staff members and students in England, the Netherlands, and France. The French educators I spoke to reported that peer pressure not to study occurred sometimes but only in some lower secondary school classes, not at the lycee serving upper-middle-class students that I visited. In lower secondary schools the pressure appeared mild by American standards. In upper secondary schools, particularly in the math-science line, the peer pressure was to excel. Discussions with Dutch and English students and educators produced similar observations.

Teacher Incentives

Most American secondary school teachers do not feel individually accountable for the learning of their students. This lack of accountability for learning stems from (1) the rarity of examinations that assess student achievement in particular subjects relative to an external standard and (2) the fact that most secondary school students receive instruction in a given subject from many teachers. Only coaches, band conductors, and teachers of advanced placement classes are exceptions. They teach in environments where student achievement is visible to parents and colleagues and, as a result, feel accountable for outcomes.

In France and the Netherlands, by contrast, upper secondary students are grouped in small classes, take most subjects together, and generally are together for two or more years. Fewer than three teachers share responsibility for preparing each class for the external exams. In the Netherlands, where schools are small, many subjects are taught by only one teacher. Since important rewards accrue to those who pass or do well on exams, everyone takes them seriously. The number of students taking and passing each exam is public knowledge within the school and among parents. Exam results influence teachers' reputations. Responding to such informal pressures, upper secondary school teachers strive to prepare their students for the external exams.

American teachers also are expected to ensure that most of their students pass, but they are free to accomplish this goal by lowering the passing standard.

Teachers who set expectations that are too high can get into trouble. For example, Adele Jones, an algebra teacher in Georgetown, Delaware, was fired because she failed too many of her students—42 percent one year and 27 percent the next. When students started picketing the school carrying "hastily scrawled signs with such slogans as 'I Failed Ms. Jones's class and It Was My Fault' and 'Just Because a Student Is Failing Doesn't Mean the Teacher Is'" (Bradley, 1993) the national news media took notice. The principal of the school justified his decision as follows:

> I have made it very clear that one of my goals is to decrease the failure rate, to make sure the kids feel good about learning, stay in class, stay in school and do well. . . . Math is just a big body of knowledge; what is Algebra II across the nation anyway?" he asks. When he taught band, he adds, he certainly didn't expect kids to finish the year as musicians—but he did want them to know more about music than . . . before. . . . The talk about preparing students for college struck him as "ludicrous." Instead the goal should be to keep students studying math. (Bradley, 1993, pp. 19, 20)

Senior Norman Kennedy said, however, that the students who flunked Ms. Jones's class "were sleeping. They don't want to learn. They goof off, and they talk." At the hearing Walter Hall, Jr., a student who had flunked the course, testified:

> I guess some of it could be attributed to a lack of study, because I wasn't really like into the books hour after hour. But in the rest of my classes, I was doing fairly well, and it was only testing that gave me a problem." He added that his parents had wondered how he could be getting such good grades in most classes without studying. (Bradley, 1993, p. 20)

A survey of teachers by Peter D. Hart Research Associates (1994) found that 30 percent reported "feeling pressure to . . . give higher grades than students' work deserves." Forty-six percent reported pressure to "pass students on to the next grade who are not ready." Thirty percent reported pressure to "reduce the difficulty and amount of work you assign."

Ms. Jones is unusual; most teachers realize that they must limit their failure rate. More commonly, the struggle over expectations plays out in the privacy of the classroom. Sizer's (1984) description of Ms. Shiffe's biology class, illustrates what sometimes happens:

> She wanted the students to know these names. They did not want to know them and were not going to learn them. Apparently no outside threat—flunking, for example—affected the students. Shiffe did her thing, the students chattered on, even in the presence of a visitor. . . . Their common front of uninterest probably made examinations moot. Shiffe could not flunk them all, and, if their performance was uniformly shoddy, she would have to pass them all. Her desperation was as obvious as the students' cruelty toward her. (pp. 157–158)

Some exceptional teachers are able, through the force of their personalities, to induce students to undertake tough learning tasks. But for all too many academic demands are compromised because the bulk of the class sees no need to accept them as reasonable and legitimate.

Administrator Incentives

External assessment changes the incentives faced by school administrators. In the United States locally elected school boards and the administrators they hire make the thousands of decisions that determine academic expectations and program quality. When there is no external assessment of academic achievement, students and their parents benefit little from administrative decisions that opt for higher standards, more qualified teachers, or a heavier student workload. The immediate consequences of such decisions—higher taxes, more homework, having to repeat courses, lower grade point averages (GPAs), less time for fun courses, a greater risk of being denied a diploma—are all negative. When student learning is not assessed externally, the positive effects of choosing academic rigor are negligible and postponed. Since college admission decisions are based on rank in class, GPAs, and aptitude tests and not externally assessed achievement in high school courses, upgraded standards will not improve the college admissions prospects of a secondary school's graduates. Graduates will do better in difficult college courses and will be more likely to get a degree, but that benefit is uncertain and far in the future. Maybe over time the school's reputation and, with it, the admissions prospects of graduates will improve because the current graduates are more successful at local colleges. That, however, is an even more uncertain and delayed result.

Few American employers pay attention to a student's achievement in high school or the school's reputation when they make hiring selections (Bishop, 1993; Hollenbeck and Smith, 1984). Those who do pay attention to school achievement use such indicators of relative performance as GPA and class rank rather than results on an external exam as a hiring criterion. Consequently, higher standards do not benefit students as a group, so parents as a group have little incentive to lobby strongly for higher teacher salaries, higher standards, and higher school taxes. Employers who recruit from a local high school are often the only group with a real interest in general increases in achievement. Since, however, they pay a disproportionate share of school taxes, they tend to support only policy options that do not cost additional money.

By contrast, in many European countries the record of each school in the external examination—the number of students who pass or get high grades—is published in local and national newspapers. Recent reforms in England and Scotland, for example, have resulted in schools publishing annual reports that contain the grades received by last year's students in each subject tested. These reports are sent to parents of current and prospective students. The school league tables have important effects on school reputations. Administrators seeking to strengthen their school's reputation are thus induced to give teaching effectiveness, as assessed by the external exam, first priority.

Competition Among Upper Secondary Schools

For generations French and Dutch upper secondary schools have faced a competitive environment that is similar in many ways to the one faced by American colleges and universities. Funding has been on a per-student basis, so schools experiencing an increase in applications have had an incentive to expand up to the capacity of their physical plant. Schools with strong reputations get more applications than they can accept and are, in effect, rewarded by being allowed to admit the "best" from their pool of applicants.

In the United States access to quality teaching and supportive peers depends on parental ability to buy or rent a home in a suburb with excellent schools. In France and the Netherlands access to the top upper secondary schools depends primarily on achievement in lower secondary school. This means that parents who want their child to attend the best upper secondary schools must make sure their child does well in lower secondary school.

The Netherlands has three types of general secondary schools—the VWO (pre-university, secondary education institution–most difficult), HAVO (senior general secondary education institution–next most difficult), and MAVO (junior general secondary education institution–least difficult)—and a system of lower vocational schools—LBO/LEAOs (junior secondary vocational education institutions) and KVBOs (agricultural junior secondary vocational education institution)—that prepare students for both occupation-specific and general education exams. The first-year curriculum is supposed to be the same in all schools, so that students can transfer between schools if necessary. In succeeding years, the curricula and rigor diverge. Rigor and workloads are greatest at the six-year VWOs, somewhat less demanding at the five-year HAVOs, and still less demanding at the four-year MAVOs. These schools also differ in the foreign languages offered and the standard to which they are taught. The LBOs devote considerable time to occupation-specific curricula, so less time is available for general studies. Advice to parents about which type of school is appropriate for their child is based on the pupil's record in primary school and in some cases standardized tests (Nijhof and Streumer, 1988). Parents have the right, however, to select the type of school and which school of that type their child will enter. In addition, there are three parallel systems of education—a locally administered public system, a Catholic system, and a Protestant system—so parents have a great deal of choice.

About a decade ago English and Scottish parents were given the right to send their children to schools outside their normal attendance areas. Two years after choice became operational in Scotland, 9 percent of pupils entering secondary school nationally (11 to 14 percent in urban areas) attended a school outside their cachement area (Adler and Raab, 1988). Scottish parents who made this choice appeared to be behaving rationally, for they tended to choose schools that were more effective than the school in their home area. An analysis of school choice in the Fife Education Authority found that the schools chosen by those leaving their cachement area had better examination results than would have been predicted given the pupil's primary school test scores and family background and the average socioeconomic status of the pupils at the school.[8] Consequently, the free choice of schools that prevails in our four European nations generates a competitive pressure on schools to excel that has no counterpart in the United States outside cities with magnet schools.

Standards of the External Exam

External examinations at the end of secondary school are probably necessary if high achievement levels are to be attained, but they are not sufficient. Effects will be small if the exams are easy, are taken by only a small minority of students, or do not generate substantial rewards for successful students. British youth have lower achievement levels than French and Dutch youth. One possible explanation for this is that the passing standard of the GCSE is lower than for the Bac and the Dutch exams, and the more difficult A-levels are taken by only a small minority.

High passing standards on external exams are clearly associated with high achievement levels. Does this reflect a cause-and-effect relationship? Yes, but causation runs both ways. High passing standards on medium- and high-stakes exams are politically sustainable only when most students taking the exam are able to meet or surpass the standard. At present, the median pupil in Britain is not expected to learn the entire multiplication table up to 10 x 10 until age 11. If the GCSE mathematics exams were made more demanding without strengthening mathematics teaching, failure rates might rise to politically unacceptable levels.

Does the passing standard also influence student effort? Yes. In data for high school and beyond, those taking more rigorous courses learned a good deal more between their sophomore and senior years, even though their GPAs suffered as a result (Gamoran and Barends, 1987). Kulik and Kulik's meta-analysis (1984) of the educational literature found that students randomly assigned to skip

---

[8]Analysis of data on out-of-cachement school selections for the Fife Local Education Authority (LEA) found that the type B school effect estimates (measures of how well each school does compared to others serving pupils of similar ability and social background) are significantly and substantially higher at the schools selected by parents choosing to leave their cachement area. My summary sentence sounds different from Willms and Echols's (1993) summary of their own results because they unaccountably base their conclusions on estimates of school effects from models that did not control for pupils' ability when entering secondary school. Luckily, they also present results based on correctly specified models with controls for initial ability in Table 3 of their paper.

a grade or to a compressed and accelerated curriculum scored 75 percent of a standard deviation higher on tests (a few years later) than the matched non-accelerated students. Repeating a grade effectively lowers learning goals and reduces the retained child's achievement a few years later by about 30 percent of a standard deviation (Holmes, 1989).

Over 100 experimental studies have been conducted of the effect of goal difficulty on various kinds of achievement. The effects are quite large. On highly complex tasks such as school and college course work, specific hard goals raised achievement by 47 percent of a standard deviation (Wood et al., 1987). In the laboratory and field settings used by psychologists conducting this research, the subjects generally accepted the goal set for them by the researcher. Achievement went up, but the probability of failing to reach the goal rose as well. In most studies more than two-thirds of those in the "hard goal" condition failed to achieve their goal (Locke, 1968). Most studies examined behavior over relatively short periods of time. One would imagine, however, that if such experiments lasted a couple of years, those who consistently failed to achieve their goal might lower their goals or give up altogether.

Stedry (1960) found that when subjects who had already set their own goals were assigned even higher ones by the study director, they rejected the assigned goal and achievement did not rise. This appears to be what happens in American secondary schools. Most students reject the goals that teachers set because the rewards for success are small. Others reject them because they appear to be unattainable.

How do European education systems induce students in upper secondary schools to set difficult learning goals and work toward them? They do not, as some have proposed for the United States, set a single high yea-nay standard that everyone is expected to meet. Young people are too different from each other for such a policy to work.[9] When exams are graded pass-fail and the same passing standard applies to all, many students are able to pass the standard without exertion and will, therefore, not be stimulated to improve by the need to pass the exam.[10] Many other students will think they are now so far behind and the effort required to achieve the standard so great that the costs of the effort are larger than the possible reward. They will reject the goal of meeting the standard. When the variance of performance is large, only a few students will find the reward attached to a single absolute passing standard an incentive to study (Kang, 1985).

---

[9]On the criterion-referenced IAEP mathematics scale, 15 to 17 percent of American 13 year olds had better mathematics skills than the average 17-year-old student, and 7 to 9 percent of 13 year olds scored below the average 9 year old (NCES, 1992). The variance of achievement is roughly comparable in Europe and East Asia (IAEP, 1992a, b).

[10]In the United States, minimum competency tests are taken in ninth or tenth grade, and most students pass them on the first sitting. Thus, for the great majority of students, such exams have no further effect on incentives to study. Incentives effects are focused on the small minority who fail the test on the first round.

External exams need to signal the level of a student's achievement, not just whether the exam was passed. Dutch external exams are graded on a scale of 1 to 10. Excellence on the Baccalaureat exams results in the award of a Mention Tres Bien, a Mention Bien, or an Mention Assez Bien. Once information on performance levels becomes available, employers and institutions of higher education will tend to base their selection decisions on it. Graduates with the strongest exam results have options not available to those with weak results, and the outcome is a system of graduated rewards. When the variance of achievement is high, incentives for effort are stronger on average under a graduated rewards system than under a single large reward attached to achieving a fixed standard (Kang, 1985).

The English GCSE and Scottish "Lowers" Examinations are taken by 90 percent of 16 year olds. As recommended by Kang's model, they generate substantial and graduated rewards for learning what appears on the exams. Indeed, the rewards for doing particularly well on these external exams appear to be larger than those in the Netherlands.[11] Why then are English and Scottish 13 year olds assigned less homework than their American and Dutch counterparts? Why is their achievement in mathematics and science at age 13 significantly lower than in the Netherlands? As the time for the exam approaches in Britain, teacher demands and student effort increase substantially. At age 13, however, standards are low. Why do the backwash effects of the secondary school graduation exams extend further back in the pupil's schooling in the Netherlands and France than in Britain?

Redoublement as Mastery Learning and an Incentive to Study

One explanation for low British standards for 10 to 13 year olds is the lack of immediate rewards for doing well in classes. The external exams are three to six years away. Students are promoted to the next grade no matter how well they do in the previous grade. Those who fall behind inevitably slow the pace of the class in succeeding years. Primary school teachers do not feel accountable for how well students do on exams taken after four years of attendance at a secondary school. Secondary schools tend to be large, and the teachers who handle the first-year students lack a sense of accountability for performance on exams that are more than three years in the future.

---

[11]In the United Kingdom, access to sixth form programs preparing for university, various vocational technical programs, and employment depend on a student's performance on the GCSE and Scottish lowers. Since A-level results are not available at the time initial university admission decisions are made, GCSE results influence which university and which field of study a student is admitted to. In the Netherlands the passing standard is high, but exceeding it by a large margin generates few rewards because the external exam results are only part of the student's overall grade, and access to the most popular university fields of study is on a first-come/first-served basis. In addition, there is much less variation in the quality and reputation of Dutch universities than of British universities.

The situation is very different in France and the Netherlands. Pupils who fail more than one of their courses are generally required to *redouble* or repeat the grade. In 1990 Dutch redoublement rates were 7.5 percent per year in academic lower secondary schools, 5.1 percent per year in LBOs (junior secondary vocational education institution), the vocational lower secondary schools, and 13.3 percent per year in academic upper secondary schools (Central Bureau Voor De Statistiek, 1993). French rates of redoublement ranged from 6.8 and 11.0 percent per year during the four years of general lower secondary education, 12.1 to 18.4 percent per year in the three-year academic upper secondary schools, and 8.4 percent per year in the first two years of vocational upper secondary schools (Ministere de l'Education Nationale et de la Culture, 1992a). According to Lewis (1985), the "basic motivation is to help the child himself, to ensure that the pupil is sufficiently well prepared so that he may fully benefit from work at a more demanding level" (p. 5). For French teachers, redoublement is a form of mastery learning, a way of allowing some students extra time to achieve very demanding learning goals. Consequently, at age 19, 31.6 percent of French and 41.5 percent of Dutch youth are still in secondary school, compared to 3.4 percent in Britain and 5 percent in the United States.

Redoublement is not something that is inflicted only on children from lower-class backgrounds. Often high aspirations can be achieved only by redoublement. The two Dutch professors with grown children with whom I have discussed this matter both had a child who was required to repeat a grade. In France selective upper secondary schools serving upper-middle-class communities have grade-repeating rates that are nearly as high as schools serving lower-income communities. For example, Lycee Charlemagne, an upper secondary school serving one of the richest neighborhoods in Paris, asked 14 percent of its entering class to repeat the year in 1992.

For French and Dutch teenagers the threat of having to repeat a grade is a strong incentive to study. When I asked how the students who must redouble feel about it, I was told that they feel "dishonored." Since redoublement is a public event, parents also feel stigmatized, so they have an incentive to see that their child studies hard. In the Netherlands, students struggling with the fast-paced VWO or HAVO curricula are often given a choice: either repeat the year or transfer to a less demanding school. At the VWO I visited in the Netherlands, one-third of the entering class transfers to a HAVO or a less demanding VWO before the beginning of the third year. VWOs offer a fast-paced six-year university preparation program. Parents who want their child to enter a VWO are generally accommodated even when primary school teachers advise against it. The child's performance in school determines whether the parents' aspirations are realized or whether a transfer to a less demanding type of school is necessary. Being forced to transfer to an HAVO or MAVO does not foreclose university attendance. With good grades at the end of the five-year HAVO program, a student can transfer to a VWO, complete the final two years, and then enter a university. In addition, numerous vocationally oriented higher education options are open to HAVO and MAVO graduates and transfers to a university are feasible with good grades.

While other routes to a university education are possible, pupils who choose the fast track in seventh grade, a VWO, do not want to be forced "to get off the train." Students in the Netherlands and France are formed into classes that take most subjects together and remain intact for two years and sometimes longer. Friendships tend to develop within this class. When I asked a Dutch student who, despite long hours of study, had been required to repeat a grade, why she had studied so hard, she responded, "I wanted to stay with my class!" Students do not want to have to repeat the grade because it threatens to sever the friendships they have made in class. Apparently, trying to keep up academically or accepting the academic goals of the school is viewed positively by peers because it is an expression of commitment to the group. Those who refuse to study are apparently seen as rejecting the group. In these two countries peer pressure seems to encourage lagging students to study, not discourage them as in the United States.[12]

Choice of Specialization as Goal Setting

All education systems give upper secondary students and their parents the right to select a specialty and the right to choose the rigor and difficulty level of either the school, the academic program, or specific courses.

In France four academic lines—literature and languages (A), economics and social sciences (B), mathematics and physical sciences (C), and biology (D)—have roughly equal numbers of students and together account for most of the Baccalaureat Generales awarded. The mathematics-physics-chemistry line (C) is the most difficult, carries the greatest prestige, and gives one the best chance of being admitted to a preparatory school for one of the elite Grandes Ecoles. Admission to the C line within a lycee is generally highly competitive. The Netherlands has a similar though less elaborate system of specialization within general

---

[12]One would not expect the study effort of primary school pupils to be influenced by the prospect of being retained. The hypothesis of significant threat-induced incentive effects applies to students in small secondary schools or large schools organized into small classes that take most subjects together and remain intact from year to year. Since most American students are in large high schools where peer relationships are not tied to taking particular courses, failing two courses does not sever peer relationships the way it does in Europe. Consequently, one would not expect the threat of failing courses to be the powerful motivator that it appears to be in France and the Netherlands. The argument against retention is that it effectively lowers the learning goals being set for the student in subsequent years. Within-school cross-sectional studies have established that subsequent learning is reduced by retention (Holmes, 1989). It also, apparently, increases the risk of dropping out before graduation (Grissom and Shepard, 1989). Consequently, it is not clear that higher retention rates would increase achievement levels at a given age in the United States

upper secondary education. As in France, the math-science line has the reputation of being the most difficult.

In France and the Netherlands, picking one's school and specialization effectively sets a specific learning goal. The prevalence of grade repeating and transfers to easier schools suggests that most students and parents initially set very difficult goals. The goal-setting literature tells us that working toward a specific and difficult goal leads to greater effort and performance than being told to "do your best" or setting easy goals. Thus, the continental European pattern of setting highly ambitious goals maximizes average achievement levels even while it increases the number of students who fail to achieve the goal they initially set. Why do French and Dutch parents select secondary schools and programs that are so challenging that many must repeat grades to keep up or transfer into easier programs and schools? There are three reasons. First, the goal selected is visible to parents, relatives, and neighbors and going for difficult goals confers prestige. Second, achieving difficult learning goals is rewarded by admission to preferred universities and fields of study and access to better jobs. Finally, the choice is generally made by the parent, not the child. Parents are better informed about the long-term benefits of achieving difficult goals, and their own prestige rises when their child attends a selective school or pursues a difficult line of study. Parents may view the extra studying necessary in a rigorous specialty as a plus not a minus.

In America, by contrast, selecting difficult goals generates much weaker rewards. Everyone in the neighborhood attends the same school. Students select individual courses, not programs or schools. Subjects are taught at vastly different levels, but the rigor of the courses is not well signaled to parents, relatives, neighbors, employers, or colleges. Admissions staff at selective colleges learn how to read the transcripts of high schools they recruit from and evaluate grades in that light. However, many colleges have, historically, not factored the rigor of high school courses into their admissions decisions. Almost no employers do. Consequently, most students not aspiring to attend a selective college avoid rigorous courses and demanding teachers. As one student put it:

> My counselor wanted me to take Regents history and I did for a while. But it was pretty hard and the teacher moved fast. I switched to the other history and I'm getting better grades. So my average will be better for college. Unless you are going to a college in the state, it doesn't really matter whether you get a Regent's diploma. (Ward, 1994, p. 1)

Another student who had avoided the harder courses even though she was sure she could do the work explained her decision with, "Why should I do it [the extra work] if I don't have to?" (Ward, 1994). Some students, the minority who want to attend selective colleges, sign up for demanding courses. Most students choose courses that have the reputation of being fun and not requiring much work to get a good grade. Teachers know this and adjust their style of teaching, assignments, and grading standards with an eye to maintaining enrollment levels.

SUMMARY AND LESSONS

In the Netherlands and France, learning in secondary school is assessed by difficult subject-specific external examinations, and doing well on the exams generates large rewards for the student. The reputations of teachers and schools are affected by student achievement on the exams. Parents base their selection of the upper secondary school their child will attend and which academic or vocational program he or she will pursue, in part, on these reputations. Parents tend to set difficult goals for their children, so most students are placed in programs of study that for them are very demanding. Students are grouped into classes that take all their subjects together, remain intact for two years or more, and become the student's circle of friends. Students who are not progressing at the rate necessary to succeed on the external exam are asked to either switch to an easier curriculum or repeat the year. Students do not want to be forced to sever the friendships they have developed in their class, so they are strongly motivated to keep up with their studies.

In the United States, students are ranked relative to their classmates, not assessed against an external criterion, so they pressure each other not to study. Teachers are expected to pass almost all students, and if the class fails to study hard, the teacher is forced to lower the passing standard of the course. Subjects are taught at vastly different levels, but the rigor of the courses and the learning achievements that result are not well signaled to parents, neighbors, colleges, or employers, so rewards for setting difficult goals are small.

The French and Dutch models of secondary education combine in one system many of the most drastic reforms that have been proposed for the United States:

• Externally set subject-specific achievement exams taken by almost all secondary school graduates that supplement not displace teacher assessments of students. Grades on the external exams need to matter to the student, but they need not be the sole or primary determinant of desired outcomes, such as college admissions and access to the best jobs.

• Parental choice of upper secondary school and special field of study with money following students.

• Mastery learning with teeth. Those who fail two subjects in secondary school are required to either repeat the grade or transfer to a less demanding school or program.

• Secondary teaching is available only to those who demonstrate very high levels of competence in their subject. High entry standards are sustained by offering high wages and good working conditions.

• High standards for admission to the next stage of education.

This system of incentives and school organization appears to work for France and the Netherlands. A similar system, lacking only the externally set exit exams, also works well in undergraduate education in the United States. At the secondary level, however, such reforms are controversial. Successful implementation of any one of these reforms would be a major political undertaking. Implementation of the whole package of reforms is not politically feasible at present. Yet the analysis here suggests that in Britain when just two elements of the package—mastery learning with teeth and attractive teacher salaries—were missing and a third element—school choice—was only recently introduced, achievement levels were substantially lower than in the Netherlands and France. Consequently, from a practical policy point of view, the message is not very positive. School climates and education standards do not change rapidly and easily. France and the Netherlands have not discovered a cheap and painless route to higher achievement.

The important lesson is that incentives, both their strength and structure, matter. There are less controversial ways of increasing the rewards for academic achievement, so the analysis here should not cause American reformers to despair. Reforms tailored to the American context have a greater chance of successful implementation than any effort to replicate the French or Dutch systems of secondary education.

President Clinton, former President Bush, and most of the nation's governors support the development of a system of European-style achievement examinations for upper secondary students. Everyone recognizes, however, that the decentralized character of American education and the controversial nature of specifying and assessing what young people should know and be able to do requires a slow, consensus-building approach. Consequently, it will probably be decades before external examinations in specific subjects are widespread in the United States. School cultures are resistant to change, so significant improvements in achievement will take even longer.

Lessons for Economic Analysis of Education Issues

Much of the economic research on elementary and secondary education has employed a production function paradigm. Conventionally, test scores measuring academic achievement are the outputs, teachers are the labor input, and students are goods in process. Even though I have written papers in this tradition myself, I am concerned that many of the inputs that conventionally appear on the right in these models are really endogenous and that severely biased findings may result.

This paper points in different directions. Schools are viewed as worker-managed organizations producing multiple products. In the classroom/school team production unit, students are as much workers as the teachers. Students are also consumers who choose which goals or outputs to focus on and how much effort to put into each goal. The behavior of each of the system's actors—teachers, administrators, school board, students, and parents—depends on the incentives facing them. The incentives, in turn, depend on the cost and reliability of the signals that are generated about the various outputs of the system. The discussion above demonstrates the relevance of agency theory, game theory, signaling theory, and other elements of economic theory to the understanding of how schools and students operate, but it only scratches the surface. Deeper plowing of these furrows will yield a large crop of new insights into education and education policy.

REFERENCES

Adler, M., and G. M. Raab. 1988. "Exit choice and loyalty: the impact of parental choice on admissions to secondary schools in Edinburgh and Dundee." *Journal of Educational Policy* 3:155–179.

Bishop, J. 1990. "Incentives to study: why American high school students compare so poorly to their counterparts overseas." Pp. 17–51 in *Research in Labor Economics*, vol. 11, D. Crawford and L. Bassi, eds. Greenwich, Conn.: JAI Press.

———. 1993. "The Impact of Academic Competencies on Wages, Unemployment and Job Performance." Carnegie/Rochester Forum, B. Malkiel, ed.

Bradley, A. 1993. "Not making the grade: teacher firing spurs debate over standards and expectations for students." *Education Week*, Sept. 13, Pp. 1, 19–21.

Central Bureau Voor De Statistiek. 1993. *Education Statistics.* The Hague, Netherlands: Central Bureau Voor De Statistiek.

Cooper, H. M. 1989. *Homework.* White Plains, N.Y.: Longman.

Costrell, R. 1994a. "A simple model of educational standards." *The American Economic Review* 84(4):956–971.

———. 1994b. Centralized vs. decentralized educational standards under pooling." Department of Economics, University of Massachusetts, Amherst.

Ehrenberg, R., and D. Brewer. 1993. Did teacher's race and verbal ability matter in the 1960's? *Coleman* revisited. School of Industrial and Labor Relations, Cornell University, Ithaca, N.Y.

Elley, W. 1992. *How in the World Do Students Read?* The Hague, The Netherlands: International Association for the Evaluation of Educational Achievement.

Ferguson, R. 1990. *Racial Patterns in How School and Teacher Quality Affect Achievement and Earnings.* Kennedy School of Government, Harvard University, Cambridge, Mass.

Frederick, W. C. 1977. "The use of classroom time in high schools above or below the median reading score." *Urban Education* 11(4):459–464.

Frederick, W., H. Walberg, and S. Rasher. 1979. "Time, teacher comments, and achievement in urban high schools." Journal of Educational Research 73(2):63–65.

Gamoran, A., and M. Barends. 1987. "The effects of stratification in secondary schools: synthesis of survey and ethnographic research." *Review of Education Research* 57:415–435.

Goodlad, J. 1983. *A Place Called School.* New York: McGraw-Hill.

Government Statistical Service. 1993. *Education Statistics for the United Kingdom: 1992.* London: Her Majesty's Stationery Office.

Graham, A., and T. Husted. 1993. "Understanding state variation in SAT scores." *Economics of Education* 12(3):197–202.

Grissom, J. B., and L. A. Shepard. 1989. "Repeating and dropping out of school." Pp. 34–63 in *Flunking Grades: Research and Policies on Retention*, L. Shepard and M. L. Smith, eds. New York: Falmer Press.

Hanushek, E. A. 1971. "Teacher characteristics and gains in student achievement: estimation using micro-data." *American Economic Review* 61(2):280–288.

Hollenbeck, K., and B. Smith. 1984. The Influence of Applicants' Education and Skills on Employability Assessments by Employers. National Center for Research in Vocational Education, Ohio State University, Columbus.

Holmes, C. T. 1989. "Grade level retention effects: a meta-analysis of research studies." Pp. 16–33 in *Flunking Grades*, L. Shepard and M. L. Smith, eds. New York: The Falmer Press.

International Assessment of Educational Progress. 1992a. *Learning Science*. Princeton, N.J.: Educational Testing Service.

———. 1992b. *Learning Mathematics*. Princeton, N.J.: Educational Testing Service.

Kang, S. 1985. "A formal model of school reward systems." In *Incentives, Learning and Employability*, J. Bishop, ed. Columbus, Ohio: National Center for Research in Vocational Education.

Kominski, R., and R. Sutterlin. 1992. *What's Its Worth? Educational Background and Economic Status: Spring 1990*. U.S. Bureau of the Census, Current Population Reports, P–70, No. 32.

Kulik, J., and C. L. Kulik. 1984. "Effects of accelerated instruction on students." *Review of Educational Research* 54(3):409–425.

Lewis, H. D. 1985. *The French Education System*. New York: St. Martin's Press.

Locke, E. 1968. "Toward a theory of task motivation and incentives." *Organizational Behavior and Human Performance* 3:157–189.

Longitudinal Survey of American Youth. 1989. Data File User's Manual. Dekalb: Public Opinion Laboratory.

Lundberg, I., and P. Linnakyla. 1993. *Teaching Reading Around the World*. The Hague: International Association for the Evaluation of Educational Achievement.

Madeus, G., and T. Kelleghan. 1991. *Student examination systems in the European Community: lessons for the U. S.* Report to the Office of Technology Assessment.

McKnight, C. C., et al. 1987. *The Underachieving Curriculum: Assessing US School Mathematics from an International Perspective*. Champaign, Ill.: Stipes Publishing Co.

Ministere de l'Education Nationale et de la Culture. 1992a. *Reperes and References Statistiques sur les enseignements et la formation*. Paris: Ministere de l'Education Nationale et de la Culture.

———. 1992b. *L'Etat de L'Ecole*. Paris: Ministere de l'Education Nationale et de la Culture.

Monk, D. 1992. Subject Area Preparation of Secondary Mathematics and Science Teachers and Student Achievement. Department of Education, Cornell University, Ithaca, N.Y.

National Center for Educational Statistics. 1992. *The Digest of Education Statistics: 1992*. Washington, D.C.: U.S. Department of Education.

———. 1993. *The Condition of Education: 1993*, vol. 1. Washington, D.C.: U.S. Department of Education.

———. 1994. *Occupational and Educational Outcomes of Recent College Graduates 1 Year After Graduation: 1991*. NCES 93–162. Washington, D.C.: U.S. Department of Education.

Nelson, H., and T. O'Brien. 1993. *How U.S. Teachers Measure Up Internationally: A Comparative Study of Teacher Pay, Training, and Conditions of Service*. Washington, D.C.: American Federation of Teachers.

Nijhof, W. J., and J. N. Streumer. 1988. "The Netherlands." In *The Encyclopedia of Comparative Education and National Systems of Education*. Oxford: Pergamon Press.

O'Leary, J. 1993. "Universities reduce A-level score needed for degree courses." *The Times*, July 12.

Organization of Economic Co-operation and Development. 1989. *Employment Outlook*. Paris: OECD.

———. 1992. *Education at a Glance*. Paris: OECD.

———. 1993. *Education at a Glance*. Paris: OECD.

Peter D. Hart Research Associates. 1994. Survey of Teachers Represented by the American Federation of Teachers.

Postlethwaite, T. N., and D. E. Wiley. 1992. *Science Achievement in Twenty-three Countries*. London: Pergamon Press.

Raffe, D. 1984. "School attainment and the labor market." Pp. 174–193 in *Fourteen to Eighteen: The Changing Pattern of Schooling in Scotland*, D. Raffe, ed. Aberdeen: Aberdeen University Press.

Robitaille, D., and R. Garden. 1989. *The IAEEA Study of Mathematics II: Contexts and Outcomes of School Mathematics.* New York: Pergamon Press.

Sizer, T. R. 1984. *Horace's Compromise: The Dilemma of the American High School.* Boston: Houghton Mifflin.

Stedry, A. C. 1960. *Budget Control and Cost Behavior.* Englewood Cliffs, N.J.: Prentice-Hall.

Strauss, R. P., and E. A. Sawyer. 1986. "Some new evidence on teacher and student competencies." *Economics of Education Review* 5(1):41–48.

Suskind, R. 1994. "Put down, kicked around, honor students struggle on." *The Wall Street Journal*, May 26.

Ward. 1994. "A day in the life." *N.Y. Teacher.* Jan.

Wiley, D. E. 1976. "Another hour, another day: quantity of schooling, a potent path for policy." In *Schooling Achievement in American Society*, W. H. Sewell, R. M. Hauser, and D. L. Featherman, eds. New York: Academic Press.

Willms, D. J., and F. Echols. 1993. "Alert and inert clients: the Scottish experience of parental choice of schools." *Economics of Education Review* 11(4):339–350.

Wood, R. E., A. Mento, and E. Locke. 1987. "Task complexity as a moderator of goal effects: a meta analysis." *Journal of Applied Psychology* 72(3):416–425.

CHAPTER 8

Public School Partnerships: Community, Family, and School Factors in Determining Child Outcomes[1]

REBECCA MAYNARD WITH MEREDITH KELSEY
The University of Pennsylvania

Public-private partnerships are now widely advocated as keys to successful educational reforms. The nature of such partnerships and their objectives vary widely, depending on which symptoms of school failure are of greatest concern—for example, low school completion rates, poor employment prospects and earnings levels of high school graduates, inadequate postsecondary education and training, low rates of school preparedness of 5 year olds, or early family formation.

Although the concept of partnerships to improve educational outcomes is gaining momentum, partnerships for this purpose are not new. The preparation of young people for the transition to adulthood has been the product of public-private partnerships, albeit generally informal ones, since the advent of public education. Families, communities, schools, and children themselves have been instrumental in defining the inputs to education, the processes through which formal education occurs, and the application of and rewards for the products of the educational process during adulthood. The current emphasis on formal partnerships is being fueled by mounting evidence that our education system is failing to keep pace with changes in the economy that have increased the skill requirements for jobs at all levels, even low-paying jobs. Moreover, it is failing to produce young adults who can maintain or improve on the social welfare of their parents and, in the aggregate, the nation.

This chapter explores one of the avenues for improving the operations and effectiveness of our schools that was highlighted in a recent report of the Panel on

---

[1]Research assistance for this paper was provided by Dan McGrath.

the Economics of Education and Reform—building stronger and more responsive partnerships (Hanushek, 1994). The chapter examines the role of partnerships in the context of what is known about relationships among the community, families, and schools in determining the educational outcomes and economic prospects of children. We first discuss evidence of the failure of the current system and its largely informal partnerships to successfully meet the educational needs of young people. The social policy issues are then framed in the context of a general model of the causes and consequences of various child outcomes. The third section describes trends in schools, families, and communities that are relevant to child outcomes and discusses policy options for mitigating those circumstances that adversely affect the chances that children will experience success in school and beyond. The final section reflects on a variety of strategies for building on the strengths of various partnerships in the education process.

EVIDENCE OF WEAK OR FAILING PARTNERSHIPS

By some measures, the American education system is holding its own. For example, dropout rates have stabilized and measured skills of graduates have remained fairly constant. By other measures, though, the system is failing not only the children it serves but also society at large. Most notably, the employment productivity (measured by real wages) of the majority of youth coming out of schools today is falling. Youth also are experiencing higher rates of single parenthood, divorce, poverty and welfare dependence, and crimes against them.

Indicators of Stable or Improving School Performance

In the aggregate, school performance has continued to improve with respect to some objectives—enrolling more children, keeping youths in school through the full 12 years of program study, and preparing young people for postsecondary education and training options. School participation rates have continued to rise, dropout rates have fallen, Scholastic Assessment Test (SAT) scores have remained stable (controlling for demographic shifts in the test-taking population), and increasing numbers of young people are enrolling in postsecondary education or training.

Our country's school system also has succeeded in extending the formal education process to younger ages for increasing numbers of children. Whereas in 1970 only 38 percent of 3 to 5 year olds were enrolled in preschool programs, by 1990 the figure had increased to nearly 60 percent (Table 8.1). In part, this trend is accounted for by the rapid rise in labor force participation of women with young children (Hayes et al., 1990; Zill and Nord, 1994). It also reflects expansions in Head Start and pre-K programs intended as "jump-start" initiatives for children from disadvantaged backgrounds.

The proportion of 14 to 17 year olds enrolled in school has remained fairly stable over this period, in the range of 90 to 94 percent (Table 8.1). However, increasing proportions of young people are completing high school by the time

TABLE 8.1 Trends in Student Outcomes, by Year

	1970	1975	1980	1985	1990	% Change, 1970-1990	% Change, 1975-1990
Percentage of 3 to 5 year olds in preschool	38	49	53	55	59	55.3	—
Percentage of 14 to 17 year olds in school	92	91	90	92	94	2.2	—
Percentage of 17 year olds who graduated high school	77	74	71	72	72	-6.5	—
Percentage of dropouts among 16 to 24 year olds	15	14	14	13	12	-20.0	—
White, non-Hispanics	13	11	11	10	9	—	-30.8
Black, non-Hispanics	28	23	19	15	13	—	-53.6
Hispanics	—	29	35	28	32	—	10.3
SAT verbal scores	455	431	424	431	422	—	-7.3
Whites	—	451	442	449	442	—	-2.0
Blacks	—	332	330	346	353	—	6.0
Mexican-Americans	—	371	372	382	380	—	2.4
Percentage of high school graduates enrolled in college	52	51	49	58	60	15.4	—

SOURCE: *Digest of Educational Statistics*, 1993, U.S. Government Printing Office, Washington, D.C.

they reach young adulthood. In 1990, 12 percent of all 16 to 24 year olds had dropped out of school prior to attaining a high school degree, down from 15 percent in 1970. Moreover, the large disparity in school dropout rates between white and black youths was reduced by 73 percent over this period. The proportion of black youth who failed to complete high school fell by over 50 percent— from 28 to 13 percent—while the proportion of white youth ages 16 to 24 who neither were attending nor had completed school declined from 13 to 9 percent. In part, this trend toward higher high school completion rates reflects the institution of alternative educational opportunities within the regular secondary education system and through alternative credentialing options, principally the General Educational Development (GED) certificate.[2]

Despite mounting evidence that many of today's youth are not well prepared for the demands of our changing economy, the educational achievement of young people has been fairly steady over the past 20 years. Performance on the National Assessment of Educational Progress, for example, has been fairly stable among all age groups. Moreover, there has been some improvement in math and science performance by children from lower socioeconomic groups relative to other students (NCES, 1994, Tables 12–18).[3] Although there has been considerable concern about declining average scores on the SAT (Haveman and Wolfe, 1994), the average performance remained stable or increased slightly among all racial/ethnic groups, except whites (Table 8.1). What has driven the trends in averages is primarily a shift in the composition of the population taking the SAT. Over the past 20 years, increasing proportions of youth from minority racial/ethnic groups, who have substantially lower average scores than white youth, have entered the pool of test-takers.

Perhaps the most encouraging trend has been the increasing rates of participation in postsecondary education, especially in the past 10 years. Between 1980 and 1990, the percentage of high school graduates enrolling in college, including two-year community colleges and vocational schools, increased 22 percent from 49 to 60 percent (Table 8.1). This increase is especially noteworthy given the strong association between postsecondary education and improved economic opportunities and the ability to better handle adverse social outcomes (Haveman and Wolfe, 1994; McLanahan and Sandefur, 1994).

Increased Educational Investments and Attention to School Improvement

Over this same period, the proportion of the gross domestic product (GDP) devoted to education has fluctuated between 6.5 percent and 7.8 percent, with the low point being in the mid-1980s (NCES, 1993a, Table 33). The share of the

---

[2]In 1990, 287,000 youths under the age of 24 earned a GED, compared with only 182,000 in 1970 (NCES, 1993a, Table 100).

[3]Average proficiency scores of children whose parents did not complete high school lag 10 to 15 percent below those of children whose parents completed more than high school (NCES, 1994).

GDP that was devoted to elementary and secondary education in 1990 was 6 percent lower than in 1970 (4.5 vs. 4.8 percent), and the share devoted to higher education has increased 14 percent (2.7 to 3.1 percent). As a result of the 68 percent expansion of the overall U.S. economy, from $2.9 trillion to $4.9 trillion, real aggregate resources devoted to education increased 60 percent. Considering that there was a 15 percent decline in the student population over this period, real resources per pupil increased even more.[4]

This increase in resources came, in large part, from states and localities. Indeed, the federal government's share of total expenditures for education declined from 11 to 8 percent of the total between 1975 and 1990, while state and local shares increased from 58 to 62 percent and private funding increased from 22 to 29 percent of the total (NCES, 1993a, Table 35).[5]

These increased aggregate expenditures have been allocated in a variety of ways intended to improve educational outcomes. For example, per-pupil expenditures increased 81 percent in real terms between 1970 and 1990, from $3,079 to $5,570 in 1992 dollars (Table 8.2). Much of the increase in expenditures was devoted to lowering the average size of classes and to higher real wages for teachers. For example, over this period, the average pupil-teacher ratio decreased 22 percent, from 20 to 17, and average teacher salaries increased by 6 percent in real terms, from $33,000 to $35,000.[6] In addition, substantial resources have been channeled into providing special services for children with learning differences or for nonacademic programs.

At the same time that the public has been increasing its financial investments in education, it has also been demanding continual improvements in the system. Some of these efforts have been in response to poor outcomes in the schools. Many others have been stimulated by a desire to keep up with technology and changes in the social and economic climate (Fuhrman et al., 1993; Committee for Economic Development, 1994). The reform movement has been directed at a variety of objectives—improving math and science education, promoting parental involvement, making better use of technology, improving teacher and staff performance, developing a curriculum that better reflects the demands of today's and tomorrow's economy, and linking school with the labor force.

The Heart of Public Concern

The high level of attention focused on schools derives from two sources. First, the stable and positive trends in educational inputs and outputs mask enor-

---

[4]Between 1970 and 1990 the student population declined from 52 to 54 million (NCES, 1993a, Table 41).

[5]The increase in private funding is due to an increase in the share of private funding for higher education, from 49 to 58 percent of all expenditures over the period 1975 to 1990 (NCES, 1993a, Table 35).

[6]One study suggests that 20 to 25 percent of the substantial cross-district variation in teacher salaries is due to ability/skill differences among teachers (Berliner, 1993).

TABLE 8.2 Trends in Educational Investments, by Year

	1970	1975	1980	1985	1990	% Change, 1970–1990
Expenditures for elementary and secondary schools (%GDP)		4.7	4.1	4.0	4.5	-6.3
Expenditures per pupil (1992–1993 $)	$3,079	$3,755	$4,171	$4,676	$5,570	80.9
Average pupil-teacher ratio in public elementary and secondary schools	22	20	19	18	17	-22.8
Average teacher salary (1992–1993 $)	$33,000	$32,000	$29,000	$31,000	$35,000	6.1

SOURCE: *Digest of Educational Statistics*, 1993, U.S. Government Printing Office, Washington, D.C.

mous and increasing variation across population subgroups, communities, and schools. Second, the youth coming out of the American secondary education system today, particularly those who do not attend college, face diminishing economic prospects.

Although nationally only 12 percent of 16 to 24 year olds are classified as school dropouts, the rate is 13 percent among blacks and 32 percent among Hispanics. Moreover, Hispanics have not contributed to the decline in the dropout rate over the past 20 years. There also are large differences in educational achievement among racial/ethnic groups with comparable years of education. For example, only 5 to 6 percent of black and Hispanic 9 year olds are able to search for information, relate ideas, and generalize from them, in contrast to 18 percent of 9 year olds nationwide (NCES, 1993a, Table 108). Although the proficiencies of all students improve as they get older, the 10 to 15 percent gap in scores between whites and other youth persists through high school, as do the gaps between youths whose parents have various levels of educational achievement (Kirsch and Jungeblut, 1986; Kirsch et al., 1993; NCES, 1993a).

Across communities there is substantial variation among those with different socioeconomic characteristics. For example, whereas nationally less than 15 percent of youths fail to complete high school, the dropout rate in urban areas often exceeds 50 percent. The proficiency levels of students also vary considerably, with reading proficiency scores in disadvantaged communities averaging 10 percent less than those in more advantaged urban communities (NCES, 1993a, Table 105). These differences can be accounted for, in part, by variations in the fiscal capacity of areas to support education and by the sociodemographic composition of student populations. Although state and federal educational support compensates for some of the disparity in wealth among communities, outputs in poorer communities still tend to seriously lag those of wealthier ones.

Of even greater public concern than the mixed record of school performance indicators is the poor record of success of youths in the workplace. The long-run economic prospects for young people have declined substantially in recent years, especially among minority groups and males (Table 8.3). Among men with various education levels, all but those with postcollege training suffered real losses in earnings potential from 1979 to 1991. Among school dropouts and high school graduates who did not go on to college, the losses exceeded 24 percent (Table 8.3). These losses have been fairly similar across racial/ethnic groups. Young women fared better relative to their male counterparts but only those completing college, and white women who pursued postcollege training realized sizable gains. It is also notable that young black women who completed only high school or less suffered losses much like their male counterparts.

There are several explanations for these trends, including the increasing proportion of the work force in higher education groups, an increase in the supply of labor due to rapidly rising rates of female labor force participation, declines in the real minimum wage, and structural shifts in the economy (Burtless, 1990,

TABLE 8.3   Percent Changes in Median Income of 25 to 34 Year Olds, 1979–1991, by Educational Attainment

	<High School	High School	Some College	College Graduate	Postcollege
Men	-36	-24	-18	-3	7
White	-32	-25	-15	-3	7
Black	-29	-23	-23	-16	0
Hispanic	-37	-28	-20	-5	0
Women	-1	-7	7	18	16
White	-1	-5	8	21	22
Black	-32	-24	-17	12	-13
Hispanic	7	-8	3	7	-12

SOURCE: Tabulations of the *Current Population Survey* data provided courtesy of Richard J. Murnane, Harvard University.

1994; Blank, 1994; Murnane and Levy, 1992). The latter explanation is the one most relevant to education and how we judge the performance of schools. There is increasing evidence that it is not enough for schools to improve incrementally on their previous performance targets. The United States is experiencing a widening skill gap between young adults coming out of the school system and the demands of the current labor market (Berryman, 1988; Berlin and Sum, 1988; U.S. Departments of Education and Labor, 1988; Committee for Economic Development, 1994; Hanushek, 1994).

Whatever the source of the declining economic prospects for the next generation of young adults, they coincide with a number of other troublesome social trends. For example, increasing numbers of young women are becoming parents during their teenage years, with low prospects of marrying the fathers of their children. This is especially true of Hispanic and black teenagers (Alan Guttmacher Institute, 1994; Zill and Nord, 1994). Increasingly, the young fathers do not share in the rearing of their children. In about half of the cases, this leaves the young mothers and their children poor and dependent on welfare (Sawhill, 1989; Zill and Rogers, 1988; Congressional Budget Office, 1990). Finally, there is evidence of substantial increases in criminal activity among young males and young adults. Nationally, 57 percent of all arrests for serious crimes are committed by persons under the age of 25. Over the 20-year period from 1970 to 1990, the arrest rate for 14 to 17 year olds increased 37 percent (from 96 arrests per 1,000 to 132), while the rate for 18 to 24 year olds nearly doubled, from 66 to 126 arrests per 1,000.

LOOKING BEYOND THE SCHOOLS TO IMPROVE EDUCATIONAL OUTCOMES

It is becoming increasingly clear that many factors are contributing to the disappointing life prospects of many of today's youth. Indeed, there is a mounting body of research that highlights the complex paths of influence at various stages from conception through the transition to adulthood.[7] Figure 8.1 summarizes this vast body of research within the context of a causal model of child development and outcomes. The literature consistently highlights the fact that most of the variation in outcomes for youths is not explained by specific measurable attributes of their families, schools, and communities. Rather, the behavioral patterns of the children themselves and their developmental status, including their innate abilities, exert powerful influences on subsequent outcomes. Of the three partners in the education process, the family has the strongest and most enduring influence on children's behaviors and outcomes. Some of these are direct influences on children throughout their preadult lives—the socioeconomic status of the family, the physical environment of the home, the amount and quality of time parents spend with their children, health and nutrition practices, and the numbers and spacing of children.

Parents have differing avenues of influence at various stages of their children's lives. For example, parents decide on the timing and spacing of children and their prenatal care, which affect the health and early development of the child. Parents make decisions regarding "mother care" versus "other care" during the preschool years. Finally, during the school years, parents convey important messages regarding the value of education through their aspirations and expectations and their involvement in school activities.

The third strongest influence on children's outcomes is that of their school. Although early studies of the impact of schools on student outcomes were discouraging (Jencks and Mayer, 1990; Coleman et al., 1966; Averch et al., 1972; Hanushek, 1989; Walberg and Fowler, 1987), other research provides more convincing evidence that schools can make a difference. At the elementary and secondary school levels, those factors that have been found to be most influential are class size, teacher quality, and peer group characteristics (Summers and Wolfe, 1977; Ferguson, 1991; Hedges et al., 1994; Odden and Kim, 1992). There is also a growing body of research indicating the power of quality preschool experiences on subsequent educational outcomes (Ramey and Campbell, 1990; Berrueta-Clement et al., 1984; McGroder, 1990). While not well substantiated, there are strong beliefs that the school's physical plant and equipment including state-of-the-art technology and laboratories, as well as nonacademic services and programs, will impact student outcomes directly.

The fourth source of direct influence on child outcomes is the community. The major sources of community influence vary over the lifespan. During the preschool years, the major source is through the quality of early care and education options. During the school years, the more powerful influences come from peer group and the alternative time use options. For example, communities differ in the opportunities they offer youths to engage in productive versus unproduc-

---

[7]Haveman and Wolfe (1994) provide an excellent review of this literature.

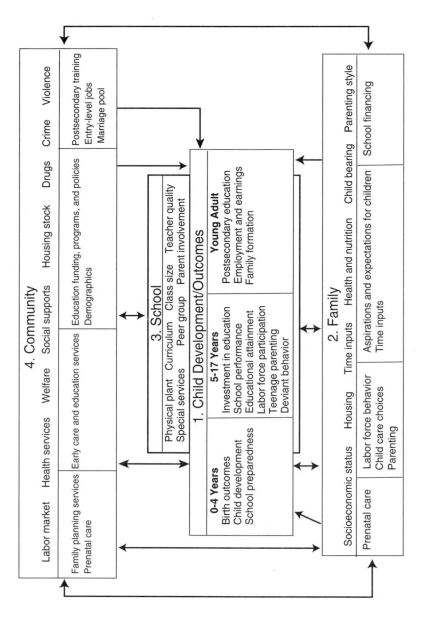

FIGURE 8.1   Educational partnerships, by stages of child development.

tive activities and in peer influences to engage in various types of school and nonschool activities. Communities also offer different levels and qualities of employment opportunities for in-school youth to complement or substitute for their school activities.

During the postsecondary period, the influence tends to be through educational and job opportunities and the social setting. For example, in tight labor markets with rising real wages for lower-skilled jobs, the proportion of youth pursuing postsecondary education, particularly community colleges, has tended to fall. Although studies have not documented the existence of a causal relationship between criminal opportunities and school retention, dropout rates are higher in areas in which there are "employment" opportunities for youth in the drug trade and where property crime rates are high (Lynn and McGeary, 1990). School participation, including enrollment in postsecondary education, has tended to rise during periods of slack labor markets providing fewer and less desirable alternatives to school.

Beyond these direct influences on child outcomes, there is a complex web of indirect paths of influence—aggregate impacts of family decisions on the community and school environments, impacts of school policies and practices on the community and on families, and impacts of children's behaviors and outcomes on the family and schools, as well as the community . For example, parents have indirect but highly important influences on their children's outcomes through their choice of community and school district. They also can influence their schools through participation in school governance, involvement in school service organizations, and formal or informal partnerships with teachers to strengthen the learning environment for children. Schools can affect communities and families through their efforts to promote parental and community involvement. Obviously, the community influences the family and the school through economic and social support for families and schools, economic opportunities, and social and political climate.

BUILDING BLOCKS FOR AND CHALLENGES TO PRODUCTIVE PARTNERSHIPS

The complexity of these relationships among the informal partners in the education process helps explain the frequent disappointments and limited success of educational reforms and bilateral partnerships designed to promote higher lifetime success rates for children. This section looks at some of the key trends in schools, families, and communities as background for examining the potential of various forms of overt partnerships to improve the general efficiency and educational performance of schools.

Trends in School Inputs

As noted above, by many standards, schools have improved over the past 20 years. They have higher levels of resources per pupil, more highly paid teachers, and more instructional support staff and specialists per pupil. In contrast, the characteristics of the student body have changed significantly in ways that pose greater challenges for the schools.

The proportion of minority students has increased substantially over the past 10 years, particularly that of Hispanics, from 9 to 12 percent of all school-age children (Table 8.4). Together blacks and Hispanics now constitute the student majority in center-city schools. By most measures of educational and life outcomes, minority youth fare poorly. Although a substantial portion of their lower performance is attributable to factors that are *correlated* with race/ethnicity, there is strong evidence of residual negative outcomes after controlling for a wide range of these other factors (Haveman and Wolfe, 1994). The proportion of youths who speak languages other than English at home has been rising with the growth in ethnic minorities. In 1990 nearly one in seven school-age children spoke another language at home (Table 8.4). One-half of these children, 7 percent, have difficulty speaking English—an increase of 26 percent from a decade earlier. Difficulty with English is a strong predictor of poor school performance and subsequent poor employment outcomes.

As a result of cultural differences between minority groups, especially minority language groups, and the dominant culture of most schools, the parenting styles of many minorities are sometimes at odds with the cultural norms in American schools. In addition, many minority children, especially those in minority groups with long histories of economic and social hardship in the United States, are likely to see few economic prospects in their future and therefore little reason to strive for academic success. Ethnographers suggest that cultural differences and perceptions of poor economic prospects account for some of the residual performance differences between some minority groups and white youth, after controlling for easily measurable socioeconomic factors (Erickson, 1987; Ogbu, 1987).

Following national poverty trends, U.S. schools are serving larger numbers of poor children. In the past 10 years alone, the percentage of public school children from low-income families increased by 40 percent (Table 8.4). Accompanying the rising poverty rates are modest (15 percent) increases in the incidence of children who have been diagnosed with learning disabilities that warrant special services. After years of decline in teenage pregnancy and birth rates following the introduction of oral contraceptives, the rates are again on the rise (Zill and Nord, 1994; Alan Guttmacher Institute, 1994). In 1990 there were 60 births per 1,000 15- to 17-year old girls in this country, a 13 percent increase from the 1980 level (Table 8.4). Even more problematic is the fact that the birth rate among unmarried young women increased by 50 percent over the same period. Motherhood increases dramatically the likelihood that a teenager will drop out of school or exhibit poor performance if she remains (Congressional Budget Office, 1990; Geronimus and Korenman, 1993; Moore et al., 1993; Nord et al., 1992).

Informal reports suggest a rising rate of school violence. However, major

TABLE 8.4   Selected Characteristics of the U.S. Student Population, by Year

	1970	1980	1990	% Change, 1980–1990
Racial/Ethnic Composition of Schools				
All schools				
% Black	15	16	18	12.5
% Hispanic	6	9	12	33.3
Urban schools				
% Black	33	35	33	-5.7
% Hispanic	11	17	20	17.7
% Students speaking English with difficulty	—	4.2	5.3	26.8
Ratio of students/special education teacher	—	18	15	-16.7
% children from low-income families	—			
Elementary school	—	13.1	18.4	40.5
High school	—	10.5	14.7	40.0
Children in programs for students with disabilities	—	9.8	11.3	15.3
% Students taking SAT	34.1	32.6	39.7	21.8
% Minority	—	17.9	26.6	48.6
Births per 1,000 school-age girls	68.3	53.0	59.9	13.0
Unmarried young girls	22.4	27.6	42.5	54.0
Minority young girls	133.4	94.9	96.3	1.4
%High school students employed	31.5	35.1	32.1	-8.5
% Seniors using drugs	—	37.2	17.1	-53.7
% Using alcohol	—	72.0	57.1	-20.7
% Seniors for whom religion is important	—	65.0	55.9	14.0

SOURCES: *The Condition of Education 1994*, National Center for Educational Statistics, Washington, D.C., NCES 94-149 (Tables 3.3, 19.1, 45.3, 45.5, 49, 49.1, and p. 122), and *Youth Indicators* 1993, National Center for Educational Statistics, Washington, D.C., (Tables 6, 7, 54).

educational statistics fail to report these data. What they do report are high rates of alcohol and drug use. In 1990 more than half of high school seniors reported using alcohol within the past 30 days and 17 percent had used drugs, including 9 percent who used drugs other than marijuana (Table 8.4). On the bright side, this figure represents less than half the rate of drug use and about four-fifths the rate of alcohol use reported by the class of 1980. There is also modest evidence to suggest that the incidence of drug trafficking in schools has declined slightly.

Smaller percentages of twelfth graders in 1992 as compared with tenth graders in 1990 were approached at school by someone offering to sell them drugs (NCES, 1994, Table 48-4).

Missing from this aggregate picture of improvements and deteriorations in school climate and resources are the widening disparities in the problems faced by schools and the resources available to them. Over the past 20 years there has been an increasing concentration of minority and poor children in center-city schools. Relative to their suburban counterparts, these schools have higher rates of reported school violence, increasing rates of children with diagnosed learning disabilities, lower resources per pupil, and, not surprisingly, much worse student outcomes.

Trends in Family Inputs

There are some trends in family characteristics that work to the advantage of children and many that work against them. On the positive side, parents, especially black parents, today have higher levels of education than was the case 20 years ago. The size of the American family also has dropped from an average of just over three children to just under two, a change most pronounced among low-income families. Furthermore, the average spacing between children has increased. Each of these factors has had a positive effect on child outcomes (Haveman and Wolfe, 1994).

Other trends have more ambiguous implications for children. One trend is the rapid increase in labor force participation by mothers (Zill and Nord, 1994; Hayes et al., 1990; Blau, 1991). Currently, a majority of children have mothers in the labor force, including more than one-half of all preschool-age children. As a result, many families, most two-parent families, enjoy higher standards of living. On the other hand, the trends in labor force participation of women also mean that children must spend substantial amounts of time in child care.[8] The best-available evidence suggests that, on balance, child outcomes either are not affected or are improved slightly by this trend (Stafford, 1986; Haveman and Wolfe, 1994).

There are several trends in the conditions of American families that are clearly associated with worse outcomes for children—especially, rising divorce rates, increases in out-of-wedlock births, rising teenage birth rates, higher child poverty rates, and higher rates of domestic violence. Whereas in 1970 only 1.2 percent of children experienced a divorce of their parents each year (double the rate in 1950), by 1988 the rate had increased 50 percent to 1.8 percent (NCES,

---

[8]Less than one-fourth of children whose mothers are in the labor force are cared for by a parent during the time the mother works. A small fraction accompany their mothers to work or have mothers who work at home. The larger portion have two parents who work different shifts (Congressional Budget Office, 1990; Hayes et al., 1990). Among poor and single-parent families, the proportion of children of working mothers cared for by a parent is very small (Kisker et al., 1989).

1993b). Half of all children today can expect to live part of their childhood in a single-parent household (Zill and Nord, 1994; Haveman and Wolfe, 1994).

Compounding the adverse consequences for children of divorce is the fact that the number of children being born to single parents is increasing at an alarming rate. Currently, 30 percent of all children in this country are born out of wedlock, more than triple the rate in 1970. Indeed, more than two-thirds of minorities and teenagers giving birth are unmarried. Similarly, over half of all births in 11 of our largest cities were to unmarried women.[9]

Although average family income has increased by about 6 percent in real terms over the past 20 years, the gain has been disproportionately enjoyed by two-parent families. The combined effect of the rising out-of-wedlock birth rate and the rising divorce rate is that today over one-fourth of all children and over one-half of black children live in single-parent households at high risk of poverty. Over half of all children in single-parent families and over two-thirds of black and Hispanic children in single-parent families live in poverty; in contrast, only about 20 percent of children in two-parent families are poor.[10]

One factor contributing to the high poverty rate is the low level of support from absent parents. Over half of single mothers receive no financial support from the absent fathers, and most who receive payments receive relatively small amounts (NCES, 1993b). Another factor is the decline in real wages, especially among low-skilled workers. Under the current wage structure, a sizable proportion of single parents, who are disproportionately low skilled, cannot escape poverty even through full-time work (Ellwood, 1988; U.S. House of Representatives, 1993).[11] A third factor contributing to the high poverty rate among single-parent families is the decline in the youth job market (Wilson, 1987; Stern, 1993), and a fourth factor is the 23 percent decline in real welfare benefits per recipient since 1970 (NCES, 1993b).

Single-parent families are not only much more likely to be poor than other families, they also have only about half the amount of time to devote to child rearing. They also have less choice about whether to use child care than do parents living together. For the vast majority of single parents, their only hope of escaping poverty is through employment. This requires them to rely on non-parental, often nonrelative, child care for significant amounts of time.[12]

---

[9]These cities are Atlanta (64 percent), Baltimore (62 percent), Chicago (54 percent), Cleveland (64 percent), Detroit (71 percent), Miami (51 percent), Newark (65 percent), Philadelphia (59 percent), Pittsburgh (52 percent), St. Louis (66 percent), and Washington, D.C. (66 percent).

[10]The poverty rate among single-parent families has remained fairly stable since 1970 (NCES, 1993b, p. 48).

[11]Labor force participation rates are higher among single parents than among women in two-parent families (Hayes et al., 1990). Moreover, the rates for minority women have consistently been substantially higher than for white women.

[12] With the rise in labor force participation rates for women, care by relatives is increasingly less often a realistic option (Hayes et al., 1990; Willer et al., 1991).

The recent upturn in the incidence of early family formation has been stimulated by both a rise in the incidence of single-parent households and by the rising child poverty rates (Nord et al., 1992; Moore et al., 1993; Zill, 1994). Teenage childbearing has numerous adverse consequences for both the educational outcomes for the teenagers who are giving birth and their children. The teenagers themselves are more likely to drop out of school and enter a life of dependency (Moore et al., 1993; Congressional Budget Office, 1990; Ahn, 1994; Geronimus and Korenman, 1993; Horowitz et al., 1991; Hoffman et al., 1993). One result is less supportive home environments for the children (Haveman and Wolfe, 1994; Zill and Nord, 1994).

Community Trends

In many respects the trends in communities mirror those in families, but communities have become much more homogeneous in terms of both their strengths and their problems. For example, poverty rates outside central cities have been falling, while those inside have been rising. As a result, there has been a near doubling of the proportion of the poor population residing in central cities (Kantor and Brenzel, 1993). Within cities the population is further segregated by neighborhood (Wilson, 1987; Kasarda, 1993; Lynn and McGeary, 1990). There has also been a trend toward higher rates of private school attendance by children from higher-income families relative to low-income families (NCES, 1993b). As a result of these trends, almost one-half of inner-city schools have a majority of the low-income students (Kantor and Brenzel, 1993). While the student population has become increasingly needy, the fiscal capacity of inner-city schools to obtain funds has declined (Kantor and Brenzel, 1993). Other community-wide trends—increases in crime rates in inner-city areas, high rates of drug use and employment opportunities in the drug industry, and decreasing job opportunities for those without postsecondary education—go hand in hand with high rates of teenage parenting, single-parent households, and high rates of school failure (Wilson, 1987; Haveman and Wolfe, 1994; Datcher, 1982; Crane, 1991; Corcoran and Datcher, 1981).

Even at the state level there is substantial variation in the community context in which children are reared (Table 8.5). Personal income per capita ranges from $11,000 in the poorest state, Mississippi, to over $23,000 in Connecticut. State child poverty rates range from 33 percent in Mississippi to 7.3 percent in New Hampshire, and the percentage of all adults who have completed high school ranges from 64 percent in Mississippi to 86 percent in Alaska. There is a tendency for these characteristics to move together and to follow per-pupil expenditures and local tax effort. For example, per-pupil expenditures range from a low of $3,187 in Mississippi to a high of $8,645 in New Jersey. Moreover, the gap in per-pupil expenditures has widened dramatically over the past 20 years, as illustrated by the fact that expenditures in the lowest-spending state, Mississippi, only

TABLE 8.5   Variations Across States in Selected Family, School, and
Community Characteristics

	Lowest State	Highest State	Highest State as % of Lowest
Personal income, 1988	$11,116	$23,059	207
% Children who speak English with difficulty [a]	0.8	14.9	1862
% 6 to 11 year olds in poverty	33.5	7.3	22
% Adults with high school diploma	64.3	86.6	135
Per-pupil expenditures	$3,187	$8,645	271
% Population completed high school	53	82	154
Tax effort index, 1988	84	127	151
Percent of Seniors Taking SAT (1990)	4	74	1850
NAEP grade 8 math score, 1990	246	281	114

SOURCES: Adapted from Odden and Kim (1992, Table 8.1) and NCES (1993a, 1994).
[a] All Children also speak a language other than English at home.

doubled in nominal terms since 1970, while those in the highest-spending state, New Jersey, increased more than eightfold (NCES, 1993a).

PARTNERSHIPS TO IMPROVE EDUCATIONAL OUTCOMES

A common theme in educational reform and improvement efforts is building partnerships—partnerships between communities and families, between families and schools, between schools and communities, and among all three groups (Figure 8.2). Such partnerships generally have a specific and fairly narrow focus and often have limited reach in terms of the proportion of the target population served.

Community-Family Partnerships

Community-family partnerships have the longest history and in some cases the broadest coverage. Yet educational improvement is generally not their primary goal. At one extreme in this category are welfare and public health programs, which offer broad coverage and spend millions of dollars annually to provide income and health security to poor families through the Aid to Families with Dependent Children and Medicaid programs. At the other extreme are small community-based family resource centers that work to strengthen individuals and families through a variety of informal supports and referrals (Weiss and Jacobs, 1988; Larner et al., 1992; Goetz, 1992). These programs vary

Community			
Family			
	School		
		Community	

Welfare
Public health
Job training
Family resource centers
Child care
	Pre-K
	Parenting/family
	  development
	Early intervention
	Teenage parent
	Adult education
	Family literacy
		School-linked family service
		  centers
		Community schools
		Community development
			School-linked
			  health centers
			Mentoring
			School-business
			  collaboratives
			Private sector
			  management

FIGURE 8.2   Types of partnerships, by key participants.

widely in terms of their missions, size, outreach, and intensity. Moreover, they tend to rise and fall with sources of financial support. In between are the many community-based job training programs designed to promote employment and the economic well-being of families. These tend to have stronger roots in the community than the family support programs as a result of their more stable funding and longer histories.

School-Family Partnerships

There are numerous examples of formal school-family partnerships that are directed specifically at improving the school outcomes of children. Head Start and the urban pre-K programs are probably the best known. There are also various early intervention programs for at-risk children, special schools and support programs for in-school teenage parents, and both adult and family literacy programs. The schools are generally the lead actors in these partnerships (Goetz, 1992; St. Pierre et al., 1994; Dryfoos, 1990, 1994; Cohen et al., 1994).

School-Community Partnerships

Prompted in large part by concerns over the quality of the work force and urban social and economic problems, many community and business groups have reached out to public schools to address some of the most pressing community problems. The resulting partnerships have included school-linked health centers, mentoring programs, work-study programs, and school-business collaboratives aimed at improving the vocational exposure and job readiness of youths. Private school management corporations are a relatively new entry into this category.

The lead partner is sometimes the school and sometimes the community agency or business (Fraser et al., 1993; Goldberger et al., 1994; Pauly et al., 1994; U.S. Departments of Education and Labor, 1988). In any case, such initiatives are generally confined to one school and, in some cases, particular curriculum areas or student groups within a school.

All-Way Partnership

The ultimate partnership is one that encompasses all points of strength and weakness in schools, families, and communities. These are rare, in large part because of their complexity in purpose and governance. The most notable examples of all-way partnerships are school-linked family service centers, community schools, university-community schools, and community development efforts (University of Pennsylvania, 1994).

Strengths and Challenges

There have been more disappointments than clear successes from the many and varied efforts to reform and improve our education system. The most common source of disappointment in these partnerships is that their designs generally are not fully implemented. Sometimes the reason is inadequate funding; sometimes it relates to a technical problem; frequently, it simply derives from the fact that the stakeholders did not share a common set of objectives. Although most of these initiatives have not undergone rigorous evaluation to assess their effectiveness, the results from existing evaluations are generally disappointing.[13] The following illustrates some of the results:

- *Income support and welfare.* Welfare reforms that have attempted to institute closer links with schools through mandating participation by teenagers who have not graduated or are parents have had modest impacts on school enrollment. Those that have required adults to participate in education or training have met with widely different levels of success at different sites. Even the most successful programs have increased employment rates by only 10 to 15 percentage points and have contributed little to the economic well-being of families.
- *Job training.* Job training programs have had small beneficial effects for adult women, but generally they have not led to increased employment rates or earnings for adult men or youth.
- *Adult education.* Adult education programs do increase attainment of the GED. However, the few studies that have measured gains in basic skills attribut-

---

[13]Maynard and McGrath (1995) review the research findings for these various types of reforms. See also the references cited earlier under the discussion of the various types of partnerships

able to the GED preparation course show no measurable gains in skills associated with the program.

- *Preschool.* Head Start and pre-K programs have been found to improve child development outcomes in the short run. However, evidence regarding the durability of those benefits is mixed.
- *Teenage parenting.* Even high-cost programs designed to mitigate the problems associated with teenage parenting have met with limited success. Only those that have truly engaged teenagers in a program with mutual obligations and services have led to increased earnings and reductions in welfare dependence. Even then, the gains are modest.
- *Adolescent health.* School-linked health centers have led to modest increases in the use of health care by adolescents. However, they do not seem to have had the hoped-for benefit of lowering the sexual activity and pregnancy rates of teens.
- *Parenting.* Programs offering parenting education and family literacy have had modest measured benefits in terms of parenting behaviors and measured literacy gains of the parents.

Other programs, such as the school-community partnerships, community development initiatives, and mentoring programs, have not been subjected to rigorous evaluation. Anecdotal evidence suggests that these initiatives have also met considerable implementation challenges that raise serious questions about whether they can reasonably be expected to make significant progress in improving school outcomes for at-risk children.

LOOKING TO THE FUTURE

It is critical that we aggressively pursue ways to improve the focus and efficiency of our education system. Increases in financial support for education in the absence of reformed goals and delivery mechanisms are likely to have limited or no impact on either the life courses of our young people or the economic welfare of the nation (Hanushek, 1994).

The United States has many experiences with educational partnerships and reform efforts to guide the crafting of improved educational models for the future. We should critically review the many lessons from these well-intentioned, but generally flawed, efforts to mitigate the adverse life consequences of growing up poor or attending a school with a high concentration of poor children. We are also searching for ways to improve all schools to enable them to better prepare noncollege-bound youngsters for the transition to the work force and enable them to earn a decent wage and strengthen our national economy. We are attempting to address large and multifaceted problems through well-intentioned but small and often ad hoc partnerships. Big complex problems require carefully planned and implemented solutions.

REFERENCES

Ahn, G. 1994. "Teenage childbearing and high school completion: accounting for individual heterogeneity." *Family Planning Perspectives* 26:17–21.

Alan Guttmacher Institute. 1994. *Sex and America's Teenagers.* New York: Alan Guttmacher Institute.

Averch, H. A., et al. 1972. *How Effective Is Schooling? A Critical Review and Synthesis of Research Findings.* Santa Monica, Calif.: RAND Corp.

Berlin, G., and A. Sum. 1988. *Toward a More Perfect Union: Basic Skills, Poor Families, and Our Economic Future.* New York: Ford Foundation.

Berliner, D.C. 1993. "Mythology and the American system of education." *Phi Delta Kappan* 74:632.

Berrueta-Clement, J. R., et al. 1984. *Changed Lives: The Effects of the Perry Preschool Program on Youths Through Age 19.* High/Scope Educational Research Foundation.

Berryman, S. 1988. *Literacy and the Marketplace: Improving the Literacy of Low-Income Single Mothers.* New York: The Rockefeller Foundation.

Blank, R. 1994. Outlook for the U.S. labor market and prospects for low-wage jobs. Paper presented at the Conference on Self-Sufficiency and the Low-Wage Labor Market: A Reality Check on the Welfare-to-Work Transition, The Urban Institute, Washington, D.C.: April 12–14.

Blau, D. ed. 1991. "Child care policy and research: an economist's perspective." In *The Economics of Child Care.* New York: Russell Sage Foundation.

Burtless, G. 1990. *A Future of Lousy Jobs? The Changing Structure of U.S. Wages.* Washington, D.C.: The Brookings Institution.

Burtless, G. 1994. Who is employable and what can the labor market absorb? Paper presented at the Conference on Self-Sufficiency and the Low-Wage Labor Market: A Reality Check on the Welfare-to-Work Transition, The Urban Institute, Washington, D.C.: April 12–14.

Cohen, M. 1991. "Key issues confronting state policy makers." Pp. 251–288 in *Restructuring Schools: The Next Generation of Educational Reform.* San Francisco: Jossey-Bass.

Coleman, J. S., et al. 1966. *Equality of Educational Opportunity.* Washington, D.C.: U.S. Government Printing Office.

Committee for Economic Development. 1994. *Putting Learning First: Governing and Managing the Schools for High Achievement.* New York: Committee for Economic Development.

Congressional Budget Office. 1990. *Sources of Support for Adolescent Mothers.* Wahington, D.C.: U.S. Government Printing Office.

Corcoran, M., and L. Datcher. 1981. "Intergenerational status transmission and the process of individual attainment." In *Five Thousand American Families—Patterns of Economic Progress,* vol. 9, M. Hill, D. H. Hill, and J. M. Morgan, eds. Ann Arbor: University of Michigan, Institute for Social Research.

Crane, J. 1991. "The epidemic theory of ghettos and neighborhood effects on dropping out and teenage childbearing." *American Journal of Sociology* 96(5):1226–1259.

Datcher, L. 1982. "Effects of community and family background on achievement." *Review of Economics and Statistics* 64:32–41.

Dryfoos, J. 1990. *Adolescents at Risk.* New York: Oxford University Press.

———. 1994. *Full-Service Schools.* San Francisco: Jossey-Bass.

Ellwood, D. 1988. *Poor Support.* New York: Basic Books.

Erickson, F. 1987. "Transformation and school success: the politics and culture of educational achievement." *Anthropology & Education Quarterly* 18(4):335–356.

Ferguson, R. 1991. "Paying for public education: new evidence on how and why money matters." *Harvard Journal on Legislation* 28(2):465–498.

Fraser, B. S., S. Hubbard, I. Charner, and A. Weinbaum. 1993. "Key elements in reforming the school-to-work transition." Washington, D.C.: Academy for Educational Development.

Fuhrman, S., R. Elmore, and D. Massell. 1993. "School reform in the United States: putting it into context." Pp. 3–27 in *Reforming Education: The Emerging Systemic Approach*, S. L. Jacobson and R. Berne, eds. Thousand Oaks, Calif.: Corwin Press.

Geronimus, A., and S. Korenman. 1993. "The socioeconomic consequences of teen childbearing reconsidered." *Quarterly Journal of Economics* 107:281–290.

Goldbeger, S., R. Kazis, and M. K. O'Flanagan. 1994. *Learning Through Work: Designing and Implementing Quality Worksite Learning for High School Students*. New York: Manpower Demonstration Research Corp.

Goetz, K., ed. 1992. *Programs to Strengthen Families: A Resource Guide*. Washington, D.C.: Family Resource Coalition.

Hanushek, E. A. 1989. "The impact of differential expenditures on school performance." *Educational Researcher* May:45–50.

————. 1994. *Improving Performance and Controlling Costs in American Schools*. Washington, D.C.: The Brookings Institution.

Haveman, R., and B. Wolfe. 1994. *Succeeding Generations: On the Effects of Investments in Children*. New York: Russell Sage Foundation.

Hayes, C., J. Palmer, and M. Zaslow, eds. 1990. *Who Cares for America's Children? Child Care Policy for the 1990s*. Washington, D.C.: National Academy Press.

Hedges, L. V., R. D. Laine, and R. Greenwald. 1994. "Does money matter?: a meta-analysis of studies of the effects of differential school inputs on student outcomes." *Educational Researcher* 23(3):5-14.

Hoffman, S., E. M. Foster, and F. Furstenberg, Jr. 1993. "Reevaluating the costs of teenage childbearing." *Demography* 30(1):1-13.

Horowitz, S. M., et al. 1991. "School-age mothers: predictors of long-term educational and economic outcomes." *Pediatrics* 87(6):862–868.

Jencks, C., and S. Mayer. 1990. "The social consequences of growing up in a poor neighborhood." In *Inner-City Poverty in the United States*, L. Lynn and M. McGeary, eds. Washington, D.C.: National Academy Press.

Kantor, H., and B. Brenzel. 1993. "Urban education and the 'truly disadvantaged': the historical roots of the contemporary crisis, 1945-1990." In *The "Underclass" Debate: Views from History*, M. B. Katz, ed. Princeton, N.J.: Princeton University Press.

Kasarda, J. 1993. "Inner-city concentrated poverty and neighborhood distress: 1970-1990." *Housing Policy Debate* 3:253-302.

Kirsch, I., and A. Jungeblut. 1986. *Literacy Profiles of America's Young Adults*. Princeton, N.J.: Educational Testing Service.

Kirsch, I., A. Jungeblut, L. Jenkins, and A. Kolstad. 1993. *Adult Literacy in America*. Washington, D.C.: U.S. Department of Labor.

Kisker, E. E., R. Maynard, A. Gordon, and M. Strain. 1989. *The Child Care Challenge: What Parents Need and What Is Available in Three Metropolitan Areas*. Princeton, N.J.: Mathematica Policy Research.

Larner, M., R. Halpern, and O. Harkavy. 1992. *Fair Start for Children: Lessons Learned From Seven Demonstration Projects*. New Haven, Conn.: Yale University Press.

Lynn, L. E., and M. G. H. McGeary, eds. 1990. *Inner-City Poverty in the United States*. Washington, D.C.: National Academy Press.

Maynard, R. A., and D. J. McGrath. 1995. "Social benefits of education: family formation, fertility, and child welfare." Paper presented at the Conference on the Social Benefits of Education sponsored by the U.S. Department of Education, Office of Educational Research and Improvement (ERI), Washington, D.C. January 3–5.

McGroder, S. 1990. Head start: what do we know about what works?" Washington, D.C.: Office of the Assistant Secretary for Planning and Evaluation (OASPE), U.S. Department of Health and Human Services.

McLanahan, S., and G. Sandefur. 1994. *Growing Up With a Single Parent: What Hurts, What Helps*. Cambridge, Mass.: Harvard University Press.

Moore, K., D. Myers, D. Morrison, C. Nord, B. Brown, and B. Edmonston. 1993. "Age at first childbirth and later poverty." *Journal of Research on Adolescence* 3(4):394-422.

Murnane, R., and F. Levy. 1992. "Education and training." Pp. 185-222 in *Setting Domestic Priorities: What Can Government Do?*, H. J. Aaron and C. L. Schultze, eds. Washington, D.C.: The Brookings Institution.

(National Center for Education Stastics). 1993a. *Digest of Educational Statistics.* Washington, D.C.: NCES.

____. 1993b. *Youth Indicators 1993.* Washington, D.C.: NCES.

____. 1994. *The Condition of Education.* Washington, D.C.: NCES.

Nord, C., K. Moore, D. Morrison, B. Brown, and D. Myers. 1992. "Consequences of teen-age parenting." *Journal of School Health* 62(7):310-318.

Odden, A. R., and L. Kim. 1992. "Reducing disparities across the states: a new federal role in school finance." In *Rethinking School Finance: An Agenda for the 1990s*, A. Odden, ed. San Francisco: Jossey-Bass.

Ogbu, J. U. 1987. "Variability in minority school performance: a problem in search of an explanation." *Anthropology & Education Quarterly* 18(4):312-334.

Pauly, E., H. Kopp, and J. Haimson. 1994. *Home Grown Lessons: Innovative Programs Linking Work and High School.* New York: Manpower Demonstration Research Corp.

Ramey, C. T., and F. A. Campbell. 1990. "Poverty, early childhood education, and academic competence: the abecedarian experiment." In *Children in Poverty*, A. Huston, ed. New York: Cambridge University Press.

Sawhill, I. 1989. "The underclass." *The Public Interest* 96:3-15.

St. Pierre, R., B. Goodson, J. Layzer, and L. Bernstein. 1994. *National Impact Evaluation of the Comprehensive Child Development Program.* Cambridge, Mass.: Abt Associates.

Stafford, F. P. 1986. "Women's work, sibling competition, and children's school performance." *American Economic Review* 77:972-980.

Stern, M. J. 1993. "Poverty and family composition since 1940." In *The "Underclass" Debate: Views from History*, M. B. Katz, ed. Princeton, N.J.: Princeton University Press.

Summers, A., and B. Wolfe. 1977. "Do schools make a difference?" *American Economic Review* 67:639-652.

University of Pennsylvania. 1994. *Universities and Community Schools.* Philadelphia: University of Pennsylvania.

U.S. Departments of Education and Labor. 1988. *The Bottom Line: Basic Skills in the Workplace.* Washington, D.C.: U.S. Department of Labor.

U.S. House of Representatives. 1993. *The Green Book.* Washington, D.C.: House Ways and Means Committee.

Walberg, H. J., and W. J. Fowler, Jr. 1987. "Expenditure and size efficiencies of public school districts." *Educational Researcher* Oct.:5-13.

Weiss, H., and F. Jacobs. 1988. *Evaluating Family Programs.* New York: Aldine de Gruyter.

Willer, B., S. Hofferth, E. Kisker, P. Divine-Hawkins, E. Farquhar, and F. Glantz. 1991. *The Demand and Supply of Child Care in 1990.* Washington, D.C.: National Association for the Education of Young Children.

Wilson, W. J. 1987. *The Truly Disadvantaged: The Inner City, the Underclass, and Public Policy.* Chicago: University of Chicago Press.

Zill, N. 1994. "Characteristics of teenage mothers." Talking points for the AIE Conference on the Costs of Teenage Child Bearing, April.

Zill, N., and C. Nord. 1994. *Running in Place: How American Families Are Faring in a Changing Economy and an Individualistic Society.* Washington, D.C.: Child Trends, Inc.

Zill, N., and C. Rogers. 1988. "Trends in indicators of academic achievement" Pp. 31-71 in *The Changing American Family and Public Policy*, A. Cherlin, ed. Washington, D.C.: The Urban Institute Press.

CHAPTER 9

Using Student Assessments for Educational Accountability[1]

DANIEL KORETZ
RAND Institute on Education and Training

A common thread runs through many recent proposals for the reform of American education: the notion of using students' performance on achievement tests—or assessments, as it is now more fashionable to say—as a basis for holding educators, schools, and school systems accountable. Indeed, in many reforms, test-based accountability is viewed as the principal tool for improving educational practice.

The proposal of the Panel on the Economics of Education Reform (PEER) (Hanushek et al., 1994) is one example of a reform approach that would rely heavily on holding educators accountable for improving students' performance, although it differs in some ways from many current assessment-based accountability systems. The PEER proposal focuses on three elements: the efficient use of resources, performance incentives for educators based on assessments of student performance, and continuous adaptation. The proposal suggests the need for new types of student assessments, although it does not clearly specify their form and cautions against too radical a departure from current assessment practice. For example, the proposal recognizes the importance of standardization, noting that "flexible measurement quickly degenerates into a collection of semi-independent observations that cannot be compared" (Hanushek et al., 1994); and it argues that it would be a mistake to discard existing standardized tests "without an operationally useful alternative." Unlike many others, however, the PEER

[1]Preparation of this chapter was supported by a grant from the Lilly Endowment. The opinions presented here are solely those of the author and do not represent the position of RAND or the Lilly Endowment.

171

proposal asserts that effective management requires that a system take into account the many sources of educational performance, some of which are not the responsibility of the school, and maintains that schools should therefore be held accountable only for value added.

To evaluate proposals of this sort and to decide how best to translate them into practice, it is essential to examine both the logic of achievement testing and the evidence pertaining to assessment-based accountability. At first, the logic seems simple and compelling: student achievement is the primary goal of education, and holding educators accountable for the amount of learning they induce can only focus and intensify their efforts. In practice, however, assessment-based accountability poses serious difficulties.

Despite the long history of assessment-based accountability, hard evidence about its effects is surprisingly sparse, and the little evidence that is available is not encouraging. There is evidence that effects are diverse, vary from one type of testing program to another, and may be both positive and negative. The large positive effects assumed by advocates, however, are often not substantiated by hard evidence, and closer scrutiny has shown that test-based accountability can generate spurious gains—thus creating illusory accountability and distorting program effectiveness—and degrade instruction. One source of these problems is limitations of tests themselves, and a primary emphasis in the current reform movement is on the development of innovative, less limited assessments. A second source is the structure of the data in which test scores are typically embedded; assessment databases are rarely of a form that would permit accurate measurement of value added or of program effectiveness. A third source is behavioral responses to accountability: holding educators accountable for students' test scores can create undesirable practices that inflate scores and may undermine learning.

This chapter sketches the recent history of assessment-based accountability and then describes some of the most important problems it entails. The final sections address the potential of innovations in testing and suggest some implications for policy. I do not wish to discourage the use of tests in accountability systems but rather want to encourage reformers to use tests in ways that take their problems into account and that are therefore more likely to improve student learning.

THE TRANSFORMED ROLE OF TESTING

Between World War II and the 1960s, achievement testing in the United States was "low stakes," without serious consequences for most students or teachers. Some tests did have serious consequences—for example, college admissions tests and tests used to place students in special education—but they were the exception rather than the rule (Goslin, 1963, 1967; Goslin et al., 1965).

The functions of testing began to change in the 1960s. The Elementary and

Secondary Education Act enacted in 1965 mandated achievement testing as a primary mechanism for monitoring and evaluating the new federal compensatory education program, Title I. Because Title I services are provided in the great majority of elementary schools, this requirement had a major influence on testing throughout the K–12 education system (Airasian, 1987; Roeber, 1988). Another important step in the transformation of testing was the establishment of the National Assessment of Educational Progress (NAEP) in the late 1960s as an ongoing program of testing to monitor achievement of our nation's youth.

Another stage in the evolution of testing was the minimum competency testing (MCT) movement in the 1970s (Jaeger, 1982). MCT programs were intended to not only measure performance but also spur its improvement through the mechanism of high stakes for students. Indeed, some of its proponents called MCT "measurement-driven instruction" (e.g., Popham et al., 1985). MCT programs relied on *criterion-referenced* rather than *norm-referenced* tests. That is, they used tests that were designed to determine whether students had reached a predetermined standard of achievement rather than to place students' performance on a distribution of performance, such as a national distribution for students in a given grade. As the term "minimum competency" suggests, the standards were low, designed only to identify students who failed to reach a standard judged to be minimally acceptable. In many states MCTs were used as an "exit exam" for high school graduation. A smaller number of states used MCTs to set "promotional gates," governing promotion between certain grades (Jaeger, 1982).

In the 1980s test-based accountability received another boost with the "reform movement" that followed the publication of *A Nation at Risk* (National Commission on Excellence in Education, 1983). The reforms of the 1980s varied from state to state, but one of the most common elements was greater reliance on testing as a policy tool. Pipho (1985) noted that "nearly every large education reform effort of the past few years has either mandated a new form of testing or expanded [the] uses of existing testing." Ambach (1987) asserted that the nation had entered a period of not only measurement-driven instruction but also "measurement-driven educational policy." Much of the new testing had high stakes, but the nature of the consequences began to change, shifting from stakes for students toward evaluations of educators or systems (Koretz, 1992).

The testing of the 1980s reform movement fell into disfavor surprisingly soon. Confidence in the reforms was so high at the outset that few programs were evaluated realistically. By the end of the decade, however, confidence in the reforms was supplanted by widespread suspicion that they had often degraded instruction and inflated test scores by inappropriate teaching to the test. Some of the evidence relevant to those negative conclusions is described below.

Despite increasing skepticism about the effects of the programs of the 1980s, few reformers questioned the basic premise that test-based accountability could be the primary impetus for better education. Rather, a growing number of reformers called for a "second wave" of programs that would continue heavy reliance on test-based accountability while changing the types of tests used. They reasoned that if tests could be designed so that they would be "worth teaching to," so that coaching for the tests would constitute good instruction, the negative effects of the test-based accountability of the 1980s could be avoided. In addition, many reformers called for linking test-based accountability to other reforms, such as improved teacher training and changes in school governance. The role of assessment, however, often remained primary. For example, the National Council on Education Standards and Testing (1992) asserted that "standards and assessments linked to the standards can become the cornerstone of the fundamental, systemic reform necessary to improve schools" (p. 5).

Advocates of this "second wave" call for replacing the conventional, multiple-choice, standardized tests of the 1980s with diverse "performance assessments." Performance assessment is a broad and poorly defined concept that includes, for example, both paper-and-pencil tests such as direct writing tests and hands-on manipulative assessments such as hands-on science experiments. It also includes both standardized, on-demand assessments and largely unstandardized assessments embedded in ongoing instruction, such as portfolio programs.[2]

The "second wave" remains a dominant force in the American school reform movement today. A number of large-scale development efforts are under way, such as the New Standards Project, and several states, such as Vermont, Kentucky, and Maryland, have been working on assessment-based reforms for several years. Evidence of the effects of these new reforms is becoming available only slowly. So far it does not appear, however, that substituting performance assessment for multiple-choice testing will be sufficient to eliminate many of the fundamental problems of test-based accountability.

WHAT TESTS ARE

For present purposes, the single most important fact about achievement tests is that most are small samples from large domains of achievement. Performance

---

[2]In popular parlance the term "standardized tests" is often used to refer to conventional, norm-referenced, multiple-choice achievement tests. Such tests are in fact standardized, but standardized tests need not resemble them. The term "standardized" does not refer to the item format (multiple-choice) or content of the tests. Rather, it refers to the fact that the test items, administrative conditions, and test scoring are uniform for all students. A performance assessment that assigns students identical performance tasks administered under uniform conditions and scored according to uniform rules also is "standardized." Current reforms employ both standardized and unstandardized performance assessments. For example, the Vermont portfolio program is unstandardized in terms of both task selection and administrative conditions. Students and teachers choose what tasks are included, and teachers decide how much time and assistance students get and whether they may revise their work before it is scored. It is standardized only in terms of scoring. In contrast, many of the components of Kentucky's well-known new performance assessment program are standardized in terms of task selection and administration as well as scoring.

on the test itself, therefore, often is or at least ought to be of little interest. Rather, what is important is students' mastery of the domain that the test is intended to represent. Thus, the results of most achievement tests are meaningful only if one can legitimately generalize from performance on the sample included on the test to mastery of the domain it is intended to represent.[3]

One reason that tests are generally small samples is that many domains of interest are simply too large to test fully. For example, although most people have working vocabularies of thousands of words, it is neither practical nor necessary to include thousands of words in a vocabulary test. A test comprising perhaps forty words can do a reasonably good job of differentiating people with strong vocabularies from those with weaker vocabularies, provided that the words included on the test are chosen carefully and the test is not used in ways that undermine its meaningfulness. In most cases, however, no one really cares about students' mastery of the few words included in a vocabulary test; rather, they are concerned about students' mastery of the broader domain that those words represent.

The degree of sampling needed to build a test therefore depends on the breadth of the inferences that it is used to support. In policy contexts the domains of achievement about which people want to draw test-based inferences are typically broad, often broader than the domains of some tests used for other purposes. For example, a relatively narrow state or district mathematics test might cover a year's work in a subject such as algebra. The traditional New York State Regents tests and the College Board Advanced Placement tests are examples. At the other extreme, many current assessments, such as NAEP and many statewide assessments, are intended to support inferences about far broader domains, such as the cumulative mastery of mathematics by eighth-grade students. Truly narrow domains that might be tested more fully, such as "using the distributive law to simplify simple algebraic expressions," are the focus of pop quizzes, not of the assessments debated by the press and policymakers. Indeed, a domain such as "using the distributive law to simplify simple algebraic expressions" is too narrow even to warrant guaranteed representation in many large-scale assessments of mathematics.

The extent to which tests are incomplete samples of domains also hinges on other factors beyond the size and complexity of many domains of interest. For example, tests may exclude important attributes that are impractical to measure, and they may either exclude or underrepresent attributes that can be measured only at a very large cost in money or testing time. For purposes of the following discussion, however, these additional factors are important but not essential. The critical fact is simply that tests are typically small samples of domains.

---

[3]One important exception is that tests are designed to predict future behavior, such as college admissions and employment screening tests. Such tests need not be designed to indicate mastery of a defined domain of knowledge or skill, although some are.

It is also essential to recognize that the domains that current assessments are designed to test are themselves only a subset of the desired outcomes of schooling. Often, the argument that measured achievement is only one of the goals of schooling is interpreted as avoidance of hard-nosed accountability, and it may often be. Nonetheless, an accountability system that fails to address outcomes beyond those typically tested is likely to be insufficient. Much of what many individuals need to learn will arise after they leave public schools—in later education, in the workplace, and in civic life. The extent to which they are successful in this later learning may depend in substantial part on the body of knowledge and skills that students have at graduation, much of which can be tested. But it is also likely to depend on attitudes and habits that are not typically measured by achievement tests—an attitude that mathematical problems are interesting and tractable, for example, or an interest in and willingness to weigh carefully conflicting evidence and competing positions underlying political arguments. Thus, an accountability system that produces high scores on tests at the price of poor performance on unmeasured outcomes may be a poor bargain (Haney and Raczek, 1994).

TYPICAL TEST DATABASES

To understand the uses and limits of test data it is also imperative to consider the types of databases in which assessment data are typically embedded. Three attributes of these databases are particularly important.

First, large-scale assessment data are usually cross-sectional. Some districts and states can track the progress of students who remain in the jurisdiction longitudinally (see, e.g., Clotfelter and Ladd, 1995), but few assessment programs are designed to do so. More typical are systems like NAEP and the assessment programs in Kentucky and Maryland, in which students in various grades are tested in a variety of subjects but scores are not linked across grades. In many instances these cross-sections are limited to a few grades. NAEP usually tests only in grades 4, 8, and 12 (in some instances, grade 11 rather than 12); Kentucky limits most parts of its accountability-oriented testing to grades 4, 8, and 11; Maryland's performance assessment program is administered in grades 3, 5, and 8. Cross-sectional data are, of course, very poorly suited to the measurement of value added and afford less opportunity to take into account statistically the noneducational determinants of achievement such as family background.

Some systems, such as the Kentucky accountability program, use repeated cross-sections only to measure *changes* in schools' scores, thus removing some of the confounding between the effects of schooling and the effects of students' backgrounds. A thorough examination of this approach is beyond the scope of this chapter, but it is important to note that it has serious limitations. One is simple imprecision: test scores provide only an error-prone estimate of a school's performance for a given year because of the limited information provided by the test itself and, often more important, year-to-year differences in the characteristics of cohorts of students.[4] Moreover, estimates of changes in school performance are more unreliable than estimates of performance in any one year. In addition to the imprecision caused by random fluctuations in the characteristics of students, some schools may undergo substantial changes in student characteristics—for example, an influx of immigrants or a change in student populations because of boundary changes—that are not taken into account by the performance measurement system.

In theory, accountability programs could use longitudinal rather than cross-sectional data, but this approach also raises practical difficulties. For example, it would require more frequent testing, most likely at least once per grade, with additional financial and time costs. Its applicability to some subject areas is also arguable. It would not be difficult to apply to subject areas in which the curriculum is cumulative, such as reading, writing, and perhaps elementary school mathematics, but it would be considerably more difficult to apply to subjects, such as high school science, in which the curriculum is not cumulative over grades.

Second, most assessment databases include only limited information on the background factors that exert powerful influences on test scores. For example, parental education, income, and ethnicity are all known to be very powerful predictors of performance on tests. Indeed, background factors are more strongly related to variations in scores than are common variations in educational practice. School districts and states, however, cannot require most parents to provide information on any of these variables. Many systems do have data on student race and ethnicity, but the data may not be reliable, especially for ambiguous ethnic classifications such as "Hispanic." Some systems have school-level data for receipt of or eligibility for subsidized school lunches, a questionable proxy for poverty. Data on parental education is rarely available.

Third, most assessment systems lack the ability to address student mobility across jurisdictions. A student who first moves into Kentucky in grade 7 will appear in grade 8 data but not grade 4 data; conversely, a student who leaves Kentucky in grade 7 will disappear from the state's data. This mobility can badly cloud the meaning of cross-sectional data at the state, district, or school level. For example, consider two hypothetical schools with similar and unusually effective mathematics programs but very different mobility rates. The school with the lower mobility rate is likely to have higher scores despite having an equally effective program. Mobility also creates serious problems for value-added models based on longitudinal data. Longitudinal records cannot be kept for many students who leave a school, and even when they can be kept, they become irrelevant as indicators of teachers' performance. Thus, longitudinal value-added

---

[4]These differences in cohorts are important sources of error because the intended inferences are about the effectiveness of schools, not about the performance of the particular cohorts of students that happen to be present in specific years.

systems are likely to be biased by the exclusion of data pertaining to mobile students, who will often be quite unlike students who remain in a single school for a considerable time.

LIMITATIONS OF TEST DATA

Partly because of the factors noted above, the information provided by tests has important limits.

Results can vary across tests. Because tests are samples of domains, their construction requires decisions about the relative emphasis on different types of content, the mix of item or task formats, the distribution of task difficulty, and other aspects of sampling. In addition, the construction of assessments requires a number of technical decisions that are largely independent of sampling, such as the choice of rubrics used to score open-response tasks and the selection of a method for scaling the results.

Given this array of decisions, it should not be surprising that alternative tests of the same domain often present different views of student performance. In the case of well-constructed traditional tests of well-defined domains, student-level cross-sectional correlations between scores on alternative tests are often very high. But even under those conditions, important results can vary markedly and in unexpected ways. For example, during the 1960s and 1970s, when achievement test scores were declining nationwide, mathematics scores of ninth-grade Iowa students on the Iowa Tests of Educational Development dropped roughly a quarter of a standard deviation, although those same students had produced a decline of nearly half a standard deviation in mathematics on the Iowa Tests of Basic Skills when they were eighth graders (Koretz, 1986, pp. 53–54). Similarly, Linn et al. (1990) showed that between the mid-1970s and mid-1980s, trends in third-grade mathematics scores varied substantially across the norming samples for commercial standardized tests, with rates of change at the median ranging from −1.0 to +2.2 national percentile ranks per year. Elizabeth Lewis Harris and I tabulated the 1986 National Assessment of Progress in Mathematics and found that the size of the black-white difference was sensitive to the relative emphasis given to content areas such as numbers and operations, algebra, and geometry.[5]

As assessment programs increasingly replace the multiple-choice format with essays and hands-on tasks, additional threats to robustness across tests arise. For example, NAEP tried scoring on-demand writing assessments using different rubrics (primary trait and holistic scoring) and found that correlations across rubrics ranged from .34 to .70, with a median of only .46 (Mullis et al., 1994, p. 308). In a more extreme case, the NAEP's first two trials of writing portfolios showed low agreement between portfolio scores and on-demand writing scores in the 1990 and 1992 assessments (Gentile, 1992; Gentile et al., 1995). In fact, one

---

[5]Unpublished tabulations.

can determine from the cross-tabulations provided by NAEP that the agreement rate was in every case only trivially higher than chance.[6]

The extent to which discrepancies among alternative tests or rubrics matters depends on how the results are used. If, for example, a test is used as one of several indicators of improvement or only to support inferences about the approximate magnitude of change, modest discrepancies among tests might be of little consequence. On the other hand, if schools are to be rewarded or sanctioned based solely on a fixed numerical criterion for changes in test scores, the underlying limitations matter far more, for they mean that decisions about test construction, often unrelated to decisions about the aspects of performance for which schools are supposed to be held accountable, will influence who is rewarded or punished.

Adjusted (partial) estimates of performance are often unstable. In many systems, school-level scores—for example, mean or median scores for students in a given grade—are the basis for accountability. Because school averages are strongly influenced by students' backgrounds, some programs adjust scores to take into account the limited background information available, such as the percentage of students from minority groups or the percentage receiving free or reduced-priced school lunches. The purpose of these adjustments is to provide a "fair" index of school effectiveness.

Controversy continues about the adequacy of indices of school effectiveness, but the evidence accumulated over the past two decades suggests wariness. First, such indices have been found in some studies to be inconsistent across grades and subject areas (e.g., Mandeville and Anderson, 1987), raising the prospect that the often limited scores available will inadequately measure school outputs and may lead to erroneous conclusions. Second, there is some evidence that the rankings of schools can be sensitive to the particular statistical model used to control for background information (e.g., Frechtling, 1982), although there is also evidence that they may be reasonably stable across variations within a given class of model (Clotfelter and Ladd, 1995). This model dependence of results may not be surprising, given the severity of the problems of omitted variables and inadequate measurement that confront such efforts. Third, school effectiveness indices are often unstable over time, a critical limitation in accountability systems that depend on measures of change. For example, Rowan and his colleagues (Rowan and Denk, 1983; Rowan et al., 1983) ranked 405 California schools on the basis of sixth-grade test scores after controlling for demographic variables and third-grade test scores. They classified the schools in the top quartile of adjusted scores as effective and then tracked their rankings over two additional years. The

---

[6]To some extent, inconsistencies between portfolio and on-demand scores could reflect unreliability of scoring rather than substantive differences. This is particularly true in the 1992 assessment (reported in Gentile et al., 1995), when the agreement rate among portfolio scorers dropped substantially compared to 1990 (reported in Gentile, 1992).

results varied from analysis to analysis, but in one fairly typical instance, of the 25 percent of schools initially classified as effective, only 10 percent remained "effective" in year 2 and only 5 percent in year 3. As many as 17 percent of schools went from the top quartile to the bottom quartile, or vice versa, between the first and third years examined. It seems hardly plausible that such dramatic shifts in "effectiveness" were real.

A primary reason for this instability is cohort-to-cohort differences in the characteristics of students attending a school. This is particularly problematic in the case of elementary schools, which typically have far fewer students per grade than do secondary schools and therefore have averages that are more influenced by a few particularly good or bad students.

In a set of schools that vary markedly in terms of background characteristics of students, the stability of those characteristics will often induce some stability of rankings in terms of raw scores. For example, schools that serve the children of highly educated parents in one year are likely to have similar student populations the next and therefore may consistently outscore schools that serve children of poorly educated parents. However, when stable differences in background characteristics are minor, or when their influence is removed or lessened statistically, the effects of cohort differences become a larger proportion of the total variability among schools, and the rankings of schools accordingly become much less stable.

Test scores are highly susceptible to corruption. In the context of accountability systems, this is probably the most serious and vexing limitation of test scores. Because tests are samples from large domains, instruction can be directed specifically toward the content emphasized on the test or the format of the test's tasks, at the expense of other important content that is either untested or given less weight on the test. In addition, instruction can be directed toward test-taking skills rather than content. That can make scores a biased estimate of mastery of the domain about which inferences are to be drawn. In other words, scores become inflated or corrupted.

Corruptible measures arise in other areas as well. For example, consider the federal budget deficit under the Gramm-Rudman-Hollings limits of the 1980s. There are many possible ways to measure the deficit, but Gramm-Rudman-Hollings focused on a particular subset. As a result, a great deal of effort went into making changes in the particular deficit measure of concern, even when the real effect on the deficit was inconsequential or nil. A good example was the movement of military paydays by a few days to put them in the fiscal year that did not count at a particular moment in the political debate.

Test scores may be unusual among social indicators, however, in the severity of their susceptibility to corruption. The following section provides evidence of the inflation of scores, as well as evidence of the contribution that test-based accountability can make to inflated scores.

EFFECTS OF ACCOUNTABILITY-ORIENTED TESTING

Although overconfidence in the test-based reforms of the 1980s resulted in a scarcity of research on their impact, there is enough evidence to paint a discouraging picture. The 1980s saw a significant inflation of scores, and there is evidence that undesirable instruction played a role in bringing it about.

Inflation of Scores

One hint that test scores were inflated in the 1980s comes from the NAEP. At least until recently, when limited comparisons among states were made possible by infrequent larger samples, no one had an incentive to "teach to" NAEP. The samples tested in most jurisdictions were too small to permit reliable estimates for them, and, in any case, NAEP did not report any results for states or localities. The smallest geographic areas for reporting were, until recently, four modified U.S. Census regions. Moreover, in recent years the structure of the test would have made it relatively difficult to teach to. First, large numbers of items are replaced on every assessment, and only items that will not be reused are released for public scrutiny. Second, the test is large and matrix sampled. That is, it comprises more items than an individual student can take in the allotted time, and students are assigned only random subsets of them.

One indication of possible corruption of scores would thus be a substantial divergence between trends on NAEP and trends on other assessments that provide more incentive and often more opportunity for coaching. Linn and Dunbar (1990) noted that over a number of two-year assessment cycles, the NAEP showed substantially less improvement than did many state and local testing programs. Although this pattern might have a number of explanations, a likely one is that the NAEP, unlike many state and local tests, was immune to the corrupting influence of teaching to the test.

A second suggestion of inflated test scores from aggregate data is the so-called Lake Wobegon phenomenon: the fact that most states with statewide data and an implausible proportion of districts in other states reported themselves to be "above the national average." This pattern was first reported by a family practitioner in West Virginia who was skeptical of his own state's scores and called around the country to get information from other states and districts (Cannell, 1987). Although Cannell's report was wrong in some of the specifics, his basic conclusion that an implausible proportion of jurisdictions were above the national average was confirmed (Linn et al., 1990). Linn et al. (1990) concluded that out-of-date norms may have accounted for part of the inflation of test scores. That is, achievement had improved nationwide, and old norms were therefore too easy and made states and districts using them appear higher-performing, relative to the nation as a whole, than they really were. However, there was also evidence of teaching to the test as well (Shepard, 1990). Moreover, the effect of old norms is not itself independent of teaching to the test. Because user districts are heavily represented in norming samples, teaching to the test could underlie some of the increasing difficulty of norms found during the 1980s (Linn et al., 1990).

A more direct evaluation of the inflation of test scores in high-stakes testing programs was provided by Koretz et al., (1991). They administered a variety of independent achievement tests to students in districts in which educators felt pressured to raise scores. Inflation of scores on the high-stakes tests would be reflected in a lack of "generalizability of performance"—that is, a lack of correspondence between performance on high-stakes tests and performance on other tests that had similar content but for which teachers had not had an opportunity or the motivation to coach. The study included three subjects—mathematics, reading, and vocabulary—in two different elementary grades in each of two districts. Randomly equivalent groups of students were administered two tests for purposes of substantive comparisons. Because the high-stakes test in each case was multiple choice, one comparison was to a competing commercial multiple-choice test. A second comparison was based on a test built to mirror the content of the high-stakes tests but that included a mix of formats. When possible, an additional randomly equivalent group was administered a "parallel form" of the high-stakes test itself—that is, a second form constructed and scaled to yield the same results as would be obtained with the primary form. This last test was used to check for biases caused by a lack of student motivation to do well on the study's tests or by differences in teachers' administration of the tests. The study tracked the scores of schools and districts for as long as five years, but the results reported here are based on cross-sectional data. In other words, the performance of individual students was not tracked over time.

The study revealed serious inflation of test scores in most, but not all, instances. Scores tended to be more inflated in mathematics than in reading. A particularly clear example is third-grade mathematics testing in the district that afforded us the strongest research design. In that district, teachers felt strong pressure to raise scores on a multiple-choice test administered district-wide. Median scores were published annually for each school in the district. For a period ending four years before the study, the district administered one test, called test C in the study. For the next four years it instead administered a competing test, test B, which to the untrained eye would look quite similar. Like most commercial norm-referenced tests, the results of both tests were reported using the same metrics, such as national percentile ranks and grade equivalents, which simplifies comparisons between them.

In the fourth year in which test B was administered, Koretz et al. administered test C—the identical test that the district had last used four years earlier—to one random sample of classrooms and the alternate tests to a second sample. A third random sample was administered the parallel form of test B, the district's current high-stakes test. Parallel-form scores in grade 3 were very similar to

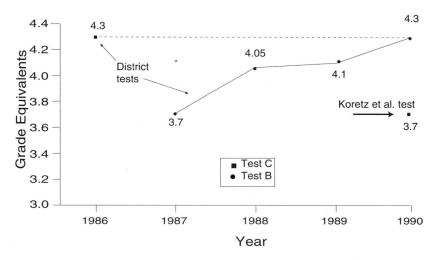

FIGURE 9.1   Performance on coached and uncoached tests, third-grade mathematics (adapted from Koretz et al., 1991).

published test B results, indicating that scores on the other tests administered in the study were unlikely to have been depressed by motivational or other artifacts.

When the district first switched from test C to test B, the median score in the district (the median of school medians) fell about half an academic year, from a grade equivalent (GE) of 4.3 to 3.7 (see Figure 9.1).[7] This corresponds to a decline from a national percentile rank (NPR) of 64 to an NPR of 52. Many factors could have contributed to this specific difference—for example, more recent and harder norms for the newer test, differences in scaling, and differences in the quality of national norming samples. But a sizable drop in scores is commonplace when one test is substituted for another because teachers are not yet familiar with the content and emphasis of the new test. In other words, some amount of decline is to be expected because of the effects of teaching to the older, familiar test.

A more clear-cut test of the generalizability of performance is provided by the comparison between Koretz, et al.'s administration of test C four years after it had last been used by the district and the results of the district's own final administration of that test. This comparison, which is not confounded with differences between tests or norms, also showed a substantial weakness of

---

[7]The grade equivalent is the median score obtained nationwide for students in a given month of a given grade. Thus, a GE of 3.7 is the median score nationwide for students in the seventh month— out of 10 academic months—in grade 3, or about average for the spring date on which this district administered its tests.

generalizability. The median score of the sample schools on test C was roughly 5 months (or 17 percentile points) lower in year 5 than in year 1, the last year in which the district administered that test itself. In year 5 the median school had an adjusted median GE of 3.8 and a median national percentile rank of 48, compared to the median of 4.2 (NPR = 65) in the last year that test C was the district's own test.[8] Indeed, performance on test C when we administered it to students who had not been coached for it was very similar to the performance in the districts' own program the first year it administered test B—that is, before anyone had an opportunity to coach for it.

Degradation of Instruction

The notion that holding educators accountable for scores on multiple-choice tests can degrade instruction was controversial less than a decade ago but is now almost axiomatic in the policy community. There are a number of ways in which degradation can occur.

Narrowing of instruction within subject areas. One form of degraded instruction is simply the flip side of inflated scores: undue narrowing of instruction to focus on the content emphasized on the test. Of course, focusing on the content of the test is not always bad; after all, one aim of test-based accountability is to accomplish precisely that end. Whether that focus is desirable or undesirable hinges on how it is brought about. To focus on the content of the test, teachers must take time from something else. The problem arises when teachers focus on the content of the test by taking time away from other parts of the domain that are excluded from or little emphasized by the test but that are nonetheless important. A number of surveys have found that many teachers knowingly take time away from other important parts of the curriculum (e.g., Darling-Hammond and Wise, 1985; Salmon-Cox, 1982, 1984; Shepard, 1988; Shepard and Dougherty, 1991). In this case, gains on the test may be seen not as improved mastery of the domain, but as a transfer of mastery from one part of the domain to another.

De-emphasis of untested subject areas. In contrast to most secondary school teachers, each of whose classes is restricted to a single subject area, most elementary school teachers teach a variety of subjects to the same students for most or all of the day. These teachers have an additional option for responding to test-based accountability, that is, to reallocate time across subject areas or other activities to maximize score gains. This is particularly problematic in the case of the many testing programs that assess only a small number of subject areas. For example, in one district some elementary teachers reported responding to test-based ac-

---

[8]Although the medians round to 3.8 and 4.2, the difference between them rounds to 5 months rather than 4.

countability by reducing the time allocated to science, which was not a tested subject area (Salmon-Cox, 1982, 1984). In this case, gains on the test can be seen as transfers of achievement from untested to tested subject areas.

Excessive drill. Once teachers know what specific skills are included on a test, they can devote large amounts of time to drilling students on them. The consequence can be boredom and the elimination of more demanding and potentially more valuable types of work.

Test preparation. Apart from focusing the content of instruction to better match the content of the test, teachers can engage in a wide variety of activities explicitly intended to prepare students for the test. Some of these activities are likely to be a waste of potentially valuable instructional time. For example, a number of companies (including but not limited to publishers of achievement tests) sell materials designed to help students prepare for specific achievement tests, and some teachers devote considerable time to using them. The impact of these materials on test scores is a matter of some dispute, just as the effectiveness of coaching for the Scholastic Assessment Test (SAT), formerly the Scholastic Aptitude Test, has been the focus of controversy. However, few would argue that students' underlying achievement, as opposed to their scores on tests, is helped more by using test practice materials than by instruction in tested subject areas.

As the material used to prepare students becomes increasingly similar to the actual test, test preparation approaches and eventually crosses the blurry, often subjective, line and becomes cheating, whether intentional or not. This can take many forms—for example, practicing problems that appear on the test or giving students hints based on the specific ways items are presented on the test. For example, in the early 1980s one California district was faced with a court order to increase scores at a specified rate in schools with large minority enrollments. The district responded by implementing a "mastery learning" curriculum that broke instructional goals into a sequence of small objectives and then allowed students to master each objective before proceeding to the next. Unfortunately, in one subject area—vocabulary—the district based its new curriculum substantially on the test that was used for accountability, incorporating the tested vocabulary words and their synonyms into the curriculum. A review found that well over half of the accountability test in vocabulary had been compromised in this fashion, and vocabulary gains appeared to be substantially inflated. On a different form of the same test there were much smaller gains. Oddly, the review found no compromise or inflated gains in other subject areas (Nagel, 1984).

Changes in the selection of students for testing. Schools and districts can improve scores by altering the pool of students tested. For example, holding low-achieving students back in the grades before those in which testing is done is likely to raise scores, and at least one study found increases in such retention following the imposition of high-stakes testing (Gottfredson, 1988). The selectivity of the tested group can also be manipulated by being lax about truancy or by excluding from testing students with limited English proficiency or certain handicaps. Although there are no systematic data on the frequency of such practices, they are widely perceived to occur and some states have imposed very strict rules to avoid them. In Kentucky, for example, only handicapped students whose conditions have removed them from a normal diploma-granting program are excluded from the regular state testing program, although other handicapped students undergo testing under special conditions consistent with their Individualized Education Plans.

THE POTENTIAL OF TECHNICAL INNOVATIONS IN ASSESSMENT

In the several years since the failings of the test-based accountability of the 1980s have become widely acknowledged, debate has focused in large part on altering tests, now generally called "assessments" to distinguish the new from the old. There are indeed steps that can be taken to lessen the problems noted above, although within practical constraints, the most that one can reasonably expect is to ameliorate them. Several of the most important steps are the following.

Methods of Reducing the Inflation of Scores

The most obvious method of reducing the inflation of scores, frequently discussed but often ignored in practice, is keeping test materials secure and changing them often. If teachers and students know only the framework of a test but have never seen the specific items that will be used in a given form of the test, they will be less able to train for the test at the expense of the domain as a whole. The Educational Testing Service traditionally has kept most SAT items secure and changed many for each new administration of the test, a procedure followed by the NAEP. Publishers of conventional achievement tests, on the other hand, tend to prepare only two highly similar forms of each edition of a test and to issue new editions only every six or seven years. School districts often use only one of the forms and keep copies between administrations of the test, with varying degrees of security.

Although test security and novelty can greatly reduce the inflation of test scores, they are not foolproof. One reason is cost. Test development is a costly process, and putting out new forms and replacing test materials every year would greatly increase the cost of testing programs. Second, if tests are to be comparable from one administration to the next to hold schools accountable for changes over time, successive forms of a test must be very similar. The more similar the test items are, the less impact replacement of test forms has on the inflation of scores.[9]

---

[9]In the study by Koretz et al., described above, students performed much the same on a parallel form of a high-stakes test and on average much worse on other tests of the same domain.

A more fundamental problem is that a test can only be an effective inducement to better instruction if teachers understand its content. Indeed, one of the axioms of advocates for accountability-based performance assessments is that the assessments can serve as models of desired student performance and instruction. To serve those functions, tasks very similar to those in the performance assessment must be publicized, and when dropped, they must be replaced by very similar tasks. Thus, accountability and test security impose competing pressures on assessment design.

Another approach to avoid narrowing of instruction and the attendant inflation of scores is to design a broad test while administering only a portion of it to each student. In theory, if a test of a given domain were made broad enough and specific items on it were secure, teaching to the test and teaching the domain would not differ. In practice, most domains are large enough that this ideal cannot be achieved within reasonable limits of expense and testing time, but it can be approximated by making a test several times as long as could be administered to any one student and giving each student a systematic sample of the test's items. In a common variant of this approach, usually called "matrix sampling," a test is broken into several different forms that are distributed randomly to students within the unit for which performance is to be reported, usually a school or district.

Matrix sampling and other sampling approaches, however, have an important limitation that forces a politically difficult trade-off. While sampling approaches can provide better estimates of group performance than can be obtained with a traditional test, they typically do not provide adequate assessments of individual students. Scores for individual students may be unreliable because of short test length, and students' scores may be dependent on the particular form they are given. In theory, one might separate the two functions, using a sampling-based assessment to provide aggregate estimates and a second, linked assessment to provide scores for individual students. In practice, however, it has been politically difficult to maintain an expensive and time-consuming sampling-based testing program that does not provide reliable scores for individual students. For example, Governor Wilson cited the lack of scores for individual students as one reason for terminating California's well-known assessment program, and both Kentucky and Maryland are now wrestling with the question of how to respond to pressure to report student-level scores from their matrix-sampled assessments.

The extent to which techniques such as test security, novel test content, and matrix sampling can avoid inflated test scores remains a matter of debate. There are as yet no good data on score inflation in accountability systems that rely heavily on all of these techniques. It seems likely, however, that they will provide only a partial solution for the foreseeable future.

The Promise (?) of Performance Assessment

A central tenet of the current "second wave" of education reform is that reliance on diverse performance assessments as the basis for school accountability will circumvent problems encountered with test-based accountability in the 1980s. This view appears to be overly optimistic.

There is some evidence, albeit limited, that shifting to performance assessments can address one of the two problems associated with test-based accountability; it can improve rather than degrade instruction. For example, Koretz et al. (1993, 1994a) found that Vermont educators reported a substantially greater emphasis on problem-solving and mathematical communication following implementation of the state's portfolio assessment program. Nevertheless, evidence about the instructional effects of performance assessment programs remains scarce. It is not clear under what circumstances these programs are conducive to improved teaching or what the effects are on student achievement.

On the other hand, there is as yet no reason to believe that test-based accountability will ameliorate the problem of inflated test scores. Indeed, there are reasons to expect that some types of performance assessments may be *more* susceptible to corruption. Because of the complexity of performance tasks, scores on them are likely to include sizable *task-specific* but *construct-irrelevant* variance—that is, variance that reflects idiosyncratic aspects of tasks rather than attributes of the latent trait supposedly being measured. For this reason, performance typically correlates only weakly across related tasks, even when the tasks are as similar as essays (e.g., Dunbar et al., 1991; Shavelson et al., 1993). Moreover, in most instances, performance assessments will comprise far fewer tasks than a corresponding multiple-choice test because of the student time required for each performance and the costs of developing them. Thus, a performance assessment is likely to comprise a relatively small number of poorly correlated tasks with substantial idiosyncratic attributes. Coaching students to do well on a small number of such tasks could easily lead to large gains in scores without commensurate real gains in mastery of the underlying areas of knowledge.

Performance assessment programs present other obstacles as well. They have been time consuming and costly to develop. Because of the amount of student time required to complete each performance, they increase the pressure to use a matrix-sampled design and to forego scores for individual students. In some cases they have proved difficult and costly to score (see Koretz et al., 1994a, b).

Finally, many innovative performance assessments have not yet been adequately validated. Although the tasks they comprise often seem appropriate, such "face validity," in the jargon of educational measurement, is not sufficient basis for judging them to be valid measures. In most cases little of the evidence needed for validation has been gathered; and in some cases the limited evidence available is discouraging. For example, it was noted earlier that the NAEP has shown essentially chance relationships between writing portfolio scores and scores on NAEP's on-demand test of writing, a pattern that raises serious doubt about the validity of the portfolio scores as a measure of writing proficiency. Koretz et al. (1993, 1994a) disattenuated relationships between portfolio scores in writing and mathematics, on-demand writing scores, and scores on a multiple-choice test of mathematics.[10] They reasoned that evidence of validity would be a finding that correlations were higher within domains (but across test formats) than across domains. For the most part the correlations did not show this pattern.

STEPS TOWARD THE APPROPRIATE USES OF TESTS

The discussion above represents a fairly discouraging assessment of test-based accountability. Traditional approaches have not worked well, and the scanty available evidence does not suggest that shifting to innovative testing formats will overcome their deficiencies. What is needed is a *better use* of tests, not just *better tests.*

What then should be done? It is neither realistic nor desirable to avoid the use of achievement tests in accountability systems. Meeting more of the goals of an accountability system and minimizing undesirable effects, however, is likely to be far more complex and difficult than many advocates of test-based accountability contemplate. It will require trial and error and many midcourse corrections. Three questions should be considered in designing an assessment program for this purpose: What attributes are important for the assessment program? How should the assessment itself be evaluated? How might achievement tests be incorporated into an accountability system?

Designing an Assessment Program

To meet the goals of many accountability systems, an assessment system is likely to need several components, each tailored to specific purposes. Tests that are used to hold teachers accountable and to induce changes in instruction may be poorly suited to providing high-quality data for comparing schools or even monitoring progress over time (see Koretz et al., 1994b). It may be important to give heavy emphasis in such tests to formats that have a large positive influence on instruction but that are inefficient or worse in terms of measurement quality. Moreover, any test used for this purpose is vulnerable to corruption, potentially distorting estimates of change.

Therefore, it may be essential to maintain a component of the assessment system that is designed specifically to monitor progress in the aggregate. This component could also serve as an audit mechanism, alerting jurisdictions to instances of egregious inflation of scores on the accountability tests. These tests

---

[10]Correlations were disattenuated for unreliability of scoring only.

would require greater protection from corruption, perhaps including higher levels of test security and more novel items per iteration than tests used for short-term accountability. In addition, monitoring tests might be constructed with more emphasis on formats, including multiple-choice items, chosen on the basis of measurement value rather than instructional incentives, although there are arguments both for and against this approach.

How to combine these two types of tests in measuring performance is likely to be a matter of debate. However, the data systems in which they are combined should be capable of supporting inferences about *school* as well as student performance. Simple cross-sectional differences in mean or median scores are unlikely to suffice. Some jurisdictions, such as Kentucky, hold schools accountable for changes in scores rather than for cross-sectional rankings that are heavily influenced by noneducational factors, but change scores present difficulties as well. Short-term change scores, particularly for small schools, can be unstable and misleading because of cohort-to-cohort differences in student characteristics. Differential student mobility remains a potentially serious source of bias, even when change rather than a cross-sectional average is the basis for accountability. Moreover, change measures may require careful scaling if they are to be fair to low- and high-achieving schools. Many of these difficulties are at least partially soluble, but in most instances solutions have not even been specified, let alone evaluated.

Evaluating Assessments

The results of accountability-oriented testing programs must themselves be assessed. Test-based accountability systems have been considered by many of their proponents to be self-evaluating, in that increases in scores on the tests used for accountability have been viewed as sufficient evidence that the policy has succeeded. Given the problem of inflated test scores, this view is clearly unfounded.

First, tests used in an accountability system should be evaluated against the conventional standards of reliability, validity, and fairness that apply to all tests, regardless of whether they are used for accountability. Second, tests used for accountability must be evaluated for inflation of scores. The monitoring tests suggested above represent one means of doing this. State-level NAEP scores, if available often enough in the same subjects and grades, might also serve as a mechanism for gauging inflation at the state level, although the NAEP is not designed to provide usable estimates at the level of individual schools and therefore would not be useful for determining whether there are specific schools in which inflation is particularly severe or modest.

Finally, the impact, often technically termed "consequential validity," of accountability-oriented testing programs should be evaluated directly. The possibility of inflated scores augments the importance of the direct assessment of impact, but even when score gains warrant confidence, direct appraisals of impact may be important. For example, some schools may achieve real gains in scores by methods that parents and communities might consider unacceptable—for example, by eliminating important activities such as instrumental music or by imposing oppressive amounts of homework that preclude extracurricular activities. Similarly, some teachers may consider it unproductive in terms of test scores to assign certain types of schoolwork such as long-term research projects or exploration of student-initiated questions. Both desirable and undesirable instructional effects of the accountability system may be distributed inequitably.

Embedding Assessments in an Accountability System

The larger question is the role of achievement tests in an educational accountability system. Achievement tests are an important but insufficient basis for holding schools accountable. "School performance" is more than the aggregate of student test scores, and the considerations above suggest that even high-quality tests do not work well enough as an accountability mechanism to warrant relying on them in isolation.

Efforts to embed tests in a broader range of indicators of school performance, however, remain rudimentary and controversial. A number of current reforms hold schools accountable for a variety of outcomes other than test scores. Both Kentucky and Maryland, for example, hold schools accountable for improving performance on a variety of other outcomes—called "non-cognitive" indicators in Kentucky and "data-based areas" in Maryland—such as drop-out rates, promotion rates, and attendance rates. The accountability systems in both states, however, mirror the national debate in giving more weight to test scores than to other outcomes, and some of the others show too little variance or change over time to have much impact.

The inclusion of school-performance indicators other than student outcomes is currently mired in controversy. Along with renewed enthusiasm for using tests to hold schools accountable has come widespread disparagement of holding schools accountable for "process" variables, such as financial and other inputs, instructional offerings, and similar factors. Few reformers endorse complete elimination of process accountability; for example, few would advocate eliminating all due process guarantees for disabled students. Moreover, some process criteria, such as "delivery standards" or "opportunity-to-learn standards," remain a part, albeit a very controversial part, of current reform debate. Nonetheless, process-oriented accountability is widely considered insufficient; and many reformers consider it a counterproductive distraction from the more important issue of outcomes.

The distinction between "process" and "outcome" accountability, however, is misleading and hinders the effort to devise an effective set of indicators for monitoring school performance. Schools produce a wide range of outcomes, some of which shade into "process."

The outcomes used in current accountability systems are often distant from teachers' day-to-day decisions. This is particularly true of some non-test indicators. For example, a fourth-grade teacher is likely to focus on issues much closer at hand than a student's potential decision, years hence, to drop out of school. Even achievement tests may not be a principal concern of many teachers given that many current accountability systems test students only in a few grades.

Teachers often establish shorter-term goals that, if met, produce important proximal outcomes that may or may not be reflected in test scores or other student-performance outcomes years later. For example, a teacher who decides to place greater emphasis on mathematics content that will be tested two grades hence may be contributing directly to higher scores. On the other hand, a teacher's decisions may be intended to increase students' interest in a subject, their intrinsic motivation to pursue it, or their willingness to take on large, self-directed projects. These efforts might be very important in terms of the broad goals of schooling, but their effect on later test scores is uncertain. Indeed, actions that are successful in terms of such proximal outcomes may even have negative effects on scores. For example, a teacher may decide to devote considerable time to a topic of unusual interest to her students to increase motivation, at the cost of reducing time devoted to other tested topics.

Proximal outcomes are often central to informal or local evaluations of schooling. For example, parents and principals often discuss whether course work is sufficiently challenging, whether homework is too heavily focused on boring drills, whether the amount of homework is appropriate, and whether students are motivated by their schoolwork and proud of their products. Centralized accountability systems, however, often give short shrift to proximal outcomes. They are complex, contextualized, very difficult to measure, and seemingly more ambiguous in meaning than test scores.

Thus, one of the major challenges in achieving better educational accountability may be deciding how much weight to give proximal outcomes and how to measure them. Some efforts have already been made to bridge the gap between distant and proximal outcomes. One rationale for large-scale portfolio assessment, for example, is that it holds teachers and students accountable for the work they produce on an ongoing basis, not just for the impact of that work on later test scores. Portfolios could also be used to monitor the quality of teachers' instructional offerings or their success in improving them rather than students' performance. The difficulties inherent in using portfolios and other nonstandardized assessment tools in a large-scale assessment, however, are formidable (Koretz et al., 1994b).

CONCLUSIONS

The notion that schools must be held accountable for their performance is compelling, and student achievement as measured by test results is clearly one of the most important components of evaluation. It is not straightforward, however, to design an accountability-oriented testing program that provides reasonable incentives for change and valid information about improvement, all at a reasonable cost in terms of money and student time. Some requirements of accountability systems are clear, but to have a reasonable chance of success, accountability systems themselves must be the subject of ongoing monitoring and evaluation. Moreover, tested student achievement should be placed in a broader constellation of desirable educational outcomes.

REFERENCES

Airasian, P. W. 1987. "State mandated testing and educational reform: context and consequences." *American Journal of Education* 95(May):393–412.

Ambach, G. 1987. Comments on "Should instruction be measurement-driven?" Invited debate, annual meeting of the American Educational Research Association, New Orleans, April.

Cannell, J. J. 1987. *Nationally Normed Elementary Achievement Testing in America's Public Schools: How All Fifty States Are Above the National Average.* Daniels, W.Va.: Friends for Education.

Clotfelter, C. T., and H. F. Ladd. 1995. Picking winners: recognition and reward programs for public schools. Unpublished paper, The Brookings Institution, Washington, D.C.

Darling-Hammond, L., and A. E. Wise. 1985. "Beyond standardization: state standards and school improvement." *The Elementary School Journal* Jan.:315–336.

Dunbar, S., D. Koretz, and H. D. Hoover. 1991. "Quality control in the development and use of performance assessment." *Applied Measurement in Education* 4(4):289–303.

Frechtling, J. A. 1982. Alternative methods for determining effectiveness: convergence and divergence. Paper presented at the annual meeting of the American Educational Research Association, New York, N.Y.

Gentile, C. 1992. *Exploring Methods for Collecting Students' School-Based Writing: NAEP's 1990 Portfolio Study.* Washington, D.C.: National Center for Education Statistics.

Gentile, C. A., J. Martin-Rehrmann, and J. H. Kennedy. 1995. *Windows into the Classroom: NAEP's 1992 Writing Portfolio Study.* Washington, D.C.: National Center for Education Statistics.

Goslin, D. A. 1963. *The Search for Ability: Standardized Testing in Social Perspective.* New York: Russell Sage Foundation.

Goslin, D. A. 1967. *Teachers and Testing.* New York: Russell Sage Foundation.

Goslin, D. A., R. R. Epstein, and B. A. Hallock. 1965. *The Use of Standardized Tests in Elementary Schools.* New York: Russell Sage Foundation.

Gottfredson, G. D. 1988. *You Get What You Measure, You Get What You Don't: Higher Standards, Higher Test Scores, More Retention in Grade.* Report #29, Center for Research on Effective Middle Schools.

Haney, W., and A. Raczek. 1994. Surmounting outcomes accountability in education. Paper prepared for the Office of Technology Assessment, U.S. Congress. Boston College Center for the Study of Testing Evaluation and Educational Policy, Chestnut Hill, Mass.

Hanushek, E. et al. 1994. *Making Schools Work: Improving Performance and Controlling Costs.* Washington, D.C.: The Brookings Institution.

Jaeger, R. M. 1982. "The final hurdle: minimum competency achievement testing." Pp. 223–247 in *The Rise and Fall of National Test Scores,* G. R. Austin and H. Garber, eds. New York: Academic Press.

Koretz, D. 1986. *Trends in Educational Achievement.* Washington, D.C.: Congressional Budget Office.

Koretz, D. 1992. "State and national assessment." In *Encyclopedia of Educational Research*, 6th ed., M. C. Alkin, ed. Washington, D.C.: American Educational Research Association.

Koretz, D. M., R. L. Linn, S. B. Dunbar, and L. A. Shepard. 1991. "The effects of high-stakes testing: preliminary evidence about generalization across tests." In R. L. Linn (chair), *The Effects of High-Stakes Testing*. Symposium presented at the annual meetings of the American Educational Research Association and the National Council on Measurement in Education, Chicago, Ill.

Koretz, D., B. Stecher, S. Klein, D. McCaffrey, and E. Deibert. 1993. *Can Portfolios Assess Student Performance and Influence Instruction? The 1991–92 Vermont Experience.* Santa Monica, Calif.: RAND Corp. (Reprinted from *CSE Technical Report 371*, National Center for Research on Evaluation, Standards, and Student Testing, Los Angeles.)

Koretz, D., B. Stecher, S. Klein, and D. McCaffrey. 1994a. *The Evolution of a Portfolio Program: The Impact and Quality of the Vermont Program in Its Second Year (1992–93).* Los Angeles: National Center for Research on Evaluation, Standards, and Student Testing.

Koretz, D., B. Stecher, S. Klein, and D. McCaffrey. 1994b. "The Vermont portfolio assessment program: findings and implications." *Educational Measurement: Issues and Practice,* 13(3):5–16.

Linn, R. L., and S. B. Dunbar. 1990. "The nation's report card goes home: good news and bad about trends in achievement." *Phi Delta Kappan* 72(2):127–133.

Linn, R. L., M. E. Graue, and N. M. Sanders. 1990. "Comparing state and district results to national norms: the validity of the claim that 'everyone is above average.'" *Educational Measurement: Issues and Practice* 9(3):5–14.

Mandeville, G. K., and L. W. Anderson. 1987. "The stability of school effectiveness indices across grade levels and subject areas." *Journal of Educational Measurement* 24(3):203–214.

Mullis, I. V. S., J. A. Dossey, J. R. Campbell, C. A. Gentile, C. O'Sullivan, and A. S. Latham. 1994. *NAEP 1992 Trends in Academic Progress.* Washington, D.C.: National Center for Education Statistics.

Nagel, T. S. 1984. Desegregation, education, or both? From the inside looking out—findings of an integration analyst. Paper presented at the annual meeting of the American Educational Research Association, San Diego, April 25.

National Commission on Excellence in Education. 1983. *A Nation at Risk.* Washington, D.C.: U.S. Department of Education.

National Council on Education Standards and Testing (NCEST). 1992. *Raising Standards for American Education: A Report to Congress, the Secretary of Education, the National Education Goals Panel, and the American People.* Washington, D.C.: NCEST.

Pipho, C. 1985. "Tracking the reforms, part 5: testing—can it measure the success of the reform movement?" *Education Week* 4(35):19.

Popham, W. J., K. L. Cruse, S. C. Rankin, P. D. Sandifer, and P. L. Williams. 1985. "Measurement-driven instruction: it's on the road." *Phi Delta Kappan* 66(9):628–634.

Roeber, E. 1988. A history of large-scale testing activities at the state level. Paper presented at the Indiana Governor's Symposium on ISTEP, Madison, Ind., Feb. 10.

Rowan, B., and C. E. Denk. 1983. *Modeling the Academic Performance of Schools Using Longitudinal Data: An Analysis of School Effectiveness Measures and School and Principal Effects on School-Level Achievement.* San Francisco: Far West Laboratory.

Rowan, B., S. T. Bossert, and D. C. Dwyer. 1983. "Research on effective schools: a cautionary note." *Educational Researcher* 12(4):24–31.

Salmon-Cox, L. 1982. MAP math: end of year one report. Unpublished, Learning Research and Development Center, University of Pittsburgh.

Salmon-Cox, L. 1984. MAP reading end-of-year report. Unpublished, Learning Research and Development Center, University of Pittsburgh.

Shavelson, R. J., G. P. Baxter, and X. Gao. 1993. "Sampling variability of performance assessments." *Journal of Educational Measurement* 30(3):215–232.

Shepard, L. A. 1988. The harm of measurement-driven instruction. Paper presented at the annual meeting of the American Educational Research Association, Washington, D.C., April.

Shepard, L. A. 1990. "Inflated test score gains: is the problem old norms or teaching the test?" *Educational Measurement: Issues and Practice* 9(3):15–22.

Shepard, L. A., and K. C. Dougherty. 1991. "Effects of high-stakes testing on instruction." In R. L. Linn (chair) *The Effects of High Stakes Testing*, Symposium presented at the annual meetings of the American Educational Research Association and the National Council on Measurement in Education, Chicago, Ill.

CHAPTER 10

Value-Added Indicators of School Performance[*]

ROBERT H. MEYER

Harris Graduate School of Public Policy Studies,
University of Chicago

Educational outcome indicators are increasingly being used to assess the efficacy of American education. Reliance on such indicators is largely the result of a growing demand to hold schools accountable for their performance, defined in terms of outcomes, such as standardized test scores, rather than inputs, such as teacher qualifications, class size, and the number of books in a school's library. Unfortunately, most schools and districts have not developed and implemented entirely suitable performance indicators. Many scholars fear that these indicator/ accountability systems could distort the behavior of educators and students, with worse results than when using no indicators at all. It is, therefore, very important to consider the attributes of an acceptable, valid performance indicator system.

CRITERIA FOR PERFORMANCE INDICATORS

Outcome Validity

The set of tests and other measures of outcomes that underlie a performance indicator system must measure the types of skills demanded by society. Otherwise, a high-stakes accountability system could induce educators to design and implement a curriculum that emphasizes skills that are of minimal social value. Many educators believe that many of the standardized multiple-choice tests are flawed because they focus almost exclusively on low-level academic content, not

*This research has been supported by the Joyce Foundation and the Smith Richardson Foundation. The author has benefitted enormously from the comments of Eric Hanushek.

on specific curriculum objectives (Smith and O'Day, 1990; Clune, 1991). As a result of this criticism, many school districts, states, and professional test developers are experimenting with new types of assessments—for example, tests with open-ended questions, performance-based assessments, graded portfolios, and curriculum-based multiple-choice tests—more closely related to educational objectives.[1] As new tests are developed, test developers and curriculum designers need to determine whether the new tests and assessments are valid, in the sense of measuring the skills that are highly valued by society.

Noncorruptability

Second, a performance indicator must accurately measure performance with respect to the outcome that it purports to measure. Test scores can be "corrupted" in various ways. For example, a test could be administered in such a way that it is easy for students and staff to cheat. Alternatively, a test form that is administered year after year could stimulate instructors to teach narrowly to the test, rather than to the broader domain of knowledge that underlies the test.[2]

Valid Measurement of School Performance

Finally, a performance indicator must accurately and reliably measure school performance, where school performance with respect to a particular test or other student outcome is defined as the contribution of the school to that outcome. In a recent paper Meyer (1994) demonstrated that the common indicators of school performance—average and median test scores—are highly flawed even though derived from valid assessments. The simulation results reported by Meyer indicate that changes over time in average test scores could be *negatively* correlated with actual changes in school performance.

The purpose of this chapter is to consider the class of educational indicators referred to as *value-added indicators* that satisfy the third criterion discussed above. For simplicity the focus here is entirely on value-added indicators derived from student test scores. The first section explains the theory and logic of value-added indicators, emphasizing the interpretation and reporting of value-added models and indicators rather than methods of estimating these models and other technical questions. The second section compares value-added and nonvalue-added indicators such as the average test score. The third part discusses policy considerations that are relevant to the use and nonuse of value-added and nonvalue-added indicators. Finally, conclusions are drawn and recommendations offered.

---

[1]See, for example, Wiggins (1989), Darling-Hammond (1991), Shepard (1991), and Koretz et al. (1994).

[2]See, for example, Haladyna et al. (1991), Nolen et al. (1992), Smith and Rottenberg (1991), and Shepard (1991).

THE THEORY AND LOGIC OF VALUE-ADDED INDICATORS

Alternative Uses of Standardized Tests and Assessments

The results of standardized tests and assessments can be used to measure the achievement of individual students, produce aggregate indicators of the level and distribution of achievement for groups of students, evaluate the efficacy of specific school policies and inputs, and measure school performance. The focus here is on the latter application, although the tasks of measuring school performance and evaluating school policies and inputs are closely related.

It is not widely appreciated that properly constructed school performance indicators differ greatly from simple aggregate indicators such as average test scores, in part because test vendors have tended to focus attention on measuring student achievement rather than school performance. Increasingly, however, schools, states, and other groups are interested in assessing the performance of schools as well as students through standardized tests. It is therefore important to draw a sharp distinction between school performance indicators and simple aggregate indicators based on test scores.

The most common aggregate indicators are average and median test scores and the share of students scoring above or below a given threshold. These "level" indicators measure some feature of the level of student achievement rather than, for example, growth in student achievement (Meyer, 1994). Level indicators are widely reported by schools, states, test vendors, and national organizations such as the National Assessment of Educational Progress. If correctly constructed and based on appropriate tests or assessments, level indicators convey useful *descriptive* information about the proficiencies of students in particular classrooms, schools, or groups. It is appropriate to use indicators of this type to target assistance, financial or otherwise, to schools that serve students with low test scores. Such indicators are not a valid measure of school or classroom performance, however.

Value-Added Indicators: An Introduction

The question of how to measure school performance is, fundamentally, a technical statistical problem, similar to the task of measuring the efficacy of school policies and inputs, and one that has been addressed in the evaluation literature for well over three decades and continues to be an active area of research.[3] The common characteristic of the value-added models used in the literature is that they measure school performance or the effect of school policies and

---

[3]See, for example, Coleman (1966), Hanushek (1972), Murnane (1975), Boardman and Murnane (1979), Raudenbush and Bryk (1986), and Meyer (1992). For studies explicitly focused on school performance indicators, see Dyer et al. (1969), Willms and Raudenbush (1989), Hanushek and Taylor (1990), and Meyer (1994).

inputs using a statistical regression model that includes, to the extent possible, all of the factors that contribute to growth in student achievement, including student, family, and neighborhood characteristics. The key idea is to isolate statistically the contribution of schools from other sources of student achievement. This is particularly important in light of the fact that differences in student and family characteristics account for far more of the variation in student achievement than school-related factors. Failure to account for differences across schools in student, family, and community characteristics could result in highly contaminated indicators of school performance.

The basic logic of a value-added model, whether it is used to measure school performance or to evaluate alternative school policies, can be illustrated by using a simple two-level model of student achievement.[4] The first level of the model captures the influences of student and family characteristics on growth in student achievement. The second level captures the effect of school-level characteristics. Given this framework, it is straightforward to define one or more indicators of school performance—for example, one that is appropriate for school choice purposes or one that is appropriate for school accountability purposes, as follows.

Let us first consider a value-added model of growth in student achievement for a particular grade—say, grade 2. A simple level-one equation is[5]

$$\text{Posttest}_{is} = \theta \, \text{Pretest}_{is} + \alpha \, \text{StudChar}_{is} + \eta_s + \varepsilon_{is}, \qquad (1)$$

where i indexes individual students and s indexes schools. Posttest_{is} and Pretest_{is} represent student achievement for a given individual in second grade and first grade, respectively; StudChar_{is} represents a set of individual and family characteristics assumed to determine growth in student achievement (and a constant term); ε_{is} captures the unobserved student-level determinants of achievement growth; θ and α are model parameters that must be estimated; and η_s is a school-level effect that must be estimated.[6] The model has been structured such that the

---

[4]See Bryk and Raudenbush (1992), Bock (1989), and Raudenbush and Willms (1991) for discussions of the application of multilevel (hierarchical) models in education. The advantage of these models is that they allow one to break down the school level into sub-levels that more realistically reflect the structure of American school systems. Models of this type could, for example, include levels representing students, classrooms, schools, school districts, and states.

[5]To simplify the notation, sets of variables and coefficients are written throughout this paper in vector form. In the equation below, for example, StudChar is a vector of student and family characteristics, α is the corresponding parameter vector, and a StudChar is a vector product that is equal to $\alpha \, \text{StudChar} = \alpha_1 \, \text{StudChar}_1 + \alpha_2 \, \text{StudChar}_2 + \alpha_3 \, \text{StudChar}_3 + \dots$, where $\alpha_1, \alpha_2, \alpha_3$, etc., are elements of the vector α and $\text{StudChar}_1, \text{StudChar}_2, \text{StudChar}_3$, etc., are elements of the vector StudChar.

[6]This model could explicitly be cast as a model of growth in student achievement by subtracting the prior achievement variable Pretest from both sides of the equation. The prior achievement variable would drop from the model if $\theta = 1$. A model that imposes the restriction that $\theta = 1$ is referred to as a linear growth model (see, e.g., Willett, 1988). One reason to consider the more general model in the text is that it applies to contexts in which the pre- and posttests are measured in different units (i.e., the tests have not been equated.) On the other hand, a model that includes a prior test as a regressor variable may require more advanced estimation techniques than a linear growth model owing to problems posed by the measurement error in the prior test (Meyer, 1992).

school effects (η_s) have an average value equal to zero in a given school year, the so-called benchmark year.

Parameter η_s is very important. It reflects the contribution of a given school (school s) to growth in student achievement after controlling for all student-level factors, pretest and student characteristics. Equivalently, it captures all of the observed and unobserved school-level factors that influence growth in student achievement. Hence, it is a measure of *total* school performance (Meyer, 1994). Willms and Raudenbush (1989) refer to this indicator as a Type A indicator.

As defined, the total performance indicator gives an unambigious ranking of schools, but the exact range and magnitude of the indicator are somewhat arbitrary. As a result, the indicator could appear to be divorced from the outcome that everyone ultimately cares about—student achievement. An alternative but equivalent strategy is to define the total performance indicator as the *predicted mean* achievement of a given school for a given *benchmark* group of students:

$$P(\text{Total})_s = \{\theta \, \text{Pretest}_{\text{BENCHMARK}} + \alpha \, \text{StudChar}_{\text{BENCHMARK}}\} + \eta_s, \qquad (2)$$

where $\text{Pretest}_{\text{BENCHMARK}}$ and $\text{StudChar}_{\text{BENCHMARK}}$ represent the mean values of Pretest and StudChar in the benchmark year and the term in brackets is a fixed number for all schools.[7] For those accustomed to interpreting test scores reported on a given scale, it may be easier to interpret the total performance indicator when it is reported as a predicted mean than as an indicator centered around zero.[8] In the remainder of this chapter the benchmark predicted mean form of the indicator is used.

The alternative predicted mean method of reporting value-added indicators opens up the possibility of reporting value-added indicators tailored to different types of students. In particular, Eq. (2) could be used to compute the predicted achievement of students given pretest scores and student and family characteristics other than those of the benchmark group. This method of reporting indicators may be termed the *conditional mean format* and has a number of advantages. First, students and families might pay more attention to indicators that are custom designed to suit their own circumstances. Second, the format provides information on the effects on student achievement of prior achievement and student, family, and neighborhood characterisitics, as well as school performance. Third, this format readily handles value-added models that are more complicated than the one considered thus far.

One possible disadvantage of reporting indicators in the conditional format is that it might be burdensome and possibly confusing to distribute multiple versions of essentially the same indicator, especially if the number of reporting

---

[7]In graphical terms, $P(\text{Total})_s$ is simply the height of the student achievement regression/prediction line at the values $\text{Pretest}_{\text{BENCHMARK}}$ and $\text{StudChar}_{\text{BENCHMARK}}$ (see Figure 10.1).

[8]Note that the term in brackets in Eq. (2) is equal to $\text{Posttest}_{\text{BENCHMARK}} = \theta \, \text{Pretest}_{\text{BENCHMARK}} + \alpha \, \text{StudChar}_{\text{BENCHMARK}}$. As a result, $P(\text{Total})_s$ can also be interpreted as the total performance indicator centered around the overall mean achievement level in the benchmark year.

categories is large. Suppose that an achievement growth model includes five control variables—prior achievement, parental education, parental income, race, and special education status. If each variable is split into five different values, the total number of reporting categories would equal $5^5 = 3,125$.[9] Clearly, it would be advantageous to find some creative ways of presenting these data without producing information overload.

How should the total performance indicator be interpreted? One interpretation is that it captures the effect at some *past* date of enrolling one additional student in a school, holding all school-level factors constant, including the composition of the student group that attends the school. If these characteristics are relatively stable from year to year, the total school performance indicator could provide reliable information on the *future* performance of schools and thus be very helpful to students and parents who are in the process of choosing a neighborhood to live in and/or a school to attend. In short, the total performance indicator is appropriate for purposes of informing school choice, but it is not the most appropriate indicator for holding schools accountable for their performance because it fails to exclude components of school performance that are external to the school.

For an indicator that serves the accountability function, let us turn to the second level of the value-added model. This equation captures the school-level factors that contribute to growth in student achievement. A simple level-two equation is:

$$\eta_s = \delta_1 \, \text{External}_s + \delta_2 \, \text{Internal}_s + u_s \tag{3}$$

where η_s is the school effect (and total school performance indicator) for school s from the level-one equation; External_s and Internal_s represent all *observed* school-level characteristics assumed to determine growth in student achievement plus a constant term; u_s is the *unobserved* determinant of total school performance; and δ_1 and δ_2 are parameters that must be estimated. To be consistent with the level-one equation, it is assumed that the internal school characteristics all have mean zero in the benchmark year.

The distinction between the external and internal variables is crucial for the purpose of measuring school performance. External_s includes all observed school-level characteristics that could be considered *external* to the school (plus a constant term), including neighborhood and community characteristics and aggregate student characteristics such as the average socioeconomic status of all students in a school. Internal_s includes all observed school-level characteristics that could be considered *internal* to the school, principally school policies and inputs.

---

[9]For example, one category would include students who are white, with average prior achievement, not in special education, and whose parents graduated from high school and earn an average income.

Given the distinction between internal and external school-level characteristics, a measure of school performance, controlling for all factors that are *external* to the school, is given by δ_2 Internal$_s$ + u_s, where the first term, δ_2 Internal$_s$, represents the component of school performance that is predictable given the observed school policies and inputs, and the second term, u_s, represents the unpredictable component of school performance. This indicator can also be written as $\eta_s - \delta_1$ External$_s$—that is, the total performance indicator minus the component of performance that is due to external school-level characteristics. This indicator may be thought of as a measure of *intrinsic* school performance; Willms and Raudenbush (1989) refer to it as a Type B indicator.

As in the case of the total performance indicator, the intrinsic performance indicator can be defined as the predicted mean achievement of a given school with benchmark characteristics:

$$P(\text{Intrinsic})_s = \{\theta \text{ Pretest}_{\text{BENCHMARK}} + \alpha \text{ StudChar}_{\text{BENCHMARK}} + \delta_1 \text{ External}_{\text{BENCHMARK}}\} + \delta_2 \text{ Internal}_s + u_s \quad (4)$$

where External$_{\text{BENCHMARK}}$ represents the mean value of External in the benchmark year and the term in brackets is a fixed number for all schools. This indicator can also be reported in the conditional mean format.

The intrinsic performance indicator can be interpreted in more than one way, depending on the types of variables that are considered external in the model and on which *individuals and institutions* are responsible for determining a school's policies and inputs at a given grade level. Let us assume that the external variables are limited to community characteristics and school-level student characteristics, such as average parental income and education. In schools where decisions are largely made by school staff, the intrinsic indicator can be viewed as a measure of the collective performance of these staff. In cases where significant school decisions are made by district staff and perhaps other parties, the indicator can be viewed as a joint measure of school and district performance. Finally, in cases where important school inputs are determined in part by state agencies or taxpayers, the indicator can be interpreted as a joint measure of the performance of the school and the institutions that affect the school's policies and inputs.

This analysis implies that it could be problematic to interpret the intrinsic performance indicator as a measure of the performance of school staff when there is substantial variation across schools in important school inputs such as class size. In this situation one alternative is to view school inputs that are determined outside the school as external school-level characteristics, along with the set of external characteristics listed above. Including these external characteristics in the value-added model would make it legitimate to compare the performance of schools that differ in these characteristics.

In any case, the intrinsic performance indicator is the appropriate indicator for the purpose of holding educational decisionmakers and providers accountable for their performance. Obviously, how this indicator is used as part of an accountability system should depend on who has authority to make decisions that determine the performance of a school and the exact specification of the value-added model used to produce the indicators.

Although the discussion here has thus far focused on deriving measures of school performance from the two-level value-added model, the *methodological similarities* between analyses designed to produce value-added indicators and analyses designed to evaluate alternative school policies and inputs, as represented by the parameter δ_2, should be apparent.[10] There are, however, some potentially important differences between the two types of analyses.

First, large-scale evaluations tend to be based on samples that include a large number of schools and districts. The High School and Beyond Study, for example, includes over a thousand high schools. In contrast, most districts have less than 50 elementary schools and even fewer middle schools and high schools. This implies that in small to medium-sized districts it might not be feasible to produce reliable estimates of the level-two slope parameters and therefore estimates of intrinsic school performances using within-district data only.[11] One possible alternative would be to estimate the slope parameters of the level-two model using data from several districts collected via some cooperative data-sharing arrangement among districts. As indicated in the next section, it is straightforward to construct estimates of total and intrinsic school performance given estimates of the slope coefficients in the level-one and -two value-added equations.

Second, when evaluating the effects of alternative policies and inputs, it is common to observe the same policies and inputs at more than one school or district, thus enabling researchers to estimate potentially small effects with a high degree of precision. In the case of value-added indicators, in contrast, the possibilities for replication are essentially eliminated because the objective typically is to estimate the performance of a single school. As a result, steps need to be taken to ensure that school performance indicators meet acceptable criteria for reliability—for example, aggregation of indicators across multiple grade levels and subject areas within a given school.

Third, the data typically used to construct school performance indicators are usually obtained from administrative records rather than extensive surveys of students and parents. As a result, the data will typically be quite limited and possibly either missing for large numbers of cases or subject to errors. This has

---

[10]The presentation in the text explicitly distinguishes the first and second levels of the value-added model. Some studies may treat the multilevel nature of the data and the analysis less explicitly, although no less rigorously. It is common, in fact, to see the first- and second-level equations combined into a single equation as follows: $\text{Posttest}_{is} = \theta \, \text{Pretest}_{is} + \alpha \, \text{StudChar}_{is} + \delta_1 \, \text{External}_s + \delta_2 \, \text{Internal}_s + u_s + \varepsilon_{is}$.

[11]In general, it is possible to obtain precise estimates of the level-one slope parameters even if the number of schools in a district is small. The key requirement is that the number of students in the data set used to estimate these parameters be reasonably large. Often it is possible to obtain a sufficiently large data set by pooling observations from several years.

important implications for the accuracy of value-added indicators, as is discussed later in the paper.

Finally, some analysts might argue that, while it is accepted practice to use statistical methods to evaluate school policies, it is problematic to use them to construct performance indicators because they may not be comprehensible to students, families, educators, and other interested parties. This is an important concern, justifying considerable effort to make value-added indicators more comprehensible—for example, by using the predicted mean achievement format. A second way to make value-added indicators more comprehensible is to provide the public with some alternative ways of understanding the logic of value-added indicators.

Value-Added Indicators: Logic

To convey the logic of value-added indicators, it is useful to think of a two-stage process of estimating the indicators. In the first stage the so-called slope parameters in Eqs. (1) and (3) (θ, α, δ_1, and δ_2) are estimated by using appropriate statistical procedures.[12] These coefficients reflect the contributions of prior achievement, individual characteristics, and school-level factors to growth in student achievement and thus can be used to *adjust* for the contributions of these factors to average differences across schools in student achievement growth. In the second stage, school performance is estimated, given estimates of the slope parameters from the first stage. Suppose that the first-stage slope parameters have already been estimated. An estimate of total school performance for a given school (school s) can then be given by:

$$\hat{P}(\text{Total})_s = \text{Mean}(\text{Posttest})_s - \text{AdjFactor}(\text{Total})_s, \tag{5}$$

where $\text{AdjFactor}(\text{Total})_s = \hat{\theta}[\text{Mean}(\text{Pretest})_s - \text{Pretest}_{\text{BENCHMARK}}] + \hat{\alpha}[\text{Mean}(\text{StudChar})_s - \text{StudChar}_{\text{BENCHMARK}}]$ and where $\text{Mean}(\text{Posttest})_s$ denotes the mean posttest for all students in school s and the other variables are similarly defined. Note that estimated parameters are indicated by placing a circumflex ($^\wedge$) over the parameter. An estimate of intrinsic school performance is similarly given by

$$\hat{P}(\text{Intrinsic})_s = \text{Mean}(\text{PostTest})_s - \text{AdjFactor}(\text{Intrinsic})_s \tag{6}$$

where $\text{AdjFactor}(\text{Intrinsic})_s = \text{AdjFactor}(\text{Total})_s + \hat{\delta}_1 [\text{External}_s - \text{External}_{\text{BENCHMARK}}]$.

The above formulas provide important insight into the meaning and mechanics of

---

[12]See, for example, Hsiao (1986), Raudenbush (1988), Meyer (1992), and Bryk and Raudenbush (1992). To estimate the parameters of the level-two equation, typically it is also necessary to estimate the school effect parameters either jointly or in an interative fashion. In the case of the level-one equation, the slope parameters can be estimated separately in a first stage using a fixed effects (ANOCOVA) model. In either case, given estimates of the slope parameters, it is straightforward to estimate the school effects, as explained in the text.

value-added indicators. The total performance indicator can be viewed as an indicator that *adjusts or controls* for average differences across schools in student and family characteristics. In particular, the value-added approach purges the average test score—Mean(Posttest) in Eq. (5)—of the component of achievement growth that represents the within-school contribution of students and families to growth in student achievement. The adjustment factor is highest for schools with students who have disproportionately high entering achievement and student and family characteristics that are positively associated with growth in achievement. It is equal to zero for schools that serve students mirroring the overall group of students in the benchmark sample. This implies that the average test score overstates the true performance of schools that have high adjustment factors and understates the true performance of those that have low adjustment factors.

The intrinsic performance indicator has a similar interpretation. The sole difference between the two is that the intrinsic indicator adjusts for differences across schools in external school-level characteristics as well as student-level characteristics. In a sense the intrinsic indicator levels the "playing field," so that it measures how much a given school *adds* to a student's achievement, controlling for all external differences across schools.

Note that the value-added indicators defined by Eqs. (5) and (6) are easy to compute, given prior estimates of the slope parameters.[13] This implies that it would be possible to implement an indicator system without placing undue emphasis on the statistical "machinery" that underlies the system—in particular, the first-stage estimation process. With sufficient training, most school administrators could learn to compute estimates of total or intrinsic school performance, resulting in a greater understanding and acceptance of the indicators.[14]

Note that the formula for computing the intrinsic performance indicator, Eq. (6), does not require data on internal school characteristics. It may be sufficient to collect this information only periodically for the sole purpose of estimating the required parameters of the value-added model, especially δ_1.[15] On the other hand, information on internal school characteristics could be useful to schools as part of a diagnostic indicator system, helping identify a school's strong and weak

---

[13]Some value-added indicators are more difficult to compute than the indicators discussed in the text—for example, indicators based on empirical Bayes methods (see, e.g., Raudenbush, 1988).

[14]A similar strategy has, in effect, been used by the testing community. Although students and families are not generally aware of it, reported test scores increasingly are the end result of sophisticated psychometric analysis, particularly in cases where there are multiple forms of the same test and where the tests are the result of computerized adaptive testing. See, for example, Lord (1980).

[15]One might ask if it is necessary to collect information on internal school characteristics at all if the primary parameter of interest in the level-two equation is the coefficient on external characteristics, δ_1. The answer depends on whether the internal and external variables are correlated. If they are correlated, excluding the internal variables would cause the estimate of δ_1 to be biased. The problem of potentially biased coefficients is especially acute for the student composition variables, such as the average parental income variable, that are typically included in the level-two equation. There is good reason to believe that these variables could be correlated with the internal determinants

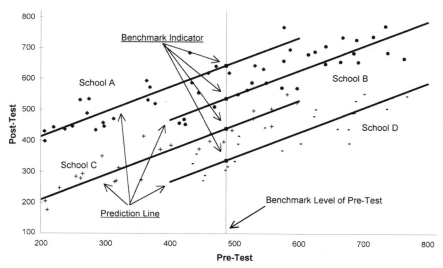

FIGURE 10.1   Plot of hypothetical test score data.

points and providing schools with a ready diagnosis of why their measured performance is high or low. To implement such a system would require a reasonably comprehensive set of school process and input indicators.[16]

Perhaps the best way to illustrate the logic and mechanics of the value-added approach is with an example. Let us consider a hypothetical dataset containing information on student achievement for students from four different schools. The data are based on a highly simplified model of growth in student achievement that contains only a single control variable—prior achievement.[17] As a result, the data can conveniently be displayed on a two-dimensional graph. For simplicity, the discussion here is limited to the total performance indicator; analysis for the intrinsic performance indicator would be similar.

To interpret properly the indicators discussed below, it is important to know something about the distribution of the pre- and posttests that underlie them. Both tests were scored in a manner similar to the Scholastic Assessment Test; scores were centered around a national mean of 500, with a range of approximately 200 to 800. Figure 10.1 plots pre- and posttest scores for 25 students from

---

of school performance. For example, affluent parents may be more able to afford housing in neighborhoods where high-performance schools are located. If so, this would induce a positive correlation between average parental income and the internal determinants of school performance. I am currently working on a model that could dispense with the need for measures of internal school characteristics.

[16]See Porter (1990) for a discussion of a system of process indicators.

[17]The data were generated by using a model of achievement growth in which the coefficient on prior achievement was equal to $\theta = 0.8$.

TABLE 10.1   Total Performance Indicator Reported as a Benchmark Predicted Mean and as a Conditional Mean, Given Selected Values of Prior Achievement

| School | Conditional Mean Indicator (Prior Achievement) | | | | | | Benchmark Indicator |
	250	350	450	550	650	750	487
A	453	533	613	693	773	853	642
B	346	426	506	586	666	746	536
C	250	330	410	490	570	650	439
D	146	226	306	386	466	546	336
Total	229	379	459	539	619	699	488

NOTE: The italicized numbers represent levels of prior achievement that are beyond the range of actual achievement in a given school.

four different schools (schools A, B, C, and D). In all four schools there is a strong positive relationship between post- and prior achievement. Moreover, for each school the data points are clustered around a centrally located, upward-sloping regression or prediction line. For each school this prediction line can be used to compute the total performance indicator, $\hat{P}(\text{Total})_s$. This indicator is simply the height of the prediction line for each school at the benchmark level of prior achievement indicated by the vertical line. The value of this indicator for each school is indicated on the graph by a black box. The total performance indicator, reported as a set of conditional mean indicators, is the height of the prediction line for each school at selected values of prior achievement. Table 10.1 reports the total performance indicator in these two alternative formats.

The total performance indicator is higher for school A than school B, even though the average test scores tend to be higher for school B. This is a consequence of the fact that the pretest scores are substantially lower in school A than in school B. School A is rated a better school than school B because it produces greater achievement growth or adds more value than school B or either of the other two schools. It is easy to see this if one compares students with similar pretest scores, for example, in the range of 400 to 600. The power of the value-added method is that it makes it possible to compare the performance of schools that differ widely in terms of their student populations.

The basic logic of this method is illustrated in Figure 10.2, which reproduces the est score data from Figure 10.1. For each school, the average test score and the total school performance rating are indicated by black squares. These two points are connected by a right triangle. The horizontal segment of the triangle represents the difference between the average level of prior achievement in a given school and the average benchmark level of prior achievement (or Mean [Pre Test]$_s$-PreTest$_{\text{BENCHMARK}}$). In the case of schools B and D, for example, this difference is positive. As a result, the average test score overstates the performance of these two schools.

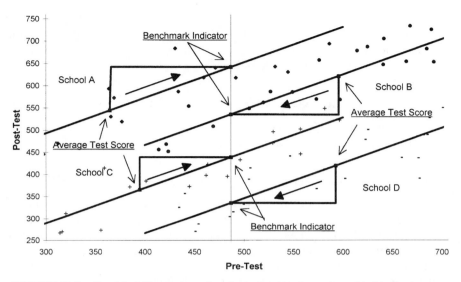

FIGURE 10.2   Graphical illustration of method of estimating value-added indicators.

As is evident in Figures 10.1 and 10.2, the value-added approach is based on two important related assumptions. First, the regression/prediction lines for all schools are linear and parallel. Second, it is possible to predict school performance, given any values of the control variables. The first assumption, in my experience, is consistent with the observed data.[18] If not, it might be appropriate to use a more complex value-added model. With regard to the second assumption, one should be very careful in interpreting predicted school performance levels in cases where the values of the control variables are substantially beyond the range of the data for a given school. One might interpret the predicted levels of performance in these cases as indicative of the level that a school could reach in the *long run*, after it has adjusted to the particular needs of new students.[19] This implies that parents should be wary of selecting schools solely on the basis of their predicted total performance if, in the past, the schools have not served students with similar individual and family characteristics. To assist school choice therefore, it is important to convey information about the composition of alternative schools. It is straightforward to incorporate this information into a report of conditional mean indicators, as indicated in Table 10.1. In the table the

---

[18]Hsiao (1986, p. 15) discusses a technique for testing the assumption that all slope coefficients in a level-one model are parallel (homogeneous). Many standard statistics and econometrics texts address the problem of testing whether a given model specification (linear or nonlinear) fits the data well in the extremes of the data.

[19]This line of argument is based on the assumption that at least some schools tailor their curriculum and instructional methods to the aptitude and prior experience of students.

predicted levels of school performance that involve extrapolation beyond existing data are italicized. For accountability purposes, the issue of extrapolation appears to be much less of a problem, since it is reasonable to evaluate schools on the basis of an indicator that reflects long-run performance potential.

Alternative Value-Added Models and Modeling Issues

As mentioned earlier, value-added modeling is an active area of research. Some of the modeling issues being addressed are discussed briefly below.

Adequacy of Control Variables

The principal obstacle to developing a high-quality indicator system is the difficulty of collecting extensive information on student and family characteristics. Value-added indicators are often implemented by using the rather limited administrative data commonly available in schools, such as race and ethnicity, gender, special education status, limited English proficiency status, eligibility for free or reduced-price lunches, and whether a family receives welfare benefits. Researchers equipped with more extensive data have demonstrated that parental education and income, family attitudes toward education, and other variables also are powerful determinants of student achievement. The consequence of failing to control adequately for these and other student, family, and community characteristics is that feasible real-world value-added indicators are apt to be biased, if only slightly, because they absorb differences across schools in average unmeasured student, family, and community characteristics.

To see this, note that the error in estimating a total performance indicator is approximately equal to[20]

$$\text{EstError}_s \approx \text{Mean}(\varepsilon)_s, \tag{7}$$

where $\text{Mean}(\varepsilon)_s$ is the average value of the student-level error term in school s. Because this error absorbs all unmeasured and random student-level determinants of achievement, including measurement error, the error in estimating a school's performance could tend to be high or low depending on whether the school has students with *systematically* high or low unmeasured characteristics. A similar problem affects the intrinsic performance indicator. In this case, however, the indicator captures all unmeasured student-level characteristics that are systematically high or low together with all unmeasured external school-level characteristics. The bottom line is that value-added models can control for differ-

---

[20]This formula ignores the precision in estimating school performance that is due to imprecision in estimates of the slope parameters θ, and α. It is generally possible to precisely estimate the level-one slope parameters (θ, and α) except in very small districts. In contrast, it is generally possible to estimate precisely the level-two slope parameters (δ_1, and δ_2) only in large school districts unless data is pooled across multiple districts.

ences across schools in student, family, and community characteristics only if they include explicit measures of these characteristics.

It would be useful for school districts and states to experiment with alternative approaches for collecting the types of information on students that are frequently missing from administrative data. One possibility is to use U.S. census block group data—for example, average adult educational attainment in the block group—as a substitute for unobserved student-level data.

Reliability

An important implication of the above equation is that value-added indicators could be subject to possible errors in estimation owing to random factors. Note that the standard error of a school performance estimate is approximately equal to

$$\text{StdError}_s \approx \text{Standard Deviation}(\varepsilon_{is})/n_s^{1/2}, \tag{8}$$

where n_s is the number of students in school s. As indicated, the magnitude of the error diminishes as the number of students in a given school or classroom increases. This implies that it could be very difficult to produce reliable estimates of school performance in a given grade or year in very small schools or at the classroom level. An alternative in such cases is to focus on indicators that are the product of aggregation across grades, years, classrooms, and possibly subject areas.[21] If school performance in these different dimensions is highly correlated, aggregation could produce substantial improvements in reliability. There are, of course, other reasons to focus on aggregate indicators. For accountability purposes, for example, a school district might prefer to focus attention on the combined performance of all grade levels at a given school (e.g., grades K–6, 6–8, or 9–12).

Models in Which School Performance Depends on Student Characteristics

As noted, the models presented thus far assume that the regression/prediction lines for all schools are parallel—that is, that the slope coefficients for all schools are identical. If this assumption is false, it could be quite misleading to report indicators that are based on it. The appropriate alternative in this case is to adopt a value-added model that allows one or more slope coefficients to vary across schools. Models of this type are often referred to as *heterogeneous slope models*.[22]

---

[21]Meyer (1994) discusses some of the conceptual issues involved in aggregating indicators across grade levels.

[22]Hsiao (1986) and Bryk and Raudenbush (1992) discuss models of this type.

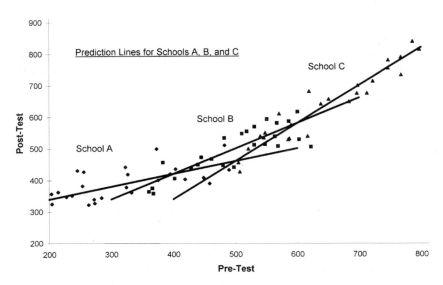

FIGURE 10.3   Plot of hypothetical test score data given heterogeneous slopes.

Figure 10.3 contains a plot of hypothetical pre- and posttest data in which the regression/prediction lines vary substantially across schools.[23] The data suggest there is no single best-performing school. School A appears to be the best for students with low prior achievement. School B appears to be the best for students with medium prior achievement. School C appears to be the best for students with high prior achievement. In this situation it is impossible to characterize school performance with a single performance rating; the relative performance of schools is a function of student characteristics. As a result, it is necessary to report school performance information in something very much like the conditional mean format illustrated in Table 10.2. As noted earlier, the major disadvantage of this format is that the total number of reporting categories could be quite large. To minimize the number, it might be advantageous to limit the number of reporting dimensions to the control variables that exhibit significant variation across schools in their coefficients.

One potential problem with heterogeneous slope models is that the coefficients tend to be less precisely estimated than in models where the slope coefficients are the same in all schools. There are fewer data to estimate the model parameters in a single school than in an entire sample of schools. It makes sense to use the heterogeneous slope model only when the variation in slope coefficients across schools is substantively and statistically significant. As mentioned

[23]As in Figures 10.1 and 10.2, the data are based on a highly simplified model of achievement growth that contains only a single control variable—prior achievement.

TABLE 10.2   NAEP Mathematics Exam Data, by Grade/Age and Year

	1973	1978	1982	1986
	Average Test Score			
Grade 3/age 9	219.1	218.6	219.0	221.7
Grade 7/age 13	266.0	264.1	268.6	269.0
Grade 11/age 17	304.4	300.4	298.5	302.0
	Average Test Score Gain			
	73 to 78	78 to 82	82 to 86	
Grades 3–7/ages 9–13	45.0	50.0	50.0	
Grades 7–11/ages 13–17	34.4	34.4	33.4	

SOURCE: Dossey et al. (1988).

previously, the assumption that slopes do not vary across schools is often a reasonable one.

Value-Added Versus Common Educational Indicators: Theory and Evidence

As discussed earlier, level indicators, such as average test scores, are frequently used to measure school performance even though they are not, in general, equivalent to either total or intrinsic performance indicators. Is the difference between level and value-added indicators substantial enough to worry about? For simplicity, consider a single-level indicator, the average test score.

The average test score, measured at a given grade level, is the product of growth in student achievement over a potentially large number of grades and years. It therefore reflects the contributions to student achievement of schools and other inputs to the learning process from multiple grades and multiple points in time. For several reasons the average test score is potentially a highly misleading indicator of how productive a school is at a given point in time. First, the average test score is, in general, contaminated by factors other than school performance, primarily the average level of student achievement prior to entering first grade and the average effects of student, family, and community characteristics on student achievement growth from first grade through the grade in which students are tested. It is likely that comparisons across schools of average test scores primarily reflect these differences rather than genuine differences in total or intrinsic school performance. Average test scores are highly biased against schools that serve disproportionately higher numbers of academically disadvantaged students.

Second, the average test score reflect information about school performance that tends to be grossly out of date. For example, the average test scores for a group of tenth-grade students reflect learning that occurred from kindergarten, roughly 10 1/2 years earlier, through the tenth grade. If the variability over time of school performance is higher in elementary school than in middle or high school, a tenth-grade-level indicator could be dominated by information that is five or more years old. The fact that the average test score reflects outdated information severely weakens it as an instrument of public accountability. To allow educators to react to assessment results in a timely and responsible fashion, performance indicators presumably must reflect information that is current.

Third, average test scores at the school, district, and state levels tend to be highly contaminated because of student mobility in and out of different schools. The typical high school student is likely to attend several different schools over the period spanning kindergarten through grade twelve. For these students a test score reflects the contributions of more than one, even several, schools. The problem of contamination is compounded by the fact that rates of student mobility may differ dramatically across schools and is likely to be more pronounced in ones that undergo rapid population growth or decline and in ones that experience significant changes in their occupational and industrial structure.

Finally, unlike the grade-specific value-added indicator, average test score fails to localize school performance to the natural unit of accountability in schools—a specific classroom or grade level. This lack of localization is, of course, most severe at the highest grade levels. A performance indicator that fails to localize school performance to a specific grade level or classroom is likely to be a relatively weak instrument of public accountability.

A simulation vividly demonstrates how the average test score is determined in large part by past gains in achievement and hence is apt to be quite misleading as an indicator of current school performance.

To focus on the consequences of variations in school performance over time assume that (1) average initial student achievement and average student characteristics are identical for all schools at all points in time, (2) school performance is identical at all grade levels in a given year, (3) growth in student achievement is determined by a linear growth model, and (4) there is no student mobility.[24] The technical details of the simulations and the simulation data reported in the figures are presented in Meyer (1994). Figure 10.4 charts average tenth-grade achievement and school performance before and after the introduction of hypothetical academic reforms in 1992. This analysis is particularly relevant in evaluating the efficacy of school reform efforts. Figure 10.4(a) depicts a scenario in which academic reforms reverse a trend of gradual deterioration in school performance across all grades and initiate a trend of gradual improvement in school performance in all grades. Figure 10.4(b) depicts a scenario in which academic reforms have no effect on school performance. The reforms are preceded, how-

---

[24]The assumption of a linear growth model is equivalent to imposing the restriction that $\theta = 1$ in Eq. (1). (See note 6.) The average error at every school at every point in time is assumed to be zero, so the issue of reliability can be ignored and we can focus entirely on the validity—or lack of validity—of the average test score as an indicator of school performance.

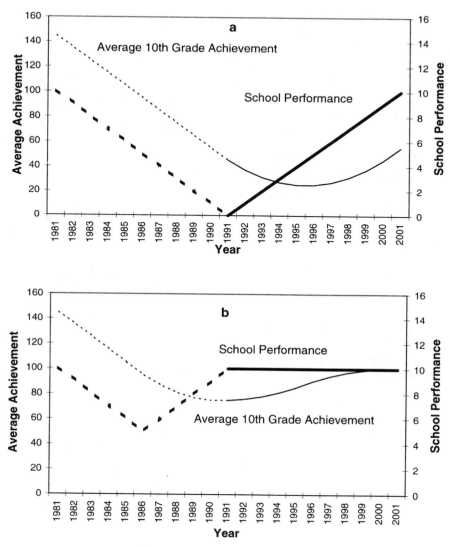

FIGURE 10.4   Average 10th grade achievement versus school performance.

ever, by an era of gradual deterioration in school performance across all grades, followed by a brief period (1987–1991) of gradual improvement.

Figure 10.4 illustrates that the average tenth-grade test score provides a totally misleading view of the effectiveness of the hypothetical academic reforms implemented in 1992. In Figure 10.4(a) the average tenth-grade test score declined for five years after the introduction of successful reforms. In Figure

10.4(b) the average tenth-grade test score increased for a decade after the introduction of reforms that have no effect on growth in student achievement. These results are admittedly somewhat counterintuitive. They arise from the fact that tenth-grade achievement is the product of gains in achievement accumulated over a 10-year period. The average tenth-grade test score is, in fact, exactly equal to a 10-year moving average of school performance. This stems from the simple assumption that school performance is identical at different grade levels in the same year. The noise introduced by this type of aggregation is inevitable if school performance is at all variable over time.

The problem of aggregation of information that is grossly out of date also introduces noise into the comparisons of different schools at the same point in time. The degree to which noise of this type affects the relative rankings of schools depends on whether the variance over time in average achievement growth is large relative to the variance across schools in achievement growth. To illustrate this point, Figure 10.5 considers the consequences of aggregation over time and grade levels for two schools that are identical in terms of school performance in the long term. In the short term, however, school performance is assumed to vary cyclically. For school 1, performance alternates between 10 years of gradual decline and 10 years of gradual recovery. For school 2, performance alternates between 10 years of gradual improvement and 10 years of gradual decline. These patterns are depicted in Figure 10.5(b). The *correct* ranking of schools, based on school performance, is noted in the graph. Figure 10.5(a) depicts the associated levels of average tenth-grade achievement for the two schools. The rankings of schools based on this indicator are also noted. The striking aspect of Figure 10.5 is that the average tenth-grade test score ranks the two schools correctly only 50 percent of the time. In short, the noise introduced by aggregation over time and grade levels is particularly troublesome if comparing schools that are roughly comparable in terms of long-term performance. On the other hand, the problem is less serious for schools that differ dramatically in terms of long-term average performance. It is also less serious if cycles of decline and improvement are perfectly correlated across schools—an unlikely phenomenon.

Example Based on Data from the National Assessment of Educational Progress

To consider whether the average test score exhibits these problems in real-world data, consider average mathematics scores from 1973 to 1986 from the National Assessment of Educational Progress (NAEP) (see Table 10.2). Unfortunately, the NAEP is not structured in such a way that it is possible to construct a value-added measure of school performance,[25] so we compare average test scores with the simple average growth in achievement from one test period to the next for the same cohort of students. This measure is typically referred to as a *gain*

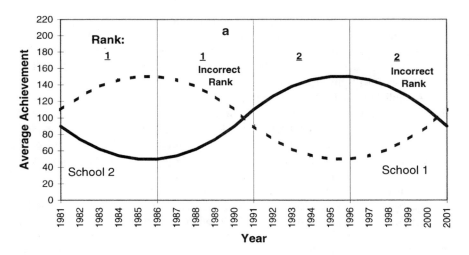

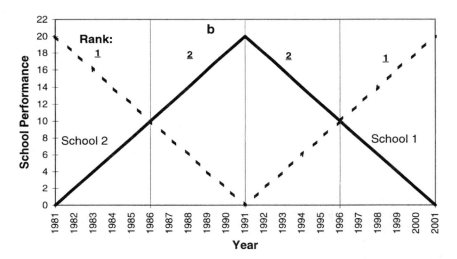

FIGURE 10.5   Average 10th grade achievement given alternative cycles of school performance.

---

[25]A value-added analysis of the NAEP is not possible because the same students are not sampled for two consecutive surveys. As a result, it is not possible to estimate the parameters of the achievement growth model. This weakness in NAEP data could be remedied by switching to a survey design that is at least partially longitudinal, although a number of technical problems would need to be addressed. For example, given that the NAEP assesses only students in grades 4, 8, and 12, it would be necessary as part of a longitudinal survey design to locate students who changed schools during the four-year intervals between tests.

indicator.[26] It differs from a true value-added indicator in that it fails to control for differences across schools and over time in average student and family characteristics. In general, it makes sense to compute a gain indicator only when the tests administered at different grade levels are scored using a common scale. The NAEP tests fulfill this criterion.

As indicated in Table 10.2, average tests scores for eleventh graders exhibit the by-now familiar pattern of sharp declines from 1973 to 1982 and then partial recovery between 1982 and 1986. The eleventh-grade data, by themselves, are fully consistent with the premise that academic reforms in the early and mid-1980s generated substantial gains in student achievement. In fact, an analysis of the data based on a more appropriate indicator than average test scores suggests the opposite conclusion. The gain indicator reveals that achievement growth during the 1982–1986 period was actually no better than that during the 1978–1982 period and that gains from grades 7 through 11 were actually slightly lower from 1982 to 1986 than in previous periods! The rise in eleventh-grade math scores from 1982 to 1986 stems from an earlier increase in achievement for the same cohort of students rather than from an increase in achievement from grades 7 through 11. In short, these data provide no support for the notion that high school academic reforms during the mid-1980s generated significant increases in test scores. Moreover, the analysis underscores that in practice, not just in theory, average test scores can be a highly fallible measure of school performance.

POLICY IMPLICATIONS

Consequences of Using Flawed Indicators

The fact that level indicators measure school performance with potentially enormous error has important implications for their use in making education policy, informing students and parents about the quality of schools, and evaluating school performance as part of an accountability system. With respect to policymaking, it is clear that level indicators potentially provide wholly incorrect information about the success or failure of educational interventions and reforms. They could lead to the expansion of programs that do not work or to the cancellation of ones that are truly effective. Similarly, level indicators are likely to give students and parents erroneous signals about which schools to attend. Either academically advantaged and disadvantaged students could be fooled into abandoning an excellent neighborhood school simply because the school served stu-

---

[25]Gain indicators were constructed by computing the change in average test scores over time for given birth cohorts. The NAEP was originally designed to permit this type of analysis. The mathematics tests have generally been given every four years at grade levels spaced four years apart, except in 1974. For the illustrative analysis here, it is assumed that average test scores in 1973 are comparable to the unknown 1974 scores.

dents who were disproportionately academically disadvantaged. At the other extreme, families whose children attend a school that serves a disproportionately higher number of academically advantaged students could be lulled into complacency about a school that is contributing relatively little to growth in student achievement. Overall reliance on average test scores or other level indicators is likely to yield lower levels of student and school performance.

The adverse effects of level indicators on the behavior of teachers and administrators are likely to be particularly acute if they are in any way rewarded or penalized on the basis of their performance with respect to a given indicator. In a high-stakes accountability system, teachers and administrators are likely to respond to the incentive to improve their measured performance by exploiting all existing avenues. It is well known, for example, that teachers may "teach narrowly to the test," although some tests are more susceptible to this type of corruption than others. For tests that are relatively immune to such corruption, teaching to the test could induce teachers and administrators to adopt new curricula and teaching techniques much more rapidly than they otherwise would. On the other hand, if school performance is measured by using a nonvalue-added indicator, teachers and administrators have the incentive to raise measured school performance by teaching only those students who rate highly in terms of average student and family characteristics, average prior achievement, and community characteristics—a phenomenon referred to as *creaming*.

The tendency toward creaming is stronger at schools that have the authority to admit or reject prospective students and to expel already enrolled students. But the problem also exists in more subtle forms. For example, schools sometimes create an environment that is relatively inhospitable to academically disadvantaged students, provide course offerings that predominantly address the needs of academically advantaged students, fail to work aggressively to prevent students from dropping out of high school, err on the side of referring "problem" students to alternative schools, err on the side of classifying students as special education students where the latter are exempt from statewide testing, or make it difficult for low-scoring students to participate in statewide exams. These practices are designed to improve average test scores in a school, not by improving school quality but by catering to high-scoring students while ignoring or alienating low-scoring ones.

Value-Added Indicators and School Performance Expectations

Some commentators have expressed the concern that value-added indicators, because they control or adjust for student, family, and community characteristics associated with growth in student achievement, reduce performance expectations for schools and states that serve disproportionately higher numbers of disadvantaged students.[27] This is obviously an important concern, but noth-

---

[27]See, for example, Finn (1994).

ing in the value-added method discourages a district or state from establishing high-performance expectations for all students. To avoid creating an incentive for schools to engage in creaming, however, it is essential to translate student performance expectations into the corresponding school performance goals. This can be accomplished by using Eqs. (5) and (6). For this application, however, Mean(Posttest)$_s$ represents the average student achievement goal rather than the actual average level of student achievement, and the performance indicators represent the school performance goals rather than the actual levels of performance.

Note that for a given student achievement goal the corresponding school performance goal will always be higher, not lower, for schools that serve disproportionately higher numbers of disadvantaged students. The reason is straightforward: to reach a given student achievement goal, it is necessary for schools that serve disproportionately higher numbers of disadvantaged students to outperform other schools. If expectations for student achievement are sufficiently high, this procedure will almost certainly produce school performance goals that are extremely ambitious for schools that serve disproportionately higher numbers of disadvantaged students—a strength rather than a weakness of the value-added approach. If the nation is serious about setting high expectations for all students, it is important to translate these performance expectations into accurate school performance goals.

A second response to concerns about lowered performance expectations is that the conditional mean format for reporting value-added indicators makes it easy to separate the tasks of measuring school performance and setting student performance expectations (see Table 10.1). It would be straightforward, for example, to augment Table 10.1 to include a separate student achievement goal for each type of student or to include a common student achievement goal for all students.

Value-Added Indicators: Data Requirements

In view of the problems associated with average test scores and other level indicators, is it appropriate to consider using value-added indicators as the core of school district, state, and national performance indicator/accountability systems? There are at least two reasons to be optimistic in this regard. First, value-added models have been used extensively over the past three decades by evaluators and other researchers interested in education and training programs. Second, a number of districts and states, including Dallas (see Webster et al., 1992), South Carolina (Mandeville, 1994), and Tennessee (Sanders and Horn, 1994), have successfully implemented value-added indicator systems.

Despite their promise, such systems require a major commitment on the part of school districts and states. Districts and states must be prepared to test students frequently, ideally at every grade level, as is done in South Carolina, Tennessee, and Dallas. They also must develop comprehensive district or state data systems that contain information on student test scores and student, family, and community characteristics.

Annual testing at each grade level is desirable for at least three reasons. First, it maximizes accountability by localizing school performance to the most natural unit of accountability—the grade level or classroom. Second, it yields up-to-date information on school performance. Finally, it limits the amount of data lost because of student mobility. As the time interval between tests increases, these problems become more acute. Indeed, for time intervals of more than two years, it may be impossible to construct valid and reliable value-added indicators for schools with high mobility rates. Mobile students generally must be excluded from the data used to construct value-added and gain indicators, since both indicators require pre- and posttest data. In schools with high student mobility, infrequent testing diminishes the prospect of ending up with student data that are both representative of the school population as a whole and large enough to yield statistically reliable estimates of school performance.[28] Less frequent testing—for example, in kindergarten[29] and grades 4, 8, and 12—might be acceptable for national purposes, since student mobility is less prevalent at the national level; but to evaluate local school performance, frequent testing is highly desirable.

CONCLUSIONS AND RECOMMENDATIONS

Average test scores, one of the most commonly used indicators in American education, are an unreliable indicator of school performance. Average test scores fail to localize school performance to the classroom or grade level, aggregate information on school performance that tends to be grossly out of date, are contaminated by student mobility, and fail to distinguish the distinct value-added contribution of schools to growth in student achievement from the contributions of student, family, and community factors. Average test scores are a weak, if not counterproductive, instrument of public accountability.

The value-added indicator is a conceptually appropriate indicator for measuring school performance. This chapter presents two basic types of value-added indicators: the total school performance indicator, which is appropriate for purposes of school choice, and the intrinsic performance indicator, which is appropriate for purposes of school accountability. The quality of these indicators is determined by the frequency with which students are tested, the quality and appropriateness of the tests, the adequacy of the control variables included in the

---

[28]In schools with extremely high rates of student mobility, it might be necessary to test students more than once a year.

[29]A kindergarten test is needed so that growth in student achievement in grades 1 through 4 can be monitored. The NAEP and recent proposals for national testing in grades 4, 8, and 12 are seriously flawed by their failure to include a test at the kindergarten or first-grade level.

appropriate statistical models, the technical validity of the statistical models used to construct the indicators, and the number of students and schools available to estimate the slope parameters of value-added models. States should consider testing students at every grade level, as is currently done in South Carolina, Tennessee, and Dallas, or at least at every other grade level, beginning with kindergarten. They should also make an effort to collect extensive and reliable information on student and family characteristics and to develop state tests that are technically sound and fully attuned to their educational goals. Further research is needed to assess the sensitivity of estimates of school performance indicators to alternative statistical models and alternative sets of control variables. In particular, it would be helpful to know more about the empirical differences between total and intrinsic school performance indicators. Finally, in order to improve the reliability of estimates of school performance, particularly intrinsic performance, small and medium-sized school districts should consider combining their data to create school performance indicator systems that serve multiple districts.

REFERENCES

Boardman, A. E., and R. J. Murnane. 1979. "Using panel data to improve estimates of the determinants of educational achievement." *Sociology of Education* 52:113–121.

Bock, R. D. 1989. *Multilevel Analysis of Educational Data*, San Diego: Academic Press.

Bryk, A. S., and S. W. Raudenbush. 1992. *Hierarchical Linear Models: Applications and Data Analysis Methods*. Newbury Park, Calif.: Sage Publications.

Coleman, J. S., and others. 1966. *Equality of Educational Opportunity*. Washington, D.C.: U.S. Department of Health, Education, and Welfare.

Clune, W. H. 1991. Systemic educational policy. Madison: University of Wisconsin, Wisconsin Center for Educational Policy.

Darling-Hammond, L. 1991. "The implications of testing policy for quality and equality." *Phi Delta Kappan* 73:220–225.

Dossey, J. A., I. V. Mullis, M. M. Lindquist, and D. L. Chambers. 1988. *The Mathematics Report Card: Are We Measuring Up?* Princeton, N.J.: Educational Testing Service.

Dyer, H. S., R. L. Linn, and M. J. Patton. 1969. "A comparison of four methods of obtaining discrepancy measures based on observed and predicted school system means on achievement tests." *American Educational Research Journal* 6:591–605.

Finn, C. E., Jr. 1994. "Drowning in Lake Wobegon." *Education Week*, pp. 31, 35.

Haladyna, T. M., S. B. Nolen, and N. S. Hass. 1991. "Rising standardized achievement test scores and the origins of test score pollution." *Educational Researcher* 20:2–7.

Hanushek, E. A. 1972. *Education and Race*. Lexington, Mass.: D. C. Heath.

Hanushek, E. A., and L. Taylor. 1990. "Alternative assessments of the performance of schools." *Journal of Human Resources* 25:179–201.

Hsiao, C. 1986. *Analysis of Panel Data*. Cambridge: Cambridge University Press.

Koretz, D., B. Stecher, S. Klein, and D. McCaffrey. 1994. "The Vermont portfolio assessment program." *Educational Measurement: Issues and Practice* 13(3):5–16.

Lord, F. M. 1980. *Applications of Item Response Theory to Practical Testing Problems*. Hillsdale, N.J.: Lawrence Erlbaum Assoc.

Mandeville, G. K. 1994. The South Carolina experience with incentives. Paper presented at the conference entitled "Midwest Approaches to School Reform," Federal Reserve Bank of Chicago, Chicago.

Meyer, R. H. 1992. Applied versus traditional mathematics: new econometric models of the contribution of high school courses to mathematics proficiency. Discussion Paper No. 966–92, University of Wisconsin-Madison, Institute for Research on Poverty.

Meyer, R. H. 1994. Educational performance indicators: a critique. Discussion Paper No. 1052–94, University of Wisconsin-Madison, Institute for Research on Poverty.

Murnane, R. J. 1975. *The Impact of School Resources on the Learning of Inner-City Children.* Cambridge, Mass.: Ballinger Publishing Co.

Nolen, S. B., T. M. Haladyna and N. S. Haas. 1992. "Uses and abuses of achievement test scores." *Educational Measurement: Issues and Practice* 11:9–15.

Raudenbush, S. W. 1988. "Educational applications of hierarchical linear models: a review." *Journal of Educational Statistics* 13:85–116.

Raudenbush, S. W., and A. S. Bryk. 1986. "A hierarchical model for studying school effects." *Sociology of Education* 59:1–17.

Raudenbush, S. W., and J. D. Willms. 1991. *Schools, Classrooms, and Pupils.* San Diego: Academic Press.

Sanders, W. L., and S. P. Horn. 1994. "The Tennessee value-added assessment system (TVAAS): mixed-model methodology in educational assessment." *Journal of Personnel Evaluation in Education* 8:299–311.

Shepard, L. A. 1991. "Will national tests improve student learning?" *Phi Delta Kappan* 73:232–238.

Smith, M. S., and J. O'Day. 1990. "Systemic school reform." Pp. 233–267 in *The Politics of Curriculum and Testing: 1990 Yearbook of the Politics and Education Association*, S. Fuhrman and B. Malen, eds. London: Taylor and Francis.

Smith, M. L., and C. Rottenberg. 1991. "Unintended consequences of external testing in elementary schools." *Educational Measurement: Issues and Practice* 10:7–11.

Webster, W. J., R. L. Mendro, and T. O. Almaguer. 1992. Measuring the effects of schooling: expanded school effectiveness indices. Paper presented at the annual meeting of the American Educational Research Association, San Francisco.

Wiggins, G. 1989. "A true test: toward more authentic and equitable assessment." *Phi Delta Kappan* 70:703–713.

Willett, J. B. 1988. "Questions and answers in the measurement of change." Pp. 345–422 in *Review of Research in Education*, E.Z. Rothkopf, ed. Washington, D.C.: American Educational Research Association.

Willms, D. J., and S. W. Raudenbush. 1989. "A longitudinal hierarchical linear model for estimating school effects and their stability." *Journal of Educational Measurement* 26:209–232.

CHAPTER 11

Economics of School Reform for At-Risk Students[1]

HENRY M. LEVIN
Stanford University

The United States faces an immense crisis in educating at-risk students, who are unlikely to succeed in existing schools. Such students comprise over one-third of all elementary and secondary school enrollments, and their numbers are rising absolutely and proportionately over time. At-risk students are about two years behind grade level in school achievement by sixth grade and are performing at about the eighth-grade level if/when they graduate from high school. More than half do not graduate. Their poor educational performance does not provide them with the skills needed for labor market success or further training, a situation with serious consequences for the nation's economy.

At-risk students are defined as those who are unlikely to succeed in school as the schools are currently constituted because they do not have the home, family, and community experiences on which school success is built. Existing curriculum and instructional practices are not neutral with respect to which students succeed. Those who come from middle-class nonminority backgrounds with both parents present and who speak a standard version of English are much more likely to be successful in school than those from poor, minority, immigrant, nonstandard English, and single-parent backgrounds. At-risk students are caught in a mismatch between their home situations and what is required for success in school. The impact of family characteristics and school achievement has been

[1]This paper was prepared under the auspices of the Panel on the Economics of Educational Reform, funded by the Pew Charitable Trusts and by a grant to the author from the Spencer Foundation. The author is the David Jacks Professor of Higher Education and Economics at Stanford University.

summarized in a recent publication of the Rand Corporation (Grissmer et al., 1994). An effective set of policies to improve the educational outcomes of at-risk students requires that both the in-school and out-of-school experiences of these children be addressed.

This chapter considers school-based strategies for improving substantially the educational outcomes of at-risk students, beginning with an overview of the crisis of at-risk students. The next section examines the prospect of improving the education of at-risk students simply by increasing educational expenditures, followed by a review of cost-benefit studies of particular investment strategies. The chapter then considers a more radical transformation of educational institutions, and a final section addresses strategies for systemic change.

THE CRISIS OF AT-RISK STUDENTS

Addressing the needs of at-risk students is important because they comprise a large and growing portion of school enrollments and their poor educational performance has significant consequences for the economy and society. High school completion represents a minimum qualification for the vast majority of jobs in the U.S. labor force and for eligibility for further training. Students from minority and low-income backgrounds are far more likely to not complete high school than are students from other groups, and the numbers of school-age minorities and children from poor circumstances are increasing.

Among 25 to 29 year olds in 1985, only about 14 percent had failed to complete high school or its equivalent (Bureau of the Census, 1987). For blacks, however, the figure was 19 percent, and among Hispanics it was almost 40 percent. For all races, students from families of low socioeconomic status have considerably higher dropout rates than those from more advantaged backgrounds (Rumberger, 1983). Similarly, children from low socioeconomic backgrounds and of minority status have considerably lower test scores than their white and nondisadvantaged counterparts (Smith and O'Day, 1991).

The heavy incidence of minorities and those from low-income families whose children are at risk is particularly ominous because it is these very populations that represent a substantial and increasing portion of school enrollments. Between 1976 and 1992 the proportion of minority students rose from 24 to 32 percent (National Center for Education Statistics, 1994). By the year 2020, minority children will represent almost half of all children 17 and under (Pallas et al., 1989), a figure that has already been reached in California and Texas. Minority students comprise three-quarters or more of the school enrollments in many of the largest cities of the nation, including New York, Chicago, Los Angeles, Philadelphia, Miami (Dade County), and Detroit (McNett, 1983). Minority enrollments have been increasing at a more rapid pace than the general population because of unprecedented birth rates and immigration, both legal and undocumented. Both factors create rapid growth, particularly among school-age populations.

When poverty is used as an indicator for "at-risk" populations, a similar pattern emerges. In 1970 less than 15 percent of children under age 18 lived in poverty; by 1992 it had risen to 21 percent (National Center for Education Statistics, 1994) and is expected to rise to 27 percent by the year 2020 (Pallas et al., 1989). Between 1984 and 2020, the number of children not living with both parents is expected to rise by 30 percent, from 16 million to over 21 million (Pallas et al., 1989). In view of the fact that real incomes of single mothers with children fell in absolute terms by 13 percent between 1970 and 1986, this is an especially ominous trend (Congressional Budget Office, 1988).

Trends for other indicators of at-risk children have been moving in the same direction. Pallas et al. (1989) project that the number of children raised in families where the mother has not completed high school will rise by 56 percent to over 21 million by 2020. Many of the immigrants who come from rural regions of some of the poorest countries in the world have low educational levels. For example, among Mexican immigrants into California, the largest national group, only 28 percent had more than an eighth-grade education in the early 1980s (Muller, 1985).

The proportion of at-risk students is high and increasing rapidly. Rough estimates derived from various demographic analyses suggest that upwards of one-third of all students in kindergarten through twelfth grade are educationally disadvantaged or at risk (Levin, 1986). When achievement is used as a criterion, the proportion of educationally at-risk students may be as high as 40 percent (Kennedy et al., 1986).

General Economic Implications

The rising numbers of at-risk students and their continuing failure to succeed educationally will have severe economic ramifications for the United States. One consequence will be a deterioration in the quality of the labor force. As long as at-risk students were a small portion of the population, they could be absorbed by low-skill jobs or fail to get jobs without direct consequences for the economy. High dropout rates, low test scores, and poor academic performance of a larger and larger portion of the school population mean that a larger portion of the future labor force will be undereducated for available jobs, not only managerial, professional, and technical jobs but even the lower-level service jobs that are increasingly important in the U.S. economy (Rumberger and Levin, 1989). Clerical workers, cashiers, and salesclerks all need basic oral and written communications skills, the acquisition of which is hardly guaranteed in the schooling of the disadvantaged (National Research Council, 1984). Test scores (Smith and O'Day, 1991) suggest that many at-risk students are not even acquiring the foundation necessary to benefit from employer training that would increase their productivity and job mobility.

As at-risk populations become an increasingly larger share of the U. S. labor force, their inadequate educational preparation will be a drag on the competitive performance of the industries and states in which they work and on the nation's economic performance. Employers will experience lagging productivity and higher training costs. The problem will be especially severe for such states as California and Texas, which have the largest growth in these disadvantaged populations, and for the industries that are dependent on these populations to fill their labor needs. State and federal governments will suffer a declining tax base and a concomitant loss of revenues that could be used to fund improvements in education and other services.

The implications are also severe for higher education. Without earlier educational interventions, at-risk students who remain in school will graduate with more learning deficits that will prevent many of them from benefiting from current levels of instruction in colleges and universities. High levels of college failures and dropouts and massive remedial interventions mean wasted time for students and wasted resources for colleges, not to mention the psychological toll of failing to "make it." Substantial remedial activities require additional faculty members. Extended periods in college will impose a greater cost in tuition and lost earnings.

A third consequence of failing to deal with the challenge of at-risk students will be the rising costs of public services, as more citizens rely on public assistance and undereducated teens and adults pursue illegal activities to fill idle time and obtain income. In a national sample of 19 to 23 year olds in 1981, 72 percent of the jobless, 79 percent of those on public assistance, and 68 percent of those arrested the previous year had scored below average on the Armed Forces Qualification Test (AFQT) measure of basic skills (Berlin and Sum, 1988). Among 18- to 23-year-old males in 1981, those with a high school diploma had a 94 percent lower probability of arrest than dropouts; among girls ages 18 to 21, the high school graduates had a 54 percent lower probability of having an out-of-wedlock baby (Berlin and Sum, 1988).

Failure to address the educational needs of at-risk students will adversely affect labor force productivity, public health status, and a variety of other important social outcomes (Haveman and Wolfe, 1984). When all of the outcomes associated with education are taken into account, it has been estimated that education has twice as high a return as when only its effect on income is measured.

MORE RESOURCES

The most frequent strategy for addressing the poor results of at-risk students is to seek more educational resources. Many public schools are inadequately funded to meet the increasing demands placed on them by rising numbers of at-risk students. Some egregious examples are described by Kozol (1991). There is little evidence, however, that higher spending by *itself* will have a profound impact on at-risk students without changes in how the resources are used. Hanushek (1986, 1989) has argued that statistical studies have shown little relationship between expenditures per student and the specific resources purchased–for example, longer teacher experience, higher teacher degrees, and smaller classes–on the one hand and student achievement on the other. Hedges et al. (1984) reanalyzed the set of studies reviewed by Hanushek and have challenged his interpretations. These challenges have been buttressed by Card and Krueger (1992), who found that statistical models, using state data, showed positive relationships between school expenditures and school characteristics of students and their later earnings as adults. However, attempts to replicate these results using data at the school and district levels have not shown similar patterns (Betts, 1994; Grogger, forthcoming).

My own interpretation is that increasing expenditures will have modest effects on student achievement unless used to support particular programs that have been shown to be effective or combined with major organizational changes in schools. The view that focusing school expenditures on the poor, as was done beginning in the 1960s, will have some positive effect is supported by recent Rand Corporation study findings of minority test scores improving in excess of what could be explained by improvements in demographic factors (Grissmer et al., 1994). Elsewhere, I have argued for greater equity in expenditures on behalf of at-risk students for reasons of fairness and social efficiency (Levin, 1991b). But additional resources will not have powerful effects unless (1) they are targeted on particularly effective learning strategies for at-risk students, such as those illustrated in the next section, or (2) school organizations are transformed to increase the general effectiveness with which they use resources. Undoubtedly, there are schools and school districts around the country that are so seriously underfunded that additional resources could make a big difference. Adequate resources are a necessary condition for meeting the educational needs of at-risk populations but not a sufficient condition (Levin, 1994). Additional resources must be combined with considerably more effective strategies than most schools are currently using (Hanushek et al., 1994).

RETURNS ON EDUCATIONAL INVESTMENT
FOR AT-RISK STUDENTS

Although there are likely to be considerable benefits from investing in at-risk student populations, there are also likely to be significant costs. To justify such investments from an economic standpoint, we need to know if the benefits exceed the costs and, if so, by magnitudes equal to or greater than alternative social investments. This section reviews the results of cost-benefit studies of educational investments for those populations.

Programs for Reducing the Number of High School Dropouts

A number of economic studies have addressed the costs and benefits of reducing the numbers of high school dropouts. In the earliest study on the subject, Weisbrod (1965) compared the impact of a St. Louis program designed to reduce dropout rates among "dropout-prone" high school students with the results of a control group of similar students who did not have such a program. The dropout prevention program was associated with a high school completion rate about 7 percent higher than that of the control group. Weisbrod estimated the cost for each of the additional graduates and contrasted it with the estimated income benefits of high school graduation for these students. He concluded that the costs of the program exceeded its benefits.

There are two reasons that more recent analyses of well-designed dropout programs show stronger benefits. Weisbrod used 1959 Census Bureau data to estimate the additional incomes of the graduates. For reasons of discrimination and other factors, the earnings of women and minorities were much lower relative to white male's earnings some 30 years ago than they are today. Since the dropout-prone group included large numbers of females and minorities, the benefits of intervention were probably understated relative to those that would be obtained with more recent data. Furthermore, the earnings advantages of high school graduates relative to dropouts has increased substantially in the past two decades (National Center for Education Statistics, 1994).

A more recent study of dropout prevention found large net benefits (Stern et al., 1989). This evaluation was based on success in reducing the number of dropouts at 11 academies created in California public high schools. These academies were special programs or schools within a larger high school setting that provided both vocational training for careers in which students stood a good chance of placement and academic training. Students were given special attention by their teachers and by local employers. When matched with a similar group of students in regular high school programs, it was estimated that the academies had graduated 29 persons who otherwise would have been expected to drop out.

The marginal costs of the academy program beyond the costs of the regular school program were compared to the additional earnings of the graduates who were "saved" from dropping out. The overall benefits of the program were found to exceed the overall costs by considerable amounts, the specifics depending on which assumptions were used regarding benefits.

In contrast to studies of a single dropout program, I undertook a national study on the economic consequences of high school dropouts (Levin, 1972). This study calculated the additional lifetime earnings and tax revenues that would have been generated if the entire cohort of 25- to 34-year old males in 1970 had graduated from high school. It was assumed that the additional earnings of dropouts who would be induced to graduate would be only 75 percent of those of conventional high school graduates. It was also assumed, however, that a portion of the induced graduates would continue into higher education, with additional earnings from that source as well.

The total loss of lifetime earnings for this group who failed to complete at least high school was estimated at about $237 billion. The additional cost of achieving this result consisted of the additional years of schooling undertaken by members of the group and the cost of enriching education to reduce the number of dropouts. It was assumed that it would have been necessary to increase annual spending on those at risk of dropping out by 50 percent a year for their entire elementary and secondary school careers to retain them until completion of high school. On this basis it was estimated that the total costs of achieving at least high school graduation for the cohort was about $40 billion, yielding a benefit of $6 to $1. The additional lifetime earnings would have generated about $71 billion in government revenue, or about $1.75 in tax revenues for each dollar in public expenditure. The study also estimated that inadequate education was contributing about $6 billion a year to the costs of welfare and crime in 1970.

Ramirez and del Refugio Robledo (1986) replicated my analysis for the cohort of Texas ninth graders in 1982-1983 who were projected to drop out before their anticipated graduation in 1986. They estimated the benefits of a dropout prevention program as those attributable to savings in public assistance, training and adult education, crime and incarceration, unemployment insurance and placement, and higher earnings associated with the additional high school graduates. Such benefits were calculated at $17.5 billion, and the costs to eliminate dropouts for this cohort were estimated at slightly less than $2 billion, for a cost-benefit ratio of nine to one. Estimates of additional tax revenues were 2.5 times greater than the costs to taxpayers.

Catterall (1987) undertook a similar analysis of children who dropped out of the Los Angeles High School class of 1985. He found that because of the dropouts, the Los Angeles class of 1985 was likely to generate over $3 billion *less* in lifetime economic activity than if all of its members had graduated. Catterall suggested that the cost of investing successfully in dropout reduction would be a mere fraction of this amount. Furthermore, he found that Los Angeles was addressing the dropout problem with specific programs that were spending the equivalent of only about $50 per dropout, or less than one-half of 1 percent of school spending, even though 40 percent of its students were not graduating.

Preschool and Higher Education

There is evidence that preschool investments in at-risk populations can deter dropouts as well as yield other benefits. Barnett (1985) undertook a cost-benefit analysis of the Perry Preschool Project in Ypsilanti, Michigan. The Perry Preschool's approach has been studied for three decades and is used as a model for hundreds of preschools for disadvantaged students across the country, including the national Head Start program. Students enrolled in the preschool project were followed until age 19. It was found that, relative to a matched control group, project enrollees experienced better school achievement, educational placement, educational attainment, and employment. Monetary values for the benefits were calculated on the basis of the apparent effect of these advantages on the value of child care during the programs; reduced school expenditures for remediation, special services, and grade repetition; reduced costs of crime, delinquency, and welfare; and higher earnings and employment.[2]

It was found that the benefits exceeded the costs by a large margin under a wide range of assumptions. The one-year program showed benefits of $7 for every dollar of costs, and the two-year program showed a cost-benefit ratio of about 3.6:1 (Berrueta-Clement et al., 1984). About 80 percent of the net benefits accrued to taxpayers in the form of higher tax contributions and lower expenditures on education, crime, and welfare and to potential crime victims in the form of lower costs for property losses and injuries.

A cost-benefit analysis by St. John and Masten (1990) of financial aid to low-income students for higher education also indicated high benefits relative to the costs. Their study compared tax revenues generated by the additional income produced by the higher levels of college participation by low-income students with the costs of financial aid that induced the higher enrollments. The net present value of additional tax revenues was four times as great as the cost of the aid program for students in the high school class of 1980. That is, from the perspective of the federal treasury, such programs had a cost-benefit ratio of 4 to 1.

These studies suggest that specific investments in at-risk students yield high social returns relative to the costs and by a margin that is competitive with or superior to that of other highly productive investments. Indeed higher tax revenues and reduced costs for social services more than compensate for the investments. In the case of the early childhood intervention program of the Perry Preschool, most of the net benefits accrued to taxpayers (Barnett, 1985).

Summary of Cost-Benefit Results

These cost-benefit results suggest that well-designed investments in the education of students who are at risk of undereducation are likely to have high payoffs to society. Although each study is based on imperfect information and entails arbitrary assumptions about both costs and benefits, the overall pattern of findings among studies is remarkably consistent.

The estimated benefits of interventions for at-risk students tend to be about three to six times as high as the estimated costs. According to Haveman and Wolfe (1984), the consideration of returns to human capital investments in the form of increases in earnings will capture only about half the total returns. Thus, most of these estimates are understated because they are limited to the effects of educational investments on earnings and do not capture the value of improvements in health, labor mobility, intergenerational effects, and reductions in the

---

[2]A more recent study followed up on students to age 27 with similar results (Schweinhart and Weikart, 1994)

cost of public services as well as a variety of other benefits. On the other hand, some recent work suggests that calculations from cross-sectional data tend to overstate the benefits of human capital investments for at-risk populations (Levin and Kelley, 1994). All of the estimates are based on cross-sectional evidence, with the exception of the preschool intervention. Because there is no direct evidence on the potential degree of overstatement or understatement of these results, a reasonable assumption is that they are offsetting and that the estimates are a first approximation of returns to investments on behalf of at-risk populations.

Several other projects have reported strong achievement results in particular subjects in existing schools, although some of the costs have been quite high and need to be reduced. In the area of early childhood reading, these programs include Reading Recovery (Pinnell et al., 1994; Hiebert, 1994), One-On-One Tutoring (Farkas et al., 1994), and Success for All (Madden et al., 1993). An approach to problem-solving and thinking skills also has reported good results (Pogrow, forthcoming). Farkas et al. (1994) have claimed that a program using graduate and undergraduate students paid at hourly rates to provide tutoring to at-risk students has yielded results comparable to Reading Recovery and Success for All at less than one-quarter of the cost.

RADICAL TRANSFORMATION OF SCHOOL ORGANIZATION

In essence, each of the investments described above is a marginal addition to an existing school organization and might be viewed as inefficient if some other form of school organization could produce considerably better overall results for at-risk students with the same resources. This dilemma was first described by Liebenstein (1966) in studying why some firms with apparently similar resources are much less productive than others. More recently it has been raised with respect to schools by Hanushek et al. (1994), Hoenack (1994), and myself (Levin, 1994).

According to this view, schools need to be redesigned to increase their efficiency in converting resources into educational results, along the lines of productive firms but taking account of the special nature of education. The goal is to identify features of efficient noneducation organizations and make those features integral to the design and operation of schools.

Economic analysis suggests that efficient firms must exhibit the following features:

- a clear, objective function with measurable outcomes;
- incentives that are linked to success on the objective function;
- efficient access to useful information for decisions;
- adaptability to meet changing conditions; and
- use of the most productive technologies consistent with cost constraints

(Levin, 1994).

Objective Function

In an efficient firm participants understand the purpose of the organization and share a collective focus on that objective. The objective must be associated with measurable outcomes in order to appraise how well the firm is doing (Cyert, 1988). Schools seem far removed from this standard. Objectives often vary from teacher to teacher, with some placing more emphasis on some subjects than others, and some pushing for rote memorization while others stress thinking skills and problem solving. Schools often set different goals for different groups of students according to their ethnicity, race, and socioeconomic origins, often through tracking or streaming of students (Oakes, 1985).

Organizational Incentives

The principal strategy for inducing employees to pursue the objectives of the firm is to link employee rewards to their performance in contributing to those objectives. In the case of schools there is little evidence of incentives tied to student success (Hanushek et al., 1994). Salary increases tend to be based on seniority and qualifications, not effectiveness. Incentives can be intrinsic (e.g., a sense of accomplishment) or extrinsic (e.g., financial rewards or recognition), individual or collective (Simon, 1991; Holmstrom and Milgrom, 1994). But even if teachers receive some intrinsic satisfaction from their individual accomplishments with students, these do not comprise a link with overall school success or assure articulation of goals from grade to grade and teacher to teacher (Little, 1990).

Information

To succeed, firms need continuous and systematic information on their overall performance to see if they are meeting objectives. They need rapid feedback on challenges, problems, bottlenecks, and impending obstacles as well as changes in market environments, productions, technologies, and prices that may affect them. Comparable information for education is not readily available at the school level. Indeed, schools rarely have accurate information on alternatives or strategies and channels to obtain that information. Even the test score data on students are usually not available until the end of the school year or the beginning of the following one, and this information is highly incomplete and restricted to a narrow set of dimensions (Office of Technology Assessment, 1991). The lack of timely and useful feedback also limits schools' ability to learn through trial and error, as suggested by Murnane and Nelson (1984).

Adaptability

Firms that are in situations where their markets, products, technologies, costs, and prices are largely stable do not need to adapt to succeed and survive. They can continue to follow the same practices that have brought them success in the past. But firms facing rapid changes must adapt to changing conditions. This becomes even more challenging when the technology of production is uncertain and requires considerable trial and error to get it right (Murnane and Nelson, 1984). Schools often face changes in student populations as neighborhoods change, precipitous changes in budgets from year to year, rapid changes in electronic technologies and their capabilities, and changes in teacher supply as relative salaries change (Murnane et al., 1991), as well as new demands such as AIDS education. Yet schools are typically obliged to follow centrally adopted curricula, rules, regulations, and mandates that are obstacles to change and generally lack internal decision-making mechanisms that could be used to adapt to change, if greater input into decision making were permitted. Schools need to have the ability to make decisions on resource allocation in order to adjust to disequilibria (Schultz, 1975).

Efficient Technology of Production

Finally, efficient firms need to adopt the most productive technologies consistent with cost constraints. Unfortunately, schools tend to follow historical approaches despite attempts to change them through educational reforms (Cuban, 1990). Although most schools still use approaches that require students to memorize material as it is presented, considerable research finds that this is an inefficient teaching and learning technique (e.g., Peterson, 1989; Gardner and Hatch, 1990; Knapp et al., 1992). A more effective approach is to enable students to build on previous experiences and engage in new activities that allow them to construct their own understanding through research, hands-on projects, and other applications. In many respects, this is the approach used for gifted and talented students, but it is becoming increasingly recognized that it works more effectively for all students (Feldhusen, 1992).

Creating Accelerated Schools for At-Risk Students

Relative to the five characteristics of efficient, productive firms, schools seem to be ill equipped to produce educational services efficiently. The Accelerated Schools Project was designed to improve school productivity dramatically by altering these five dimensions. Starting with only two pilot schools in 1986-1987, the project comprised more than 700 elementary and middle schools in 37 states by 1994-1995. It was designed to transform public schools with high concentrations of at-risk students into organizations that will make all students academically able by the end of elementary school and sustain high levels of achievement through middle school to prepare such students for academically demanding high schools. In the past the schools relied primarily on remedial education, which slows the pace of learning and reduces learning expectations.

These schools have been notoriously unsuccessful in bringing their students into the educational mainstream.

Accelerated schools undergo a process of organizational transformation that embodies the five organizational dimensions. Space limitations do not permit a detailed explanation here of the application of these ideas and the transformation process, but details can be found elsewhere (Finnan, 1994; Hopfenberg, 1993; Levin, 1994). Accelerated schools acquire a unity of purpose among staff, parents, and students that is directed at accelerated academic outcomes for all children. This unity is buttressed with a system of decision making that gives all participants incentives to engage in problem-solving methods that will lead to those outcomes building on concepts found in Simon (1991) and Holmstrom and Milgrom (1994). In addition, school staff members along with students and parents acquire training in problem solving and group dynamics, with a focus on assessment of results and the use of powerful learning strategies (Hopfenberg, 1993). Thus, schools develop an objective function, collective incentives to address that objective, shared information, and an ability to adjust to disequilibria. In addition, schools acquire a more powerful technology of learning, usually reserved only for the most gifted and talented students in traditional schools, that is based on constructivist learning approaches (Brooks and Brooks, 1993).

To induce these profound changes in organization and operations, schools are introduced to a philosophy and set of practices that require substantial changes in the values and expectations of all participants. The accelerated school undergoes a substantial cultural transformation (Hopfenberg, 1993). Although attempts at such change have been judged to be problematic in the past (Sarason, 1990), evaluations of accelerated schools indicate impressive improvements in student achievement, attendance, and parent participation and reductions in costly policies such as students retained in grade and special education placements. One study found that prior to its transformation into an accelerated school, fifth graders at a Houston school had achievement that was two years below average (McCarthy and Still, 1993). Within three years they were exceeding the national average. A comparison school in the same district with similar students showed declines in achievement over the same period. Evaluations of many schools have shown equally impressive results (see summaries in English, 1992; Knight and Stallings, 1995; Wong, 1994). The costs of this organizational transformation and results have been exceedingly modest, about $30 to $40 per student in the first year of school transformation and less in ensuing years.

The transformation of school organizations, or school restructuring (Fullan, 1991), is a promising way to improve the educational outcomes of at-risk students, largely within available resources. The School Development Project (Comer, 1988) and the Coalition of Essential Schools (Sizer, 1992) also represent models of school restructuring, although with less emphasis on the economic model of productive organizations. Such changes will require major policy alterations in the education system, whether reforms are undertaken in the public sector or shifted to a market environment through exit or choice mechanisms (Hirschman, 1970), decentralization, and a supportive infrastructure to provide information, technical assistance, and assessment of results.

GETTING THERE

The evidence suggests that there are both effective strategies for conventional schools to address certain educational outcomes and more far-reaching organizational changes to address the needs of at-risk students. The Accelerated Schools Project has had considerable success in getting conventional public schools and parochial schools to adopt its model, but that does not ensure adequate supporting systems at the district and state levels to induce schools to meet the needs of at-risk students (Hanushek et al., 1994).

Some reformers believe that only through a market system or public choice mechanism will schools address the needs of at-risk students, and indeed all students, because of competition to attract enrollment. There are few empirical studies to rely on in resolving conflicting claims about the effects of educational markets generally and educational vouchers in particular (Levin, 1991a, c; West, 1991a, b). Only in Milwaukee, Wisconsin, has a voucher plan been adopted for students from low-income families. An evaluation after three years showed that voucher students in private schools were performing no better than similar students in public schools (Witte et al., 1993).

At the same time, it is clear that states and school districts need to consider whether they have appropriate systems of educational finance, performance incentives, accountability, information, and flexibility to achieve the changes that have proven effective in schools under the right conditions. Decentralization in Chicago, state reform in Kentucky, and semiautonomous charter schools in many states represent attempts to change the politics of education. It is too early to determine the effects of these changes, but it is clear that new institutional supports must be implemented at higher levels to support the changes that are required in individual schools (Clune, 1993, 1994).

REFERENCES

Barnett, W. S. 1985. "Benefit-cost analysis of the Perry Preschool Program and its long-term effects." *Educational Evaluation and Policy Analysis* (3):333–342.

Berlin, G., and A. Sum. 1988. Toward a more perfect union: basic skills, poor families. Occasional Paper No. 3. Ford Foundation Project on Social Welfare and the American Future, The Ford Foundation, New York.

Berrueta-Clement, J. R., L. J. Schweinhart, W. S. Barnett, A. S. Epstein, and D. P. Weikart. 1984. *Changed Lives: The Effects of the Perry Preschool Program on Youths Through Age 19.* Monograph No. 8. Ypsilanti, Mich.: High/Scope.

Betts, J. R. 1994. "Does school quality matter? Evidence from the National Longitudinal Survey of Youth." *Review of Economics and Statistics.*

Brooks, J. G., and M. G. Brooks. 1993. *The Case for Constructivist Classrooms.* Alexandria, Va.: Association for Supervision and Curriculum Development.

Bureau of the Census, U.S. Department of Commerce. 1987. "Educational attainment in the United States: March 1982 to 1985." *Current Population Reports,* Ser. P–20, no. 415. Washington, D.C.: U.S. Government Printing Office.

Card, D. E., and A. B. Krueger. 1992. "Does school quality matter? Returns to education and the characteristics of public schools in the United States." *Journal of Political Economy* 100:1–40.

Catterall, J. S. 1987. "On the social costs of dropping out of school." *The High School Journal,* 71:19–30.

Clune, W. H. 1993. "The best path to systemic educational policy: standard/centralized or differentiated/decentralized?" *Educational Evaluation and Policy Analysis* 15(3):233–254.

——— ed. 1994. Equity and Adequacy in Education: Issues for Policy and Finance, A Special Issue. *Educational Policy* 8(4).

Comer, J. P. 1988. "Educating poor minority children." *Scientific American* 259(5):2–8.

Congressional Budget Office, U.S. Congress. 1988. *Trends in Family Income: 1970–1986.* Washington, D.C.: U.S. Government Printing Office.

Cuban, L. 1990. "Reforming, again, and again and again." *Educational Researcher* 19(1):3–13.

Cyert, R. 1988. *The Economic Theory of Organization and the Firm.* New York: New York University Press.

English, R. A. 1992. *Accelerated Schools Report.* Columbia: University of Missouri, Department of Educational and Counseling Psychology.

Farkas, G., J. Beron, K. Vicknair, and D. Walters. 1994. Reforming compensatory education with reading one-one. Paper prepared for annual research conference of the Association for Public Policy Analysis and Management at the University of Texas, Dallas, Oct. 27.

Feldhusen, J. F. 1992. *Talent Identification and Development in Education (TIDE).* Sarasota, Fla.: Center for Creative Learning.

Finnan, C. 1994. "Studying an accelerated school." Pp. 93–129 in *Pathways to Cultural Awareness: Cultural Therapy with Teachers and Students,* G. Spindler and L. Spindler, eds. Thousand Oaks, Calif.: Corwin Press.

Fullan, M. G. 1991. *The New Meaning of Educational Change.* New York: Teachers College Press.

Gardner, H. and T. Hatch. 1990. "Multiple intelligences go to school: educational implications of the theory of multiple intelligences." *Educational Researcher* 19:4–10.

Grissmer, D. W., S. Nataraj Kirby, M. Berends, and S. Williamson. 1994. *Student Achievement and the Changing American Family.* Santa Monica, Calif.: Rand Corp.

Grogger, J. Forthcoming. "School expenditures and post-schooling wages: evidence from high school and beyond." *Review of Economics and Statistics.*

Hanushek, E. A. 1986. "The economics of schooling: production and efficiency in public schools." *Journal of Economic Literature* 24:1141–1177.

———. 1989. "The impact of differential expenditures on school performance." *Educational Researcher* 18:45–51.

———. et al. 1994. *Making Schools Work.* Washington, D.C.: The Brookings Institution.

Haveman, R., and R. Wolfe. 1984. "Schooling and economic well-being: the role of nonmarket effects." *The Journal of Human Resources* 19(3):377–407.

Hedges, L. V., R. D. Laine, and R. Greenwald. 1984. "Does money matter? A meta-analysis of studies of the effects of differential school inputs on student outcomes." *Educational Researcher* 23:5–14.

Hiebert, E. H. 1994. "Reading recovery in the United States: what difference does it make to an age cohort?" *Educational Researcher* 23(9):15–25.

Hirschman, A. O. 1970. *Exit, Voice, and Loyalty.* Cambridge, Mass.: Harvard University Press.

Hoenack, S. A. 1994. "Economics, organizations, and learning: research directions for the economics of education." *Economics of Education Review* 13(2):147–162.

Holmstrom, B., and P. Milgrom. 1994. The firm as an incentive system." *The American Economic Review* 84(4):972–991.

Hopfenberg, W., H. M. Levin, et al. 1993. *The Accelerated Schools Resource Guide*. San Francisco: Jossey-Bass.

Kennedy, M. M., R. K. Jung, and M. E. Orland. 1986. *Poverty, Achievement, and the Distribution of Compensatory Education Services*. Interim report from the National Assessment of Chapter I. Washington, D.C.: U.S. Department of Education, Office of Educational Research and Improvement.

Knapp, M. S., P. M. Shield, and B. J. Turnbull. 1992. *Academic Challenge for the Children of Poverty, Vol. 1-2*. Washington, D.C.: Office of Policy and Planning, U.S. Department of Education.

Knight, S., and J. Stallings. 1995. "The implementation of the accelerated school model in an urban elementary school." Pp. 236–251 in *No Quick Fix: Rethinking Literacy Programs in American Elementary Schools*, Richard Allington and Sean Walmsley, eds. New York: Teachers College Press.

Kozol, J. 1991. *Savage Inequalities*. New York: Crown.

Levin, H. M. 1972. *The Costs to the Nation of Inadequate Education*. Report prepared for the Select Senate Committee on Equal Educational Opportunity, 92nd Congress. Washington, D.C.: U.S. Government Printing Office.

———. 1986. *Educational Reform for Disadvantaged Students: An Emerging Crisis*. West Haven, Conn.: NEA Professional Library.

———. 1991a. "The economics of educational choice." *Economics of Education Review* 10:137–158.

———. 1991b. "The economics of justice in education." Pp. 129–148 in *Spheres of Justice in Education*, D. A. Verstegen and J. G. Ward, eds. New York: HarperBusiness.

———. 1991c. "Views on the economics of educational choice: a reply to West." *Economics of Education Review* 10:171–176.

———. 1994. "The necessary and sufficient conditions for achieving educational equity." In *Outcome Equity in Education*, R. Berne and L. O. Picus, eds. Thousand Oaks, Calif: Corwin Press.

———. Forthcoming. "Accelerated schools after eight years." In *The Contributions of Instructional Innovation to Understanding Learning*, R. Glaser and L. Schauble, eds. Garfield, N.J.: Ablex Publishing Co.

Levin, H. M., and C. Kelley. 1994. "Can education do it alone?" *Economics of Education Review* 13(2):97–108.

Liebenstein, H. 1966. Allocative efficiency and X-efficiency. *American Economic Review* 56:392–425.

Little, J. W. 1990. "The persistence of privacy: autonomy and initiative in teachers's professional relations." *Teachers College Record* 91(4):509–536.

Madden, N., R. Slavin, N. Karweit, L. Dolan, and B. A. Wasik. 1993. "Success for all: longitudinal effects of a restructuring program for inner-city elementary schools." *American Educational Research Journal* 30:123–148.

McCarthy, J., and S. Still. 1993. Hollibrook Accelerated Elementary School. Pp. 63–83 in *Restructuring Schools: Learning from Ongoing Efforts*, J. Murphy and P. Hallinger, eds. Newbury Park, Calif.: Corwin Press.

McNett, I. 1983. *Demographic Imperatives for Education Policy*. Washington, D.C.: The Urban Institute Press.

Muller, T. 1985. *The Fourth Wave: California's Newest Immigrants*. Washington, D.C.: The Urban Institute.

Murnane, R. J., and R. R. Nelson. 1984. "Production and innovation when techniques are tacit." *Journal of Economic Behavior and Organization* 5:353–373.

Murnane, R. J., J. D. Singer, J. B. Willett, J. J. Kemple, and R. J. Olsen. 1991. *Who Will Teach? Policies That Matter.* Cambridge, Mass.: Harvard University Press.

National Center for Education Statistics. U.S. Department of Education. 1994. *The Condition of Education 1994.* NCES 94–149. Washington, D.C.: U.S. Government Printing Office.

National Research Council. 1984. *High Schools and the Changing Workplace.* Report of the Panel on Secondary School Education for the Changing Workplace. Washington, D.C.: National Academy Press.

Oakes, J. 1985. *Keeping Track: How Schools Structure Inequality.* New Haven, Conn.: Yale University Press.

Office of Technology Assessment, U.S. Congress. 1991. *Testing in American Schools.* Washington, D.C.: U.S. Government Printing Office.

Pallas, A., G. Natriello, and E. L. McDill. 1989. "The changing nature of the disadvantaged population: current dimensions and future trends." *Educational Researcher* 5:16–22.

Peterson, J. M. 1989. "Remediation is no remedy." *Educational Leadership* 46(6):24–25.

Pinnell, G. S., C. A. Lyons, D. E. DeFord, A. S. Bryk, and M. Seltzer. 1994. "Comparing instructional models for the literacy education of high-risk first graders." *Reading Research Quarterly* 29:8–39.

Pogrow, S. Forthcoming. "Lessons about reform that can be learned from the success of HOTS." *Educational Leadership.*

Ramirez, D., and M. del Refugio Robledo. 1986. *Texas School Dropout Survey Project: A Summary of Findings.* San Antonio: Intercultural Development Research Association.

Rumburger, R. W. 1983. "Dropping out of school: the influences of race, sex and family background." *American Educational Research Journal* 20:199–220.

Sarason, S. B. 1990. *The Predictable Failure of Educational Reform.* San Francisco: Jossey-Bass.

Schultz, T. W. 1975. "The value of the ability to deal with disequilibria." *Journal of Economic Literature* 13:827–846.

Schweinhart, L. J., and D. P. Weikart, eds. 1994. *Significant Benefits: The High/Scope Perry Preschool Study Through Age 27.* Ypsilanti, Mich.: High/Scope Press.

Simon, H. A. 1991. "Organizations and markets." *Journal of Economic Perspectives* 5(2):25–44.

Sizer, T. 1992. *Horace's Compromise.* Boston: Houghton Mifflin.

St. John, E. P., and C. L. Masten. 1990. "Return on the federal investment in student aid: an assessment of the high school class of 1972." *Journal of Student Financial Aid* 20(3):4–24.

Smith, M., and J. O'Day. 1991. "Educational equality: 1966 and now." Pp. 55–100 in *Spheres of Justice in Education,* D. A. Verstegen and J. G. Ward, eds. New York: Harper Business.

Stern, D., C. Dayton, I-W. Paik, and A. Weisberg. 1989. "Benefits and costs of dropout prevention in a high school program combining academic and vocational education: third year results from replications of the California Peninsula Academies. *Educational Evaluation and Policy Analysis* 11(4):405–416.

Weisbrod, B. A. 1965. "Preventing high school dropouts." Pp. 117–148 in *Measuring Benefits of Government Investments,* R. Dorfman, ed. Washington, D.C.: The Brookings Institution.

West, E. G. 1991a. "Public schools and excess burdens." *Economics of Education Review* 10:159–170.

———. 1991b. "Rejoinder." *Economics of Education Review* 10:177–178.

Witte, J. F., A. B. Bailey, and C. A. Thorn. 1993. *Third Year Report, Milwaukee Choice Program.* Report to the Department of Public Instruction, Milwaukee Public Schools. Madison: University of Wisconsin-Madison.

Wong, P. 1994. *Accomplishments from Accelerated Schools.* Stanford, Calif: National Center for the Accelerated Schools Project, Stanford University.

CHAPTER 12

Staffing the Nation's Schools with Skilled Teachers[1]

RICHARD J. MURNANE
Harvard University

Students who are taught by effective teachers learn much more in school than students who are taught by ineffective teachers. This judgment by most parents is also the conclusion of many research studies.[2] Devising strategies to provide all children with skilled teachers, both by improving the effectiveness of teachers already working in schools and by attracting a greater number of talented new teachers to the nation's classrooms, should be at the center of school reform efforts. These goals are related; providing opportunities for growth and learning on the job is important in attracting and retaining talented college graduates who seek not only good compensation but also rewarding work.

This chapter addresses the second objective, attracting a greater number of skilled teachers to the nation's classrooms. It considers the role of incentives in determining who trains to teach, who becomes a teacher, which teachers change districts, who leaves teaching, and who returns to teaching. It is through changes in incentives that public policies can influence which college graduates staff our nation's schools. Designing incentives to attract talented college graduates to teaching will be especially important over the next 15 years as an increase in retirement rates among the existing teaching force increases the opportunities for new hiring.

---

[1]The author would like to thank Dominic Brewer, Linda Darling-Hammond, Eric Hanushek, and Michael Podgursky for helpful comments on drafts of this paper.
[2]For a summary of the evidence, see Hanushek (1986).

MEASURING TEACHER QUALITY

The lack of reliable indicators of teacher quality has hindered researchers' attempts to answer the central policy question: How do alternative policies affect the supply of effective teachers? Most studies have focused on the role of incentives in the occupational decisions of *all* teachers, potential teachers, and former teachers and on how their decisions affect the total pool of college graduates willing to teach. These studies are useful in that they document that incentives do affect career decisions, but they do not directly address the central question of how policies affect the *quality* of the stock of teachers.

One assumption used in many studies of teachers' career patterns is that academic talent is a good indicator of teaching effectiveness. The assumption rests on the results of studies showing that measures of teachers' academic talent are positively related to their students' test score gains. Some of these studies use teachers' scores on standardized tests as the measure of academic talent; others use indicators of the quality of the undergraduate college the teacher attended (Ehrenberg and Brewer, 1994, 1995; Ferguson, 1991; Hanushek, 1972; Summers and Wolfe, 1977; Winkler, 1975).

The value of the assumption that college graduates' academic talent predicts their effectiveness as classroom teachers is that many databases that track college students' careers contain measures of academic talent. The assumption makes it possible to interpret the results of studies exploring the career decisions of academically talented college graduates as evidence of the factors affecting the career decisions of effective teachers.

This assumption has intuitive appeal. Teaching is a complex job, and it makes sense that academically talented college graduates have an advantage in learning the many skills required to teach well. However, one should be cautious in equating academic talent with teaching effectiveness. The evidence supporting this assumption comes from databases in which academically talented teachers went through the same type of preservice training that other teachers did. There is no reason to believe that the preservice training received by the academically talented teachers in these studies was less intensive than that received by teachers with lower levels of academic talent. In fact, it might have been of higher quality since the academically talented teachers tended to attend colleges with more financial resources than the colleges attended by less academically able teachers.

In recent years public and private policies have been introduced to attract academically talented college graduates to teaching, in part by reducing the amount of preservice training that participants must undergo before beginning classroom teaching. Examples include alternative certification (licensing) programs in a number of states and the highly publicized private program, Teach for America (TFA). These programs are attractive to academically talented college graduates who intend to teach for a few years and then pursue other, more lucrative careers because they provide an opportunity to enter teaching without taking a large number of preservice teacher preparation courses.

The question of whether alternative licensing programs improve the quality of teaching in the nation's schools is highly controversial. In a strongly worded critique of the TFA program, Darling-Hammond (1994) argues that it hurts children in urban schools by providing them with teachers who have little knowledge of the techniques needed to teach effectively. She cites the statement of one former TFA participant, a Yale graduate:

> I—perhaps like most TFAers—harbored dreams of liberating my students from public sector mediocrity and offering them as good an education as I had received. . . But I was not ready. . . . As bad as it was for me, it was worse for the students. . . Many of mine . . . took long steps on the path toward dropping out. . . . I was not a successful teacher and the loss to the students was real and large. (Schorr, 1993)

At the center of Darling-Hammond's criticism is the belief that good preservice training is critical to effective teaching.[3] I think she would agree that in the best of all worlds academically talented people who have participated in high-quality preservice programs are attracted to teaching. Later in this chapter strategies for accomplishing this are considered. However, no inferences about the value of programs that attract academically talented graduates to teaching by reducing training requirements can be made from studies in which academically talented teachers had preservice training that was at least as good as that of teachers with less academic talent.

Studies examining the career decisions of academically talented college graduates are useful because, holding quality and quantity of training constant, academically talented teachers do seem to be more effective in the classroom. Learning about the factors that influence the career decisions of academically talented college graduates may provide ideas for policies to attract more of them to teaching. Nevertheless, these studies tell nothing about the efficacy of policies designed to attract talented college graduates to teaching by reducing training requirements.

FACTORS AFFECTING CAREER DECISIONS

The evidence on factors that affect college students' teaching career decisions can be organized according to the sequence of those decisions: whether to begin work as a teacher, whether to switch districts, how long to stay in teaching, and whether to return to teaching after a career interruption.

---

[3]See Darling-Hammond (1990) for a summary of evidence supporting the importance of preservice training.

Obtaining a Teaching License

To examine trends in the number of college graduates who obtain teaching licenses, data from individual states are needed. As job opportunities in teaching fell during the 1970s, the number of college students who were training to become teachers declined dramatically. In North Carolina the number of new teaching licenses granted by the state fell from 6,538 in 1975 to 2,830 in 1984, a period during which enrollments in North Carolina colleges and universities were quite stable (Murnane et al., 1991). Data from New York show a decline in the number of teaching licenses from 34,770 in 1974 to 16,002 in 1985 (Gilford and Tenenbaum, 1990). This decline is attributable to the decline in job opportunities in teaching, the fall in teachers' salaries relative to those of other occupations, and improved job opportunities for women and minorities in fields outside education.[4]

It is often observed that Scholastic Assessment Test (SAT) scores of college freshmen who intend to major in education are low, both in absolute terms and relative to the scores of freshmen planning to major in other fields; but two studies have found that the SAT scores of freshmen who plan to become teachers are poor predictors of the scores of those college students who actually complete education majors. Many freshmen with low scores drop out of college before completing degree programs, and more able students switch fields of study during their college years. Studies show that the academic skills of students who complete education majors are higher than those of students who announce as freshmen that they intend to major in education (Nelson, 1985; Hanushek and Pace, 1994), although probably not as high as those of college graduates not preparing to teach.[5]

A recent study shows that college students are less likely to complete education majors in states that require candidates for teaching licenses to complete a relatively large number of education-related courses (Hanushek and Pace, 1994), which raise the cost of obtaining a teaching license, especially for college students who either plan to teach for a few years before moving to another occupation or want to obtain a teaching license as "insurance" in case opportunities in other fields prove unattractive. This finding points to a dilemma in designing licensing requirements for teaching. Schools have always relied heavily on teachers who intend to teach only for a few years. It is important to develop licensing requirements that do not discourage college students from considering teaching

---

[4]Given the limited time series evidence, it is not possible to compare the relative importance of these complementary explanations.

[5]See Ballou and Podgursky (1994), Hanushek and Pace (1994), and Nelson (1985). An exception to this pattern is a 1990 study reporting that newly qualified teachers had higher grade point averages than did all college graduates as a group (Gray et al., 1993). While provocative, it is difficult to interpret this pattern given the variation in grading practices among colleges and universities.

even if they do not plan to make it their life's work. At the same time, teachers need to acquire skills to teach effectively. As elaborated on below, basing licensure on the demonstration of teaching competence rather than on completion of course work is a strategy for reconciling these objectives.

Among the factors affecting the number of college students who seek teaching licenses the role of standardized testing in licensing requirements has been the subject of a good deal of analysis. As part of attempts to raise entry standards over the past 20 years, several states have required that candidates for teaching licenses achieve scores above threshold values on certain standardized tests, primarily the NTE, formerly known as the National Teacher's Examination, developed by the Educational Testing Service. Until recently the NTE included a "Core Battery," which tested communication skills, general knowledge; and professional knowledge; 49 specialty-area tests that measured knowledge of specific academic subjects or fields; and the Pre-Professional Skills Tests, which measured basic reading, writing, and mathematics skills.[6] As of 1994, 34 states used at least part of the NTE in their teacher licensing requirements. Other states use different standardized multiple-choice tests, such as the SAT or the California Achievement Test.

Several studies have shown that requiring applicants for teaching licenses to score above a prespecified cutoff on the NTE reduces the number of college students who train to become teachers and the number of college graduates who obtain teaching licenses. The effect is particularly great on minority students, who tend to score lower on standardized tests such as the NTE (Murnane et al., 1991; Hanushek and Pace, 1994).

The use of standardized multiple-choice tests in teacher licensing programs is controversial. Critics point to the low correlation between scores on these tests and measures of teaching effectiveness. One comprehensive review summarized the evidence as follows:

> The available evidence is none too good, but it indicates that teacher tests have little, if any, power to predict how well people perform as teachers, whether that performance is judged by ratings of college supervisory personnel, ratings by teachers, student ratings, or achievement gains made by students. (Haney et al., 1987, p. 199)

Defenders of these tests argue that the lack of correlation between test scores and measures of teaching effectiveness is not the issue. They argue that the tests screen out applicants who lack the basic literacy skills necessary to serve as successful role models to students and to write grammatically correct and coherent prose. This argument has considerable merit, but the underlying issue is

---

[6]See Educational Testing Service (1988). The number of NTE specialty-area tests was counted from a table entitled "NTE Programs: Table of User Qualifying Scores and Validity Study Status Information," provided by Carol Dwyer of the Educational Testing Service.

whether the use of multiple-choice tests in state licensing procedures increases the likelihood that our nation's children will be taught by effective teachers of varying backgrounds. One reason for doubt is that multiple-choice tests of "professional knowledge" do not reliably measure whether applicants possess the knowledge needed to teach effectively because the test items rarely provide the rich contextual information needed to respond thoughtfully to a problem situation. Nor do multiple-choice questions allow applicants to offer creative responses. These are critical limitations because the answer to almost all questions about how an effective teacher should respond in a particular classroom situation is "it depends."[7]

Given the lack of evidence relating scores on multiple-choice tests of knowledge to measures of teaching effectiveness, how has the use of these tests survived legal challenge? The courts have ruled that use of the NTE tests in licensing is justified because they measure "the content of the academic preparation of prospective teachers" (*South Carolina*, 1989, p. 241). In other words, it is argued that the tests measure particular types of knowledge and are not intended to measure teaching effectiveness. This is an exceedingly weak defense in view of the questionable validity of multiple-choice questions about professional knowledge and the demonstrable negative impact that the testing requirements have on the racial composition of the teaching force.

A challenge in revising licensing requirements is to ensure that potential teachers do possess the skills necessary to communicate effectively with students and their parents and to provide incentives and opportunities for candidates deficient in basic skills to improve their skills. In response to this challenge, the Educational Testing Service recently made dramatic changes in the structure of the NTE. The new Praxis system has three components. Praxis I, which assesses reading, writing, and basic math skills, is designed to be taken by college students *before* entering a teacher education program. The idea is that students should be made aware of any deficits in their basic skills before they prepare to become teachers. Praxis II tests subject matter knowledge and is designed to be taken after college seniors have completed their course work. Unlike the old subject matter tests, Praxis II does not consist solely of multiple-choice items. It also includes constructed-response questions. Praxis III assesses teacher competence through interviews, classroom observations, and examination of documents; it is designed to be used with teachers in their second or third year of teaching as part of their licensing requirements (Forbes, 1995). As states are just beginning to make the transition from the old NTE to the new Praxis system, there is as yet no evidence on its effectiveness in keeping ineffective teachers out of the classroom or on the number of minorities becoming teachers.

---

[7]See Wise and Darling-Hammond (1987, p. 22).

Entering Teaching

In the late 1960s, one out of every three students who graduated from college in the United States taught in either a public or private school within five years of graduation. By the early 1980s, only one in 10 new graduates entered teaching (Murnane et al., 1991). This trend reflects a decline in teaching opportunities accompanying declines in student enrollment. Between 1971 and 1984 the number of students attending elementary and secondary schools fell from 46 million to 39 million.

The decline in the number of college students preparing to teach and entering teaching is simply a response to declining demand, but changes in the *composition* of the pool of college graduates choosing to teach are disturbing. One striking change is the decline in minorities. In the late 1960s, approximately 60 percent of all black female college graduates entered teaching within five years of graduation; less than 40 percent of white female graduates made the same decision. During the 1970s, the percentages of black and white graduates who became teachers not only declined but converged. In the early years of the 1980s, black graduates were less likely to enter teaching than were white graduates (Murnane et al., 1991).

In recent years the percentages of black and Hispanic teachers have increased slightly. In the 1987-1988 school year, 8 percent of the nation's public school teachers were black, and 2.6 percent were Hispanic (NCES, 1992). In the 1990-1991 school year the comparable figures are 8.3 and 3.4 percent, respectively (NCES, 1993). These percentages do not reflect the racial/ethnic composition of the public school student body, 16.1 percent of which was black and 11.1 percent Hispanic in the 1990-1991 school year (NCES, 1993).

Another disturbing trend is the decline in the representation of the most academically able college graduates. In the late 1960s, college graduates with IQ scores of 130 were only slightly less likely to become teachers than graduates with IQ scores of 100. By 1980 a college graduate with an IQ score of 100 was more than four times as likely to become a teacher than was a graduate with a score of 130.[8] In other words, throughout the 1970s the number of new entrants to teaching who were among the most academically able of all college graduates became smaller and smaller.

In the 1990s the demand for new entrants to elementary and secondary school teaching has been rising for two reasons, both demographic. First, the teacher retirement rate is rising as the large group of teachers hired during the 1950s and 1960s, the baby boom years, reach retirement age. Second, school enrollments of the children of the last baby boom are rising moderately. There is little question that enough warm-bodied adults will be found to staff the schools,

---

[8]See also Murnane et al. (1991). Hanushek and Pace (1994) show that this trend did not reverse itself over the 1980s.

but unless recent trends change, a declining proportion will be the nation's most academically able college students.

Will salary increases attract skilled teachers in the years ahead? Although the evidence is scanty, one study showed that the occupational decisions of college graduates in England were extremely sensitive to relative salaries in teaching and other professions (Dolton, 1991). A second study showed that the higher the teaching salaries, the larger the pool of college graduates who enter teaching (Manski, 1987). But the study concluded that salary increases, by themselves, do not have a marked effect on the ability distribution of the set of college graduates who enter teaching. Higher salaries attract graduates with low SAT scores, the measure of ability in this dataset, as well as graduates with high SAT scores. Moreover, some school districts do not choose to hire the most academically able candidates.

There are various reasons why many school districts do not value academic talent (Ballou and Podgursky, 1994). Explanations include patronage, the weight attached to skills other than teaching ability such as coaching skill, and the possibility that academically strong candidates lack thorough teacher preparation. The pattern complicates strategies to staff all of the nation's schools with skilled teachers, suggesting that incentives to attract skilled teachers may not be sufficient. It may also be necessary to ensure that the most effective applicants are hired or that ineffective teachers are removed from applicant pools.

Changing Districts

The evidence on factors influencing teachers' decisions to change school districts, although scanty, supports the notion that opportunities matter. Teachers who are "underpaid" (defined as receiving a salary lower than that predicted from a model in which teachers' salaries are a function of personal characteristics) have a relatively high probability of changing districts (Baugh and Stone, 1982). Male teachers are more likely to remain in a school district greater the number of administrative positions to which they can be promoted, and the higher the salaries in these administrative positions. Male teachers are also more likely to leave a school district the higher the salaries of administrators in neighboring districts. Administrative opportunities apparently do not affect the mobility decisions of female teachers (Brewer, 1994).

How Long to Stay in Teaching

Decisions about how long to stay in teaching are influenced by salaries and opportunity costs. A $2,000 difference in annual salary is associated with a difference in median employment duration of approximately one year for teachers in Michigan and approximately two years for North Carolina teachers. In both states, differentials are more likely to induce teachers to leave during the first years on the job (Murnane et al., 1991). A study based on data from Indiana produced similar findings (Grissner and Kirby, 1992). Another study shows that the turnover rate of mathematics and science teachers in California is negatively related to teachers' salaries (Rumberger, 1987).

Not only do teachers' salaries affect career decisions, so do opportunity costs. Murnane et al. (1991) used two measures of opportunity cost in studying the determinants of employment duration in teaching. The first was a teacher's score on the NTE, on the assumption that teachers who achieve high scores on the NTE are also likely to achieve relatively high scores on other tests, such as the law boards, that determine entry to relatively high paying occupations. The second measure of opportunity cost was a teacher's subject specialty, on the assumption that teachers with disciplinary specialties are likely to command higher salaries in fields outside education than are elementary school teachers who teach basic skills in many subject areas. Among secondary school teachers, those in such fields as chemistry and physics, which command relatively high salaries in business and industry, are likely to have the shortest teaching spells, especially since virtually all U.S. public school districts have a uniform salary scale that takes no account of variations in opportunity cost by field.

In North Carolina 56 percent of white teachers with NTE scores at the 90th percentile remained in teaching for at least five years, compared with 71 percent with scores at the 10th percentile of the sample distribution (Murnane et al., 1991). In both North Carolina and Michigan, the median employment duration for secondary school teachers was two or more years shorter than that of elementary school teachers. Among secondary school teachers in both states, chemistry and physics teachers had the shortest teaching careers. The median length of time that chemistry and physics teachers in Michigan stayed in teaching was 2.2 years, compared to 4.0 years for social studies teachers, and 3.7 years for English teachers (Murnane et al., 1991).

Other evidence concerning the role of salaries and opportunity costs in teachers' decisions to shift occupations comes from the first administration of the School and Staffing Survey, administered by the National Center for Education Statistics. White male teachers who left teaching within their first three years in the classroom to work full time in another industry earned $3,300 more, on average, in their new jobs, than they did in their last year teaching. The comparable numbers for nonwhite men and white women are increases of $6,200 and $300, respectively. The one exception to this pattern is nonwhite women, who earned $300 less in their first jobs in other industries than they did in their last year teaching. This helps explain why only 2.8 percent of nonwhite women left teaching in their first three years compared to 7.5 percent of white women, 9.0 percent of white men, and 18 percent of black men.[9]

---

[9]These tabulations were conducted at my request by the National Data Resource Center, National Center for Education Statistics, in February 1991.

Whether to Return to Teaching

One of the surprises from recent research on teacher supply is the increase over the past 20 years in the proportion of new hires who come from a "reserve pool" of people who were neither teaching the previous year nor engaged in full-time study. In 1966, three out of 10 newly hired teachers came from the reserve pool; in 1991 the proportion was seven out of 10.[10] It is therefore a mistake to think of newly minted college graduates as the only or principal source of teachers, an assumption behind many projections of teacher shortages in the years ahead. The reserve pool has been the principal source of new hires in recent years when demand has been low and relatively few college students have prepared to teach.

What is not known is how large a source of supply the reserve pool will be in the years ahead when the demand for new hires will grow. Undoubtedly, the answer depends on the attractiveness of teaching salaries and working conditions relative to those in other occupations. It also likely will depend on the costs associated with licensing requirements of moving from other occupations into teaching. As yet there are no data on the sensitivity of mobility decisions to these factors.

There is some information on the behavior of members of the reserve pool who left teaching and then returned to it. Approximately one in four teachers who leave the classroom return within five years. The teachers most likely to return are those with subject area specialties that provide limited opportunities for better-paying employment outside teaching (Beaudin, 1993; Murnane et al., 1991). This pattern supports the hypothesis that decisions to return to teaching are sensitive to opportunity costs.

POLICIES FOR STAFFING THE SCHOOLS WITH SKILLED TEACHERS

Evidence on the career decisions of potential teachers, teachers, and former teachers show that they do respond to incentives. Salaries and opportunity costs influence who goes into teaching, who stays in teaching, and who returns to teaching after a career interruption. At the same time, some school districts do not hire candidates with the most promise for helping children acquire critical skills. Thus, the policymaking challenge is not only to design incentives to attract effective candidates and former teachers to the pool of those who want to teach but also to exclude from the pool those who lack the skills to teach.

---

[10]See National Education Association (1992). The percentages of newly hired teachers drawn from the reserve pool in 1966 and 1991 were calculated by using information from Table 13.

Ill-Advised Policies

The mandatory master's degree

Several states, including New York and California, require that teachers earn a master's degree within a specified period of time after initial hiring. Teachers who fail to do so lose their positions. This policy is ill advised for two reasons. First, the preponderance of evidence is that teachers with master's degrees are no more effective than teachers who do not hold these degrees.[11]   Second, the requirement raises the cost of choosing teaching as a career and may have the effect of dissuading potentially effective teachers from entering the profession.

Some recent evidence indicates that "fifth-year" programs are successful in attracting academically talented college graduates to teacher preparation. These programs enable college graduates who did not prepare to teach to obtain teacher training and a master's degree in teaching. Graduates of the fifth-year program at the University of New Hampshire were more academically talented than graduates of the university's undergraduate education program, were more likely to enter teaching, and were more likely to remain in teaching. Graduates of the fifth-year program believed that their preparation for teaching was better than did graduates of the undergraduate program (Andrew, 1990).

Master's degree programs can play a significant role in providing schools with academically talented, well-prepared teachers, but the evidence does not support a policy of requiring all teachers to complete a fifth-year program. Fifth-year programs probably attract talented college graduates in part because they want to distinguish themselves from graduates of undergraduate teacher education programs.   Education schools certainly have incentives to make their programs effective in order to compete for students who can enter teaching without continuing in school for a fifth year. If a state mandates that all prospective teachers must complete a master's degree program, the incentives change markedly, and the education schools then have captive student bodies and, worse, face pressures to lower standards to produce enough graduates to staff the schools.

Paying a premium for master's degrees

The uniform salary schedules of almost all public school districts in the country pay teachers with master's degrees premiums ranging from a few hun-

---

[11]For a summary of this evidence, see Hanushek (1986). One exception to this general pattern is a study by Ferguson (1991), which found that students in Texas schools taught by teachers with master's degrees had higher achievement scores than students taught by teachers without master's degrees. Ferguson made creative use of available data in conducting this study; however, the data have important limitations. First, it is not possible to match students to individual teachers. Second, it is not possible to measure the achievement *gains* of individual students taught by teachers with different characteristics.

dred to several thousand dollars. To obtain these premiums, more than half of the nation's teachers have earned master's degrees. In view of the lack of evidence of the superior effectiveness of teachers with master's degrees, this is a poor use of scarce resources.

High quality teacher training is important in helping graduates learn to teach effectively. As Shulman (1987) observed, "Our question should not be, Is there really much one needs to know in order to teach? Rather, it should express our wonder at how the extensive knowledge of teaching can be learned at all during the brief period allotted to teacher preparation." The problem is that the automatic premium for the master's degree gives teachers an incentive to seek a degree program that makes as few demands on their time and energy as possible. Teacher education schools, to maximize enrollments, have an incentive to design undemanding programs. The salary premium gives both teachers and education schools the wrong incentives.

Merit pay based on supervisors' evaluations

Merit pay systems reward teachers with higher compensation for superior supervisor assessments of teaching quality. In principle, merit pay appears to be a good way to improve the performance of public schools. Does it not attract talented college graduates to the profession and give all teachers an incentive to teach as well as possible? Unfortunately, the results of extensive research are clear—merit pay based on supervisors' performance evaluations simply does not work. In the vast majority of cases where school districts have adopted merit pay plans for teachers, they have dropped them within five years. This is as true in districts without teachers' unions as in districts with unions. It was as true in the 1920s as it is in the 1990s. There is no example of a troubled district that has successfully used merit pay to improve its performance (Murnane and Cohen, 1986).

A COMBINATION OF POLICIES WITH PROMISE

The challenge is to attract academically able college students to the teaching profession, give aspiring and veteran teachers an incentive to undertake high-quality training, and adopt licensing requirements that discourage those who lack the skills necessary to teach effectively. A two-part strategy holds promise for making progress toward these goals.

Performance-Based Teacher Licensing

In most states a college graduate obtains a teaching license by documenting that he or she has completed a program of prescribed study at an accredited institution of higher education and by scoring above threshold levels on a series of multiple-choice tests. These requirements are ill advised for several reasons. First, the prescribed courses are often of low quality. As a result, participants do not learn the critical skills needed to teach effectively, and some college students may decide not to teach because they do not want to take courses they perceive to be of little value. Second, scores on the multiple-choice tests keep many minorities from obtaining a teaching license and provide no assurance that graduates who do obtain teaching licenses possess the skills needed to teach effectively.

Several changes would improve the effectiveness of licensing procedures in keeping incompetent teachers out of schools without discouraging talented college students from trying teaching. First, the multiple-choice tests should be replaced with constructed-response tests that assess whether candidates can perform certain tasks related to teaching, such as writing a lucid letter to parents advising them of a problem with their child. Aspiring teachers should be able to take these tests as early in their training as they desire so as to eliminate the uncertainty that deters many minorities from training to teach and provide the maximum possible time for remediation.

Second, compulsory training requirements should be replaced with a system of performance assessments, under which candidates would obtain a long-term teaching license only after demonstrating that they can teach effectively.[12] A system of performance-based assessments is much more costly than current licensing procedures but has the potential for improving the quality of teaching. A system of comprehensive, high-quality performance assessments should improve teacher training by focusing instruction on the critical skills needed to pass the assessments and giving aspiring teachers an incentive to seek the best training in the skills needed to pass the assessments. Ensuring that the skills needed to pass the assessment are closely related to the skills needed to help children learn is a serious challenge because there is little consensus, but there has been progress in designing performance-based assessment systems.

Teachers' Salaries

Attempts to improve the quality of the teaching profession cannot succeed unless talented college graduates want to teach. A salary schedule that attracts academically talented graduates to teaching and makes it worthwhile to acquire the skills needed to teach effectively is a necessary condition of improving the quality of teachers. The question is how to structure salaries to achieve these goals efficiently.

The salary schedules in the vast majority of the nation's school districts reward longevity and advanced degrees. They do not pay premiums for subject specialties with shortages of teachers or provide incentives for teachers to invest

---

[12]See Murnane et al. (1991, Chap. 7) for a detailed discussion of alternative designs for performance-based assessments.

in improving their skills, for example, through collaborative exploration of teaching strategies. Most salary schedules reward teachers for taking university-based graduate courses, but the reward is as large for undemanding courses quite unrelated to teachers' day-to-day work as it is for a demanding one that tries to help teachers change how they teach. Moreover, the best university-based courses may be no better than alternative forms of professional development that are not rewarded in most teachers' contracts.

Over the past 20 years the funds available for increases in teachers' salaries have gone disproportionately to experienced teachers (Monk and Jacobson, 1985; Murnane et al., 1989). This "backloading" of pay increases reflects the increased power of experienced teachers, who became a majority in most districts, but as a result the salary structure becomes increasingly unattractive to college graduates interested in teaching for several years but not for an entire career.

Across-the-board salary increases may not improve the average quality of the teaching force at all. Although higher salaries do attract more talented graduates to teaching, they induce teachers to stay on the job longer, reducing opportunities to upgrade the teaching stock by hiring talented new applicants. The lower probability of receiving a teaching offer induces candidates with the best alternatives outside teaching, often the more academically able graduates, to choose a different occupation.[13]

A number of changes in the structure of teachers' salary schedules would make it easier to recruit talented college graduates in every subject field and would encourage them to obtain the training needed to learn to teach effectively.

• *Flexible salaries for teachers in fields with shortages of teachers.* College graduates trained in specialties with the best salaries outside of teaching are the least likely to enter teaching, the most likely to leave teaching after only a very few years in the classroom, and the least likely to return to teaching after a career interruption. This evidence that career decisions are related to opportunity cost suggests that a policy of paying premiums to teachers in fields with shortages is an efficient strategy for attracting skilled teachers in all subject areas (Kershaw and McKean, 1962). Fortunately, teacher union opposition to this policy has weakened in recent years (AFT Task Force on the Future of Education, 1986).

• *Large pay increase for passing the performance-based licensing exam.* With performance-based licensing, teachers with provisional teaching licenses, or "interns," would take the licensing examination after one or two years of supervised teaching. The payment of a large salary increase for passing the performance-based licensing exam serves two related purposes. It encourages apprentice teachers to seek training that will best help them pass the exam, and it encourages them to stay in teaching for at least a few years after passing the test.

---

[13]This paragraph is a paraphrasing of the conclusion to Ballou and Podgursky's (1995) paper.

This is important because the effectiveness of teachers tends to increase markedly during their first years in the classroom (Murnane and Phillips, 1981).

• *Incentives for licensed teachers to improve their teaching skills.* Giving all teachers an incentive to invest in improving their performance is a major challenge for the nation's education system. Merit pay based on supervisors' assessments of individual teachers' performances was thought to be the answer, but it is not. The problem remains.

In January 1995, as part of a long-term project in which a talented group of educators sought to define what good teaching is and devise a set of strategies to measure teaching effectiveness, the National Board for Professional Teaching Standards (NBPTS) provided board certification to 81 middle school teachers who had demonstrated a remarkably high degree of teaching skill over a year of difficult, performance-based assessments. In the years ahead the NBPTS plans to expand its scope markedly and develop assessment programs that will provide experienced teachers of every subject and grade level the opportunity to apply for board certification. Although it is not yet known whether the benefits of board certification will be sufficient to justify the enormous amount of work needed to prepare for and complete the NBPTS assessment, initial reactions are promising. A number of states and school districts have agreed to pay the approximately $1,000 fee to go through the assessment process and to provide substantial salary bonuses to teachers who become board certified (NBPTS, 1994).

The NBPTS program has several attractive characteristics. By defining good teaching in concrete terms and developing methods of measuring teaching success, it may stimulate improvements in teaching training. Second, it may provide experienced teachers with incentives to seek help to improve their teaching. Third, it may provide financial rewards and enhanced status that will help keep extremely effective teachers in the classroom.

LEARNING FROM NEW INITIATIVES

Research has provided a great deal of information about the factors that influence who staffs the nation's schools. A variety of studies confirm that incentives matter. Incentives influence who goes into teaching, where teachers teach, how long teachers stay in teaching, and whether teachers return to the classroom after a career interruption. To conclude that incentives matter is not the same as knowing what set of incentives will best contribute to staffing the nation's schools with skilled teachers. In fact, many policy initiatives designed to improve the quality of the teachers in our nation's schools have had negative results. Examples include merit pay for individual teachers and extra pay for earning a master's degree.

Getting the incentives right is difficult. Responses to policy initiatives, even ones that in theory seem promising, cannot be predicted. This is especially the case for initiatives that increase risk. For example, performance-based licensing increases the risk of preparing to teach. A person might find that he or she is unable to demonstrate satisfactory teaching performance and is barred from public school teaching after having spent several years preparing for it. Offering a sizable salary increase to teacher interns who pass a performance-based licensing exam should compensate for this risk, but as yet there is no evidence of the size of the salary increase that would be needed to make teaching attractive to talented college graduates under a performance-based licensing system.

The decentralized nature of the nation's education system provides many opportunities to test the effectiveness of alternative policies. Many of the 50 states and 15,000 school districts in the United States are experimenting with policies to increase the quality of teachers. These initiatives represent natural experiments from which a great deal can be learned, but only rarely are policy initiatives accompanied by systematic evaluations (Hanushek, 1994). Careful research on the consequences of policy initiatives is critical to improved knowledge of the policies that will contribute to staffing all of the nation's schools with highly skilled teachers.

REFERENCES

AFT Task Force on the Future of Education. 1986. *The Revolution That is Overdue*. Washington, D.C.: American Federation of Teachers.

Andrew, M.D. 1990. "Differences between graduates of 4-year and 5-year teacher education programs." *Journal of Teacher Education* 41(2):45–51.

Ballou, D., and M. Podgursky. 1994. Do public schools hire the best applicants? Working paper, Department of Economics, University of Massachusetts, Amherst.

Ballou, D., and M. Podgursky. 1995. "Recruiting smarter teachers." *Journal of Human Resources*, 30(2):326-338.

Baugh, W. H., and J. A. Stone. 1982. "Mobility and wage equilibrium in the educator labor market." *Economics of Education Review* 2(3):253-274.

Beaudin, B. Q. 1993. "Teachers who interrupt their careers: characteristics of those who return to the classroom." *Journal of Policy Analysis and Management* 15(1):51-64.

Brewer, D. J. 1994. "Career paths and quit decisions: evidence from teaching." Working paper, Rand Corporation, Santa Monica, Calif.

Darling-Hammond, L. 1990. "Teaching and knowledge: policy issues posed by alternative certification for teachers." *Peabody Journal of Education* 67(3):123-154.

Darling-Hammond, L. 1994. "Who will speak for the children? How 'Teach for America' hurts urban schools and students." *Phi Delta Kappan* 76(1):21-34.

Dolton, P. 1991. "The economics of UK teacher supply: the graduate's decision." *Economic Journal* 199(4):91-104.

Educational Testing Service. 1988. *Guidelines for Proper Use of NTE Tests*. Princeton, N.J.: Educational Testing Service.

Ehrenberg, R. G., and D. J. Brewer. 1994. "Do school and teacher characteristics matter? Evidence from *High School and Beyond*." *Economics of Education Review* 13(1):1-17.

Ehrenberg, R. G., and D. J. Brewer. 1995. "Did teachers' verbal ability and race matter in the 1960s? *Coleman* Revisited." *Economics of Education Review* 14(1):1-21.

Ferguson, R. F. 1991. "Paying for public education: new evidence on how and why money matters." *Harvard Journal on Legislation* 28:465-498.

Forbes, E. 1995. "Statement about the Praxis series: professional assessments for beginning teachers." Princeton, N.J.: Educational Testing Service.

Gilford, D. J., and E. Tenenbaum, eds. 1990. *Precollege Science and Mathematics Teachers*. Washington, D.C.: National Academy Press.

Gray, L., and others. 1993. *New Teachers in the Job Market: 1991 Update*. Washington, D.C.: Office of Educational Research and Improvement, U.S. Department of Education.

Grissner, D. W., and S. Nataraj Kirby. 1992. *Patterns of Attrition Among Indiana Teachers, 1965-1987*. Santa Monica, Calif.: Rand Corp.

Haney, W., G. Madaus, and A. Kreitzer. 1987. "Charms talismanic: testing teachers for the improvement of American education." *Review of Research in Education* 14:169-238.

Hanushek, E. A. 1972. *Education and Race*. Lexington, Mass.: Heath-Lexington.

———. 1986. "The economics of schooling." *Journal of Economic Literature* 24:1141-1177.

———. 1994. *Making Schools Work: Improving Performance and Controlling Costs*. Washington, D.C.: The Brookings Institution.

Hanushek, E. A., and R. R. Pace. 1994. "Understanding entry into the teaching profession." In *Choices and Consequences: Contemporary Policy Issues in Education*, R. G. Ehrenberg, ed. Ithaca, N.Y.: ILR Press.

Kershaw, J. A., and R. N. McKean. 1962. *Teacher Shortages and Salary Schedules*. New York: McGraw-Hill.

Manski, C. F. 1987. "Academic ability, earnings, and the decision to become a teacher: evidence from the national longitudinal study of the high school class of 1972." In *Public Sector Payrolls*, D. A. Wise, ed. Chicago: University of Chicago Press.

Monk, D. H., and S. L. Jacobson. 1985. "The distribution of salary increments between veteran and novice teachers: evidence from New York state." *Journal of Education Finance* 11:157-175.

Murnane, R. J., and D. K. Cohen. 1986. "Merit pay and the evaluation problem: why most merit pay plans fail and a few survive." *Harvard Educational Review* 56(1):379-388.

Murnane, R. J., and B. Phillips. 1981. "Learning by doing, vintage, and selection: three pieces of the puzzle relating teaching experience and teaching performance." *Economics of Education Review* 1.

Murnane, R. J., J. D. Singer, and J. B. Willett. 1989. "Changes in teacher salaries during the 1970s: the role of school district demographics." *Economics of Education Review* 6(4):379-388.

Murnane, R. J., J. D. Singer, J. B. Willett, J. J. Kemple, and R. J. Olsen. 1991. *Who will teach? policies that matter*. Cambridge, Mass.: Harvard University Press.

National Board for Professional Teaching Standards (NBPTS). 1994. "State Action Supporting National Board Certification." Detroit: NBPTS.

National Center for Education Statistics (NCES). 1992. *Schools and Staffing in the United States: A Statistical Profile, 1987-88*. Washington, D.C.: U.S. Department of Education, Office of Educational Research and Improvement.

National Center for Education Statistics (NCES). 1993. *Schools and Staffing in the United States: A Statistical Profile, 1990-91*. Washington, D.C.: U.S. Department of Education, Office of Educational Research and Improvement.

National Education Association (NEA). 1992. *Status of the American Public School Teacher: 1990-91*. Washington, D.C.: NEA.

Nelson, F. H. 1985. "New perspectives on the teacher quality debate: empirical evidence from the National Longitudinal Study," *Journal of Educational Research* 78(3):133-140.

Rumberger, R. W. 1987. "The impact of salary differentials on teacher shortages and turnover: the case of mathematics and science teachers." *Economics of Education Review* 6(4):389-399.

Schorr, Jr. 1993. "Class action: what Clinton's National Service Program could learn from 'Teach for America.'" *Phi Delta Kappan* (Dec.):315-318.

Shulman, L. S. 1987. "Knowledge and teaching: foundations of the new reform." *Harvard Educational Review* 57(1):1-22.

South Carolina. 1989. 445 F. Supp. 1094 (D.S.C. 1977, aff'd; 434 U.S. 1026 (1978),1108.

Summers, A. A., and B. L. Wolfe. 1977. "Do schools make a difference?" *American Economic Review* 67(4):639-652.

Winkler, D. R. 1975. "Educational achievement and school peer group composition." *Journal of Human Resources* 10(3):189-204.

Wise, A. E., and L. Darling-Hammond. 1987. *Licensing Teachers: Design for a Teaching Profession*. Santa Monica, Calif.: Rand Corp.

Index

A

Accelerated Schools Project, 235-237
Access, 117-118
    college enrollment, 150
    minority enrollment trends, 158, 226
    preschool enrollment, 148
    quality schools, 134
    secondary school enrollment, 148-150
    trends, 148
Accountability
    assessment-based, 171, 188-189,
        191-192
    average test score assessment, 213-214,
        221
    of school administration, 133-134
    in school-based management, 76,
        100-101
    of teachers, 131-133, 137
    test design and analysis for, 176-178
    unmeasured outcomes and, 176
    value-added assessment, 202
Active learning, 235
Adaptability, 234-235
Advanced Placement tests, 16
Algebra, 16

Assessment of schools
    classroom-specific, 24
    criteria for performance indicators,
        197-198
    cross-school comparison, 18, 207-210
    dependent/independent variables, 23-25
    examples of school-based management,
        79-93
    gain indicator, 216-218
    implementing performance-based
        system, 48-49
    implications of flawed practice,
        218-219
    inadequacies in, 21-22
    management factors, 106-108
    measures for, 148
    reform outcomes, 21
    standards for, 7-8, 12
    for systemic reform, 5, 24-25
    techniques, 199
    See also School performance;
        Value-added assessment
Assessment of students
    adjustment of test scores, 179-180
    as basis for educational reform,
        173-174

259

conceptual and technical development, 172-174
for educator accountability, 171-172, 191-192
evaluation of system for, 190-191
improving test design for, 186-189
level indicators, 199
limitations, 103-104, 172, 178-180
negative effects on teaching, 184-186
role of achievement tests, 174-176
system design, 189-190
in systemic school reform, 5
test design and analysis, 176-178
thinking skills, 176
At-risk students
accelerated schools for, 235-237
cost-benefit analysis, 229-233
definition and characteristics of, 225-226
patterns of poverty, 227
preschool interventions for, 231-232
resource allocation for, 228-229
significance of, 226
social outcomes, 227-228
trends, 227

B

Board certification for teachers, 255
Britain
access to education, 117-118
examination system, 128-129, 137
secondary school admissions, 134-135
spending on education, 121-122
student achievement in, 112-116
student body diversity, 116-117
teacher accountability, 137
teaching practice, 122-125
teaching profession, 118-121

C

Class size
international comparison, 121
resource efficiency and, 6-7
spending to decrease, 151
student performance and, 22, 38

Clinton administration, 9-14
College(s)
admission standards for teachers, 119
admissions criteria, 129, 133
attainment trends, 1, 2-3
employment outcomes related to, 55-73
enrollment trends, 150
student loans, 9-11
Cost-benefit analysis, 6, 8, 41
dropout prevention, 229-231
interventions with at-risk populations, 232-233
preschool programs, 231-232
Creaming, 185-186, 219, 220
Criminal behavior, 154
prospects for at-risk students, 228
school trends, 158-160
Curriculum design
depth of content, 16
in performance-based incentive systems, 49
in school-based management, 77
student capacity to learn, 15-16

D

Dade County, Florida, 82-90
Dropout rate, 148-150, 153, 226
economic outcomes, 230-231
high school interventions, 229-231
preschool intervention, 231-232
Drugs in schools, 159-160

E

Economic analysis
as basis for reform effort, 29-30
of educational issues, 142-143
of human capital, 1-2
implications of at-risk student populations, 227-228
lack of, in reform effort, 8
measures for school assessment, 23
outcomes for high-school dropouts, 230-231
potential for crisis in school system, 35

research support for systemic reform, 5-6, 8
school governance models, 75-76
See also Investment in education
Educational attainment
of at-risk students, 226, 227
benefits of, 31
earnings correlated with, 31, 32, 53
macroeconomic effects, 32-33
market trends vs., as employment factor, 62-73
of parents, and participation in educational system, 101
preschool education and, 231-232
prospects for at-risk students, 227-228
relative wage correlations, 55-62
of teachers, student performance and, 22-23
trends, 1, 2-3, 53-54, 73, 150
Elementary and Secondary Education Act (ESEA), 3, 4, 6, 172-173
academic standards, 13-14, 20
reauthorization, 12-14, 18-19
state autonomy, 19
systemic school reform and, 5
Title I, 13-14, 173
Employment and income
career decisions of teachers, 242-250
cohort patterns, 57-58
educational attainment and, 31, 32, 53, 73
employer hiring behaviors, 133
employment opportunities for teachers, 247, 248
income trends, 161, 162
labor market shifts, 54, 153-154
occupational shifts related to educational attainments, 66-72
prospects for at-risk students, 227-228
prospects for high-school dropouts, 230-231
quantification of human capital investment, 2
relative wages related to educational attainments, trends in, 55-62
student preparation for labor market, 153-154
trends, 53-54
working mothers, 160
ESEA. See Elementary and Secondary Education Act

F

France, 141
access to education, 117-118
examination system, 128-129
repeating a grade in, 138, 139
secondary school admissions, 134
spending on education, 121-122
student achievement, 112-116
student body diversity, 116-117
student specialization, 139, 140
teaching practice, 122-125
teaching profession, 118-121

G

Gender issues, 58-59, 153
General Educational Development (GED) certificate, 150
Goal setting
adaptability in, 234-235
choice of specialization, 139-140
goal achievement and, 30, 135-137
for performance-based incentives, 103-104, 105
qualities of efficient organizations, 234
for systemic reform, 5
Goals 2000, 6
academic standards, 12, 20
criticism of, 3-4
goals of, 3, 12
rationale, 18-19
resource allocation, 14
systemic school reform and, 5
underlying assumptions of, 46-47
Grading on curve, 12, 130

H

Head Start, 148, 164, 166
Health care, school-based, 166
High school

attainment trends, 1, 2-3
competitive admissions, 134
enrollment trends, 148-150
international comparison, 111, 141-142
interventions with at-risk students,
    229-231
occupational education and training,
    11-12
teacher compensation, 119
teacher training, 119, 121

I

Improving America's Schools Act, 12-14
Information management
    data needs for value-added assessment,
        204-205, 206-207, 210-211, 220-221
    needs of efficient organizations, 234
    for school-based management, 106
International Association for the
        Evaluation of Educational
        Achievements, findings of, 112-116
International comparisons
    access to quality education, 134
    economic competition, 32-33
    educational spending, 121-122
    examination systems, 128-129
    extent of student performance
        differences, 111, 112-116
    external assessment, 133-134
    possible causes of student performance
        differences, 116-125
    redoublement/repeating a grade,
        137-139
    secondary school admissions, 134-135
    significant features of European
        practice, 141-143
    standard setting for external exams,
        135-137
    student assessment, 112
    student engagement, 124-125
    student performance, 35-36
    student time on task, 122-124
    teaching environment, 131-133
    teaching profession, 118-121
    See also Britain; France; Netherlands
Investment in education

benefits for individual, 31
community economic status and,
    162-163
cost-benefit analysis, 6
distribution of spending, 121-122, 151
expenditures per pupil, 23, 33, 35, 121,
    151, 162-163
international comparison, 121
as investment in human capital, 1-2
macroeconomic considerations, 32
policymaking environment, 4
preventive interventions with at-risk
    students, 229-233
scope of economic analysis, 31
significance of at-risk population, 226
social rationale, 31, 151-154
trends, 30, 33-40, 150-151
Investment in human capital
    vs. investment in tangible assets, 2

J

Jones, Adele, 132

L

Language issues, 158
Level indicators, 199, 218-219

M

Minimum competency testing, 173
Monroe County, Florida, 90-92
Motivation to learn
    peer group norms, 130-131
    standards of external exams and,
        135-137
    teacher qualities related to, 17
    threat of repeating a grade, 138-139

N

National Board for Professional Teaching
        Standards, 255
National Education Goals. *See* Goals 2000
National Teacher's Examination (NTE),
    245-246, 249

Netherlands, 141-142
  access to education, 117-118
  examination system, 128-129, 137
  repeating a grade in, 138-139
  secondary school admissions, 134
  spending on education, 121-122
  student achievement, 112-116
  student body diversity, 116-117
  student specialization, 139-140
  teaching practice, 122-125
  teaching profession, 118-121
NTE. *See* National Teachers' Examination

O

Occupational education and training,
  11-12

P

Panel on the Economics of Education
  Reform (PEER), 4, 6, 8, 171
Parents and families of students
  characteristics of at-risk students,
    226-227
  community-family partnerships,
    163-164
  ethnic differences, 158
  influence on child outcomes, 154-155,
    157
  participation in educational system,
    99-102
  school-based training programs for, 166
  school-family partnerships, 164
  single parent families, 161-162
  trends related to school performance,
    160-162
  in value-added assessment model,
    200-201
  working mothers, 160
PEER. *See* Panel on the Economics of
  Education Reform
Performance-based incentives, 7, 41-43
  basic features, 42-43
  with disadvantaged students, 46
  distortion problems, 104
  in efficient organizations, 234
  evaluation of effectiveness, 44, 45

  goal-setting, 103-104, 105
  implementation, 44-45, 47-50
  management structure for, 48-49
  measurement problems, 103-104
  merit pay systems, 252
  performance standards for, 47, 103
  potential problems of, 103-105
  quality of assessment data for, 219
  rationale, 41, 46, 105
  research support for, 48
  school-based management with, 93, 98,
    103, 105-106
  for teacher licensing, 252-253, 254-255,
    256
Performance standards
  achievement related to difficulty of,
    135-137
  for assessment of schools, 7-8, 12
  conceptual and technical development,
    173
  criteria for, as assessment indicators,
    197-198
  criterion-referenced/norm-referenced,
    173
  current conceptualization, 174
  decentralized decision-making for, 126
  equality in implementation, 20
  in ESEA, 13-14, 20
  federal guidelines, 20
  in Goals 2000, 12, 20
  high-quality examples, 20
  incentives to lower, 131-132
  performance-based incentives and, 47,
    103
  political environment, 135
  prospects for, as assessment indicators,
    188-189
  school administrator behaviors, 133-134
  signaling effects, 125-129
  state and local autonomy, 7-8, 14-15,
    19, 20
  for systemic reform, 20
  for teacher training, 253
  for Title I students, 13-14, 173
Philadelphia, Pennsylvania, 92
Policymaking
  assessment-based, 173

attracting skilled teachers, 250-256
based on flawed indicators, 218-219
Clinton administration, 9-14
economic considerations, 4
implementation through incentive, 7-8
political environment of standard
 setting, 135
value-added assessment, 204
Praxis I/II, 246
Preschool enrollment, 148, 155, 166
long-term benefits, 231-232
Primary school
international comparison of student
 performance, 111, 116
teacher compensation, 120
Private-public partnerships
community-family, 163-164
effectiveness, 165-166
objectives, 147
in performance-based incentive
 systems, 49
prospects, 166
rationale, 154-157
school-community, 164-165
school-family, 164
tradition, 147
trends, 147
Production function. *See* School
 performance
Productivity
educational factors in, 32-33
implications of at-risk student
 populations, 227-228
international comparison, 32
Property rights, 1

Q

Quality of education
access, 134
economic outcomes and, 32-33

R

Race/ethnicity
academic performance, 36-37, 150, 153
at-risk populations, 226-227

diversity of student body as
 performance factor, 116-117
dropout rate, 150, 153, 226
economic trends, 161
education majors, 247
English as second language, 158
income related to educational
 attainment, 58-59
labor market correlations, 54
minority enrollment trends, 158, 226
parenting styles, 158
peer group influences on academic
 performance, 130
Reform efforts
assessment-based accountability as
 basis for, 173-174
assessment systems for, 171-172
of Clinton administration, 9-14
community-family partnerships for,
 163-164
community involvement, rationale for,
 154-157
economic analysis for, 8, 29-30
effects on educational outcomes, 21
experimental research for, 44
goal setting, 5
incentive-based, 7-8, 41-43
obstacles to, 18, 45-46
political context, 142
prospects, 49-50, 142
recent history, 3-4, 29
school-based management, 76-79
school-community partnerships for,
 164-165
school-family partnerships for, 164
significance of European practice,
 141-143
spending reform for, 50
spending trends, 151
See also Systemic school reform
Repeating a grade, 137-139
Resource allocation and use
adaptability, 234-235
for at-risk populations, 228-229
class size and, 6-7
current inefficiency, 30, 40-41
economic analysis of schools, 6

educational spending trends, 150-151
for implementing school-based
management, 78, 81
meaning of efficiency in, 41
measurement techniques, 23
motivation for efficiency, 39
non-instructional salary expenditures,
35, 121-122
qualities of efficient organizations,
233-235
recommendations for reform, 50
school performance and, 23-24
for special needs students, 4-5
state and local decision-making, 14, 15
for systemic reform, 5
use of teacher's time in school-based
management, 102

S

SATs
performance trends, 150
scores of education majors, 244
School administration
accountability, 133-134
adaptability, 234-235
autonomy, 8
cost of, 35
limitations of decentralized
decision-making, 98-103
local political environment, 107
obstacles to assessment, 106-108
parental involvement, 99-102
participatory decision-making, 17,
44-45
performance-based contracts for
teachers, 7
performance-based incentives for
improving, 7
qualities of efficient organizations,
233-235
rationale for district-level governance,
75
student performance linkage, 107
See also School-based management
School-based management
accountability in, 100-101

authority structure, 77-78, 80-81
evaluation criteria, 93, 106-107
examples of implementation, 79-80
expertise of participants in, 99-100
information needs, 106
objectives, 79, 81
parental participation, 99-102
participants in decision-making, 99
performance-based incentives in, 93,
98, 103, 105-106
rationale for, 75-76, 98-103
research needs, 93, 97-98, 106-108
resources for implementation, 78, 81
socioceconomic setting, 100-102, 107
student outcomes, 80, 81-93, 98, 102,
103
teacher autonomy in, 99
teacher participation in, 99, 100
School choice
at-risk students and, 237
effects of flawed assessment data,
218-219
as incentive for student performance, 7
student performance and, 134-135
School performance
class size and, 6-7, 22
community inputs, trends in, 162-163
community outcomes affected by, 157
economic analysis, 142-143
family inputs, trends in, 160-162
incentives for, 7, 40
measurement, 7, 21-25
outcome-based incentives for, 41-43
public knowledge, 133-134
social trends related to, 157-160
student outcomes affected by, 155
teacher training and, 7
trends, 148-150, 157-158
See also Assessment of schools;
Value-added assessment
School-to-Work Act, 11-12
Single-parent families, 161-162, 227
Sociocultural factors
commitment to education, 111-112
discouragement of student performance,
112

public knowledge of school
performance, 133-134
threat of repeating a grade, 138-139
Socioeconomic factors
in analysis of standardized test
performance, 177
at-risk populations, 226, 227
in child outcomes, 154-157
community trends, 162-163
minority student performance, 158
parent participation in educational
system, 100-102
rationale for investing in education, 31
in school-based management outcomes,
100-102, 107
in student performance, 23-24, 36-37,
153-154, 226
students in poverty, 158, 227
Special needs students
expenditures, 23
in performance-based incentive
systems, 46, 49
resource allocation, 4-5
See also At-risk students
Specialization, student, 139-140
Standardized testing
achievement related to difficulty of,
135-137
adjustment of test scores, 179-180
aggregate/average scores, limitations of,
199, 213-218, 221
appropriate use of, for assessment,
189-193
assessment goals, 174-176
conceptual and technical development,
172-174
control of test-taking pool, 185-186,
219
corruptibility, 180, 198
curriculum-based, 126
degradation of instruction as result of,
184-186
design and analytical methods, 176-178
improving design and administration of,
186-189
inflation of scores, 181-184, 186-187

as instrument of accountability,
171-172
limitations, 178-180
as measure of school performance,
23-24, 199
prospects for external exams, 142
racial/ethnic differences, 36-37
signaling effects, 125-126
socioeconomic variables, 177
student performance related to system
of, 125-129
in systemic discouragement of student
performance, 112
for teacher licensing, 245-246
teaching to the test, 173-174, 181-184,
185, 219
validity, 188-189, 197-198
variation across tests, 178-179
State and local decision-making
for implementing incentive-based
system, 48-49
implementing value-added assessment,
220-221
rationale for centralized school
governance, 75
regulatory relief, 14
resource use, 14
for setting performance standards, 7-8,
14-15, 19, 20
student performance outcomes and, 21
in systemic school reform, 13, 14-15,
18-19
Statewide Systemic Initiative, 19
Student aid, 9-11
Student performance
academic standards for Title I students,
13-14
academic standards of Goals 2000, 12
access to education and, 117-118
achievement related to external
standards, 135-137
capacity to learn, 15-16
causes of international disparities,
116-125
class size and, 22, 38-39
classroom engagement and, 124-125
college acceptance criteria, 129

determinants of, 39-40, 44, 107, 154-157

examination system as factor in, 125-129

extent of international disparities, 111, 112-116

external factors, 23-24

graded on curve, 130

incentives for, 7, 40, 43

inter-school comparison, 18

international comparison, 35-36

limitations of assessment, 103-104, 112, 172

peer group norms, 130-131

quality of teaching and, 17

racial/ethnic differences, 36-37, 158

in school-based management systems, 80, 81-93, 98, 102

school choice and, 134-135

school management linkage, 107

school reform and, 21

school spending and, 35, 37, 38-40

sociocultural factors, 111-112

specialization as factor in, 140

spending trends targeted to, 151

student body diversity and, 116-117

systemic pressures for discouragement of, 112

teacher accountability, 131-133

teacher incentives based on, 41-43, 121

teacher training and, 22-23, 38-39

time on task and, 122-124

trends, 35, 150

value-added assessment model, 200-201

See also Assessment of students

Student-teacher ratio. *See* Class size

Systemic school reform

assessment techniques for, 24-25

basic concepts, 4-5, 14-15

conditions for success, 19-20

implementation, 15, 19

policymaking environment, 6

program coordination for, 13

rationale, 5, 18-19

research base for, 5-6, 15-18

state and local autonomy, 14-15

T

Teach for America, 242-243

Teacher compensation/incentives

attracting skilled teachers, 250-256

career decisions of teachers, 242-250

competitiveness with other sectors, 34

employment duration and, 248-249

for fields with shortages, 254

flexibility in, 254

international comparison, 119-121

market demand for teachers, 247-248

master's degree in education and, 251-252

merit pay systems, 252

objectives, 241, 252

opportunities for research, 255

performance-based approaches, 7, 42-43, 48

for professional development, 255

salaries, 248, 253-255

student performance and, 121

teacher mobility and, 248

trends, 7, 33-34, 35, 151

Teacher-student ratios. *See* Class size

Teacher training

board certification, 255

enrollment trends, 243

international comparison, 119

licensing requirements, 242-243, 244-246

master's degrees, 22, 38, 251-252

minority enrollments, 247

performance-based licensing, 252-253, 254-255, 256

as predictor of teacher effectiveness, 242

quality of trainees, 247-248

student performance and, 22-23, 38

subject matter expertise, 119

for systemic school reform, 5, 17, 20

trends, 7

Teaching practice

accountability of teachers, 131-133, 137

active learning, 235

employment trends, 247

international comparisons, 122-125

measures of quality, 242-243

negative effects of test-based
accountability, 184-186
participation in administration, 17
in performance-based incentive
systems, 104
predictors of effectiveness, 242
in school-based management system,
99, 100, 102
student engagement, 124-125
student performance and, 17, 22, 241
student time on task, 122-124
support for, 20
for systemic school reform, 17-18
teacher autonomy, 99
teaching to the test, 173-174, 181-184,
185, 219
work loads, international comparison,
120-121
Teen pregnancy/parenting, 154, 158, 162
school-based programs for, 166
Title I program, 13-14, 173

V

Value-added assessment, 7, 44, 172,
221-222
analytical method, 205-210
benchmark measures, 201
conditional mean format, 201-202
control variables, 210-211
current implementation, 220
data collection for, 204-205, 206-207,
210-211, 220-221
external school inputs, 203
heterogeneous slope models, 211-214
intrinsic performance indicators,
202-204, 206
predicted mean method, 201
public understanding of, 205
rationale, 172
reliability, 211
role of, 198
sample size, 204
school performance expectations and,
219-220
standard error, 211
statistical techniques, 199-205
total performance indicator, 201, 202
Type A indicator, 201
underlying assumptions, 209-210
vs. average test score assessment,
213-216
Violence in schools, 158-159